W0081854

THE FIGHT FOR
SEX ED

THE FIGHT FOR
SEX ED

THE CENTURY-LONG BATTLE
BETWEEN TRUTH AND DOCTRINE

MARGARET GRACE MYERS

BEACON PRESS, BOSTON

BEACON PRESS
Boston, Massachusetts
www.beacon.org

Beacon Press books
are published under the auspices of
the Unitarian Universalist Association of Congregations.

© 2025 by Margaret Grace Myers

All rights reserved
Printed in the United States of America

28 27 26 25   8 7 6 5 4 3 2 1

This book is printed on acid-free paper that meets the uncoated paper
ANSI/NISO specifications for permanence as revised in 1992.

Text design and composition by Kim Arney

*Library of Congress Cataloguing-in-Publication
Data is available for this title.*
Hardcover ISBN: 978-0-8070-0806-5
E-book ISBN: 978-0-8070-0805-8
Audiobook: 978-0-8070-2088-3

The authorized representative in the EU for product safety and compliance
is Easy Access System Europe 16879218, Mustamäe tee 50,
10621 Tallinn, Estonia: http://beacon.org/eu-contact

To my dad, the physician,
whose best explanation for the
HPV vaccine was, tersely,
as we walked across the parking lot
on the way to my appointment:
"It's for warts."

And to my mom,
always my first editor.

CONTENTS

THEN AND NOW

When I first got the idea that would become this book, it was 2017. *Roe v. Wade* still stood, critical race theory had not yet been weaponized in schools, and the book-banning movement had yet to reach its chilling peak. As for myself, I was not yet thirty, I was in a nonfiction MFA program, and I believed I knew exactly what I wanted to write about.

I was conducting research about my great-grandparents, who had worked in Baltimore as biologists at the turn of the twentieth century. I was planning to center my MFA thesis on them, but my attention quickly shifted. I became drawn into their world—they had been close friends with a number of "social hygienists": people who were dedicated to eradicating the "social evil," the euphemism of the day for sex work.* In Baltimore, as in many American cities at this time, brothels were legal but were confined to a red-light district. The people in my great-grandparents' circles—doctors and suffragists, motivated by what they saw as the dangers of both the health and moral aspects of sex work—generally believed that the women who were employed in brothels were victims of a complex matrix of factors, including industrialization,

---

* Throughout this book, I use the terms *sex work* and *sex worker*. These terms are anachronistic for most of the narrative but have become, in the past few years, preferred (though highly contested) because they center a person's work and distance it from criminality and shame. As it is with many identity-signifying labels with contentious histories, no term is a perfect solution, but these are the ones I have chosen.

isolation, and boredom. They also believed that sex work was the root cause of the burgeoning epidemic of sexually transmitted infections (STIs) that was ravaging their city.

One of the ways they hoped to end sex work, and so this epidemic, was by undertaking an educational campaign about the many and varied risks of extra- and premarital sex. But even among allies, there was very little agreement about whom, exactly, should be educated, or what that education should consist of.

When reading about debates on the topic from more than a century prior, I realized that many of the questions felt familiar; even in my own context I had heard all of the questions in my own life: At what age should a person be taught about sex? Does instruction on how to prevent pregnancy and infection encourage promiscuity? What are the right qualities of a sex educator? Where, ideally, should sex ed take place? At home? At church, or in school? These questions felt alive and present in my own reality.

The seed of this book came to me then, but it grew when I realized how very expansive the story of sex ed is. The history of the subject contains stories of American public schools, of the Red Scare, and of the religious right. It is also a narrative about politics, protest, social change, children, science, and medicine. Above all, it is a story of how difficult it is to solve real problems that have no clear answers in a highly politicized atmosphere.

This book is also very much about our society today. In the introduction to his book *Postwar America*, Howard Zinn wrote, "Any book of history is, consciously or not, an interpretation in which selected data from the past is tossed into the present according to the interest of the historian. That interest, no matter how much the historian's mind dwells on the past, is always a present one."[1] I carried this thought with me as I worked on *The Fight for Sex Ed* and watched as a pandemic unfolded in front of me, as *Roe v. Wade* was reversed, and as school districts became battlegrounds over not just sex ed but also critical race theory, transgender students on sports teams, and book bans targeting work on climate change.

The science fiction author Robert Heinlein once posited that every generation believes that they invented sex. After writing this book, I also think it's fair to say that each generation also thinks they invented sex ed. And, as Heinlein continues, "each generation is totally mistaken."[2] As I researched and wrote this book, I was at first bemused and then almost laughably frustrated by the way the debates about sex ed repeated themselves across time and space with uncanny similarity. This may be in part due to the fact that our culture has crafted no overarching narrative about the history of sex ed: no story about when it emerged, why it was first needed, what early advocates thought it could accomplish; and no popular understanding that sex ed has long been the subject of intense political and religious debate. There is therefore a sort of cultural amnesia around sex ed—little sense of the real work that has been done on it or the long history in which it is situated.

This is why, in school districts across the nation, sex ed is *still* often perceived as an experiment, just as it has been for more than a century—partly the result of purposeful efforts by those who want young people to remain ignorant of their bodies and of sex.

All of this amnesia and obfuscation has made the job of constructing this narrative pretty difficult. I probably made it more difficult by my love of diving deeply into primary sources. I constructed most of the action in this book from newspaper archives—grateful every day for the wonders of the internet—from which I plumbed the most interesting, maddening, and compelling instances of fights about sex ed. From there, a narrative began to come into focus. With the help of secondary sources—books and articles on history, religion, politics, and sexual health—I hope I have been able to put forth a convincing, and accurate, story of the fight for sex ed. Jeffrey P. Moran's 2000 book *Teaching Sex*, Janice Irvine's 2002 *Talk About Sex*, and Kristin Luker's 2006 *When Sex Goes to School* were all especially helpful.

If my book does nothing else, I hope it can tell the story of American sex ed for readers in the 2020s, a time as unique as any other. Because how we talk about sex, public health, and reproductive justice is a live wire, present and hot and very real. And tied up in it all is the history of sex ed.

I feel lucky to have carried this work with me for so long—and, in the process, to have read and watched and asked questions; to have had my ideas challenged and to have arrived at genuinely new conclusions. Now I feel lucky to get to share the result with readers.

CHAPTER 1

DR. PRINCE MORROW AND THE BIRTH OF SEXUAL HEALTH ADVOCACY IN AMERICA

New York City in 1901 had no Woolworth Building, no Chrysler Building, no Empire State Building, no Grand Central Terminal, no Pennsylvania Station. There was no New York City subway, no Williamsburg or Manhattan Bridge. Immigration was flourishing, and the city's total population stood at 3.5 million. The Statue of Liberty had not yet completely turned from copper brown to oxidized green. Men donned suits and hats; women wore long dresses.

It would be easy to assume that the people in the dapper crowds who walked the cobblestone streets—stopping to buy an oyster from an open cart, scandalized by the sight of a woman's ankle—had sexual lives as prim as their topcoats. But the truth was very different.

SYPHILIS AND MARRIAGE

In 1882, Prince Albert Morrow—a New York City doctor whose practice specialized in sexually transmitted infections (STIs)*—published his English translation of a French book entitled *Syphilis et mariage*, written by physician Jean Alfred Fournier. In it, Fournier described the troubling phenomena he was witnessing as a doctor who treated STIs. His male

---

* Throughout the book, I use the term *sexually transmitted infection* or *STI*. Like the term *sex work*, this term is largely anachronistic, but it reflects up-to-date thinking, and, as the Cleveland Clinic explains, it is "more accurate and comes with less historical and political baggage" than the generally more common term *STD*.

patients were coming to him with complicated questions: If a man had had a past infection but hadn't been symptomatic in years, could he, in good conscience, now marry? Would future children be affected by present infections? Some of the questions medicine alone couldn't solve: If a patient contracted an infection outside of marriage, could he take steps to prevent its spread without his wife knowing? What information about his condition did the patient owe his wife? And what information, for that matter, did the doctor owe his patient's wife? These were complicated human and moral conundrums. Morrow was evidently quite moved by Fournier's writing, and in his translator's preface he wrote: "There is scarcely a subject in the entire domain of medicine of greater practical importance to the profession and to the public."[1]

In 1899, seventeen years after translating *Syphilis and Marriage*, Morrow paid his own way to attend the International Conference on Syphilis and Venereal Diseases in Brussels.[2] There, medical experts from twenty-nine countries convened to discuss the STIs ravaging their countries.[3] Such infections—syphilis in particular—were running rampant globally. The British Army was admitting 122 of every 1,000 men to the hospital for an STI. In the Norwegian city of Kristiania (now Oslo), 3,525 cases of gonorrhea and syphilis were recorded, affecting 1.56 percent of the population.[4] The conference assumed that syphilis and other STIs were being spread primarily by sex work. As such, much of the work there was concerned with models of regulating, reducing, or abolishing the sex trades. A smaller section of the conference was dedicated to "measures affecting the civil population." Participants from several countries suggested establishing public lectures or printed "warnings." Professor Fournier himself called for free state-run hospitals.[5]

There was little agreement among the delegates, however, when it came to functional resolutions. They did decide one thing, however: to create a permanent International Society of Sanitary and Moral Prophylaxis, to be headquartered in Brussels.

We can imagine Dr. Morrow listening as these experts reported on the rates of STIs in their countries, on their current mitigation efforts, and on their future plans. Then he returned to the United States, where there were no such data, no plans, and no measures in place to prevent infections. There was no way to know how the United States was faring in comparison to other countries. Was it possible that New York, Morrow's own city, was experiencing numbers as high as cities abroad?

MORROW'S COMMITTEE OF SEVEN

Morrow was not alone in his burgeoning curiosity about the prevalence of sex work and infection in New York City. In 1900, a group of well-to-do New Yorkers formed the "Committee of Fifteen," which sought to incite authorities to repress "vice"—particularly sex work and gambling—and also look into their root causes. As a direct result of the Committee of Fifteen, at least one physician closely involved theorized, "The medical profession [was stirred] into action," and in 1901, the president of the Medical Society of the County of New York appointed "a Committee of Seven for the 'study of measures for the prophylaxis of venereal diseases'" in the Greater New York area.[6] Dr. Morrow served as chairman.

The committee's first goal was to attempt to quantify the number of STIs in the area—a tricky task because, as their December 1901 report noted, "There were no statistics regarding the prevalence of venereal diseases in this city."[7] To attempt to gather data, they sent surveys to 4,750 private physicians and to public hospitals and outpatient clinics, asking them to report how many cases of gonorrhea and syphilis they had treated that year. In the end, the committee received responses from only about 20 percent of the physicians.[8] Even so, the data was troubling. These private physicians reported a total of 23,196 cases of STIs in their practices in 1901.[9] Meanwhile, thirty-seven public institutions (of forty-five solicited) reported 22,256 cases of gonorrhea and syphilis, as well as 9,452 other cases referred to as "venereal diseases," for a total of 31,708 infections.[10] Combining the numbers made for a total of 54,904 named cases of gonorrhea and syphilis in the New York City area in 1901.

Morrow and the committee also knew that, in reality, the city was home to far more cases than these records showed. The clinics had noted, for example, "3,907 cases of chancroid, 898 cases of epididymitis and orchitis, 332 cases of cystitis, 414 cases of bubo, 261 cases of venereal warts, 172 cases of balanitis and phimosis, 523 cases of ophthalmia, 142 of ophthalmia neonatorum, 19 of vulvovaginitis in children."[11] Most, if not all, of these cases were merely iterations of syphilis or gonorrhea that had morphed into ailments with different names.

Then there were the many sufferers who chose not to seek treatment, or who did not know they were infected, as well as those who sought care only from "quacks"—swindlers peddling useless "medicine" and false hope. The numbers also didn't include statistics from specialists like ear, nose, and throat doctors; eye doctors; gynecologists; and neurologists who did not record illnesses under the category of "venereal disease."

The committee estimated that if the physicians who had not reported statistics were seeing similar numbers to those who had, there were probably about 162,372 cases of gonorrhea and syphilis in private practices alone. Then, taking into account public institutions as well, Morrow estimated a venereal morbidity of about 225,000 in the New York City area.[12]

If this was correct, STIs vastly outnumbered other infectious diseases. New York City in 1900 had reported just 12,530 cases of measles, 11,001 of diphtheria, and 7,387 of scarlet fever. Yet, syphilis and gonorrhea were going unrecorded and unacknowledged. This did not have to be the case—the city knew how to make public health information available to its citizens.

Seven years earlier, in 1893, the New York Department of Health had made tuberculosis—an infectious bacterial respiratory disease spread by coughing and sneezing—a reportable condition. This meant that any healthcare provider who treated a case of it had to report the incidence to the state.[13] Because of this registry, officials knew how many people had tuberculosis and where it was spreading. Increased screening and facilities were made available where it was needed most, and the health department was empowered to quarantine infectious individuals. Voluntary groups formed dedicated to the prevention and cure of tuberculosis, and in 1896, public spitting—one way that tuberculosis was spread—was banned in New York City.[14] Pamphlets, posters, and placards about the illness, its cause, and treatment were plastered throughout New York (and, following suit, other cities across the nation). Notification, treatment, and educational campaigns like this became the hallmark of a robust public health program.

Morrow proposed a similar campaign for gonorrhea and syphilis. However, unlike with tuberculosis, educating New Yorkers on STIs required publicly acknowledging the reality of sex. A recommendation not to spit was far different, in the public mind, from a recommendation not to have pre- or extramarital sex. At the time, American culture regarded sex as something deeply private that happened only within marriage. Though a doctor *might* talk to a patient about their genitals, reproduction, or childbirth, there were few other venues in which to discuss the topic. The assumption was that "good" people simply had no need to discuss sex, or even to really know the basics of how reproduction worked. On this point, Morrow indicted the "entire system of our educational machinery" as "organized upon a basis of silence and secrecy in regard to the reproductive function."[15]

Looking up even the most basic information about sex and reproduction would have been a daunting task during this time. A young reader flipping through *Anatomy, Physiology and Hygiene for High Schools*—a standard textbook published in 1900—might reasonably conclude that humans had no means of reproduction, as the textbook did not once mention *reproduction*, nor *genital*, nor *sex*, nothing so profane as *penis* or *vagina*—and certainly not *gonorrhea* or *syphilis*.

Part of this all-encompassing "silence and secrecy" stemmed from the fact that the United States had been built on Christian norms that permitted sex only within marriage. These norms had been reified by laws that criminalized adultery, fornication, and cohabitation. And though other countries also claimed Christian heritage, a number of factors—including plain pragmatism and time—had allowed them to recognize the reality of pre- and extramarital sex in a way that the US had not. In reality, Americans regularly had sex before and outside of marriage, but to admit this would be to pull a brick from the edifice of proper society and risk it crumbling entirely. Morrow argued that it was a necessary risk.

In 1901, Morrow and his committee released a set of recommendations for how best to lower rates of STIs, but since they all required frank acknowledgment of sex, there was little response. The *Therapeutic Gazette*, a monthly journal out of Detroit, reported in 1902 that Morrow's committee had "not excited the interest or received the comment which such a study would seem to warrant." It went on in even more drastic terms: "It is safe to predict that all these recommendations will be neglected, that a population which will cheerfully spend millions for the elimination of smallpox will adopt no active measures directed toward the lessening of diseases infinitely more lethal."[16]

MORROW'S CALL FOR PROPHYLAXIS

In September 1902, Prince Morrow attended the second International Congress for the Prophylaxis of Syphilis and Venereal Disease. The gathering concluded with a call for the creation of individual prophylactic societies in each country represented. Some countries, like France and Germany, already had such groups. Morrow was charged with creating one in the United States.[17]

Before assembling an organization of his own, Morrow wrote a book, released in 1904: *Social Diseases and Marriage: Social Prophylaxis*. In many ways, the book was similar to Fournier's. Morrow covered the medical mechanisms of STIs, the quandaries of medical etiquette, and the complicated relationship between sex work and infection. Dermatologist Edward Bennet Bronson described the book as having "excellence in style and elevation in tone," and noted that it deserved "to rank as a medical classic."[18]

It was a common belief that STIs were contracted only by the morally corrupt: philanderers, sex workers, and the like. Accordingly, in this view, an STI could be seen as a deserved punishment for sin. But Morrow's book showed that it was not just the impure who could contract STIs. He noted that it was not uncommon for recently married young women—who may never have had sex before—to contract an STI from their new husbands. Often, this was due not to maliciousness on the part of the husband, but ignorance. As Morrow explained: "While many men are fully aware that the chancre is a source of contagion [for syphilis], they know nothing of the multitudinous methods of contagion independent of the chancre."[19]

Moreover, Morrow explained, if a woman with gonorrhea gave birth, the infection could easily be passed from mother to infant, resulting in ophthalmia neonatorum, now known as neonatal conjunctivitis. In 1909, one doctor would calculate that ophthalmia neonatorum accounted for 15 to 50 percent of cases of blindness in the country.[20] The condition was entirely preventable, but treatment, naturally, was only available to those who knew they were infected. Even more troublingly, there was a mistaken belief that an STI could be cured by having sex with a young virginal partner. This led to children as young as two being infected with gonorrhea and syphilis, victims of horrific sexual abuse.

In highlighting these tragedies, Morrow argued that caring about STIs was a means of defending the very backbone of American society: the family. (The family was understood to be, of course, a married mother and father with at least one child.) Healthy families meant a healthy country, and so protecting them was a civic duty. And, at its core, this protection began with one step—education: "The true remedy to modify or lessen the appalling evils, moral and physical, which flow from venereal diseases," Morrow wrote, "is the general dissemination of knowledge."[21]

FOUNDING THE AMERICAN SOCIETY OF SANITARY AND MORAL PROPHYLAXIS

On February 8, 1905, Morrow assembled a small group at the New York Academy of Medicine for the first meeting of the American Society of Sanitary and Moral Prophylaxis (the ASSMP). The first meeting may have been modest, but the attendees were impressive. They included Dr. Sigard Adolphus Knopf, tuberculosis expert; Felix Adler, founder of the Ethical Culture movement; Abraham Jacobi, "father of American pediatrics"; Edward Robert Anderson Seligman, economist; Edward Thomas Devine, social welfare advocate; and a slew of other gynecologists, public health advocates, and interested parties. The doctors and medical reformers present would represent the "sanitary" aspect of preventing STIs, while the religious and social reformers would focus on the "moral" aspect.

At the time, this was an easy partnership, because the sanitary and moral ways of preventing STIs were one in the same: Don't have sex before you get married. Marry young, and only have sex with that person. This fit in perfectly with Christian morality, but it was also medical advice. There were no antibiotics to prescribe for the treatment of infections, and though condoms and condom-like devices had existed for centuries, they were not widely available.

Condoms existed in the United States, certainly—they had made their way to America in the nineteenth century and were usually made of linen or animal bladder or intestine. Then, in 1837, when Charles Goodyear discovered how to stabilize rubber, that became the material of choice.[22]

Until 1873, condoms could be purchased through the mail and were advertised in newspapers. In that year, however, politician and moralist Anthony Comstock's eponymous law was enacted. The Comstock Law prohibited, among other things, the mailing of "every obscene, lewd, or lascivious, and every filthy book, pamphlet, picture, paper, letter, writing, print, or other publication of an indecent character, and every article or thing designed, adapted, or intended for preventing conception or producing abortion, or for any indecent or immoral use."[23] After the Comstock Law was passed, twenty-four states passed their own laws restricting access to contraception, often known as "little Comstock" laws.[24]

Under the Comstock Law, condoms became unmailable—although many condom manufacturers simply became more evasive. But they were far from respectable and were regarded as illegal. And so, while at the turn of the century some Americans may have had access to condoms, many did not—and in a world where sex before and outside of marriage was summarily dismissed as immoral, to seek out a condom was to admit one's immorality. So, doctors were left with only one surefire medical suggestion for how to prevent STIs: monogamy with a partner who was free of infection.

In addition to the goal of reducing rates of STIs, Morrow also wanted the ASSMP to break the silent dictates of American decency and talk more openly about sex and its myriad risks.

At fifty-nine years old, Morrow was described as "a man of striking appearance, large build . . . fine proportions [and] an air of self-reliance and reserve force."[25] He addressed the small group with his big plans: to be the ones to face, head-on, with all their power, the epidemic that no one else would even admit existed. He proposed three main areas of focus: treatment, legislation, and wide-ranging education. Morrow urged the members of his new group to cast as wide a net as possible in seeking allies: "We should enlist the co-operation of the heads of schools and colleges, of the clergy . . . of jurists . . . of sociologists . . . of philanthropists and public-spirited men generally." The prevention of STIs, he explained "is pre-eminently a socio-sanitary problem, complicated with all the complex interests of our social life."[26]

The records of the ASSMP's early years reflect the holistic and wide-ranging aims of the group. They hosted doctors working to treat and prevent STIs, who shared papers like "Gonorrheal Arthritis in Children" and "The Prevention of Blindness Resulting from Ophthalmia of the New-Born," as well as people like Colonel Valery Havard on "Venereal Diseases in the Army." They heard talks about stopping sex work, which was seen as the root source of STIs. The turn of the twentieth century had seen a rise in sex work in part due to industrialization, which tended to drive young girls and women out of the home and into big cities, looking for work. And sex work was, undoubtedly, an important factor in the spread of infections—if one sex worker became infected, she could quickly spread the infection to her clients.

But the relationship between sex workers and STIs was often exaggerated. As suffragist Edith Houghton Hooker would write in *The Arbitrator* in 1919, "Many people have come to believe that the responsibility for the dissemination of venereal disease rests solely upon the prostitute."[27] This view did not account for a male who may have hired a sex worker and given her an infection. Historian Allan Brandt, in his landmark 1985 book, *No Magic Bullet*, further explains "this [theory of a] uni-directional mode of transmission reflected prevailing attitudes rather than any bacteriologic reality."[28] But this understanding was largely lost to the ASSMP, and so they focused on educating those whom they thought would be most likely to hire sex workers—young men and teenage boys.

TOWARD A BLUEPRINT FOR SEX ED

Morrow proposed two phases of sex education. The first would be "constructive," focusing on reproduction, parenthood, and eugenic ideals. In 1905, eugenics did not yet have the rightfully earned negative connotations that it has now, and instead was regarded as a new branch of science that experts believed would improve humanity. Introduced in 1883 by English statistician Francis Galton, eugenics had started with a simple premise: children were the benchmark for the well-being of the human race, and so their health needed to be prioritized. This meant closely examining the health of prospective parents. Some of these factors were truly medically significant, like being free from disease; others were junk-science opinions about race and gender. Eugenicists believed that science and society should evaluate potential parents on those "scientific" factors that would produce the "best" children. At its most shameful, eugenics advocated forced sterilization of some groups. But as far as the ASSMP was concerned, eugenics was mainly—though not entirely, and certainly not unproblematically—about teaching young people to stay healthy in service of their presumed future parenthood. This constructive phase would also seek to build up, in Morrow's words, "what may be termed the 'sexual character' of the individual upon the foundations of sound knowledge, self-reverence, respect of woman and for good morals."[29]

The second phase, Morrow wrote, had "perhaps a more important bearing upon the specific object of this society's work—the prevention of venereal diseases." These lessons would involve frank explanations of anatomy and sex, and they would tacitly concede that some people had sex outside of marriage. This second phase was far more controversial than the first, and skeptics—many within the ASSMP itself—were convinced that openly teaching the realities of one's body and potential sexual activity would lead young people to sexual deviance. Many adults believed if they kept children ignorant, they could protect their innocence.

But Morrow, as well as other educators, knew that this was not the case. He knew that the mind of a young person was never as blank or innocent as his critics wished to believe. Even if parents never told their child about gonorrhea or syphilis, even if they never uttered the word *sex* in their home, never explained where babies or puppies came from, or even how flowers blossomed—the child would still learn about sex. They would learn from classmates or from books; they would overhear conversations or come across a pamphlet or article. Information learned in this way was often misguided, misinterpreted, or downright wrong.

But even people who agreed that young people needed information disagreed about how it should be given. Many were convinced that parents alone should educate their children about sex. Morrow conceded that in a perfect world, a parent would be the primary sex educator. This would allow information to come from a trusted source. It would also permit one-on-one teaching, which many experts believed was optimal, and it left private conversations in private life. But Morrow noted that parents were often too embarrassed, or didn't have the information they needed to fully educate their children. So, the group discussed the possibilities of enlisting churches, doctors, and—most controversially—schools.

Within the ASSMP itself, the idea of school-based sex ed was highly contested. Yale-trained urologist E. L. Keyes was skeptical, claiming that the prospect of teaching about sex in school "is a powder magazine and the instructor is smoking a pipe." Even comparative anatomist Burt Green Wilder, who gave special sex hygiene lectures to seniors at Cornell University, was wary of expanding that education to younger students. "If to-day I advocate any degree of instruction upon the subject in the schools," he said, "it is because so few parents of to-day have both the ability and the disposition to import it, and because I hope the pupils so enlightened may, in their turn, do better by their own children."[30]

Even if there had been a widespread consensus that sex ed should be taught in schools, there were structural difficulties in bringing such lessons to them. In April 1906, Morrow lambasted the "existing system" for having "no provision for imparting this particular knowledge."[31] There were a few established school subjects in which the lessons of sex might be incorporated, however: anatomy, domestic science, and "hygiene" courses. Teachers also seemed amenable to the idea: one survey, conducted by gynecologist Helen Putnam, found that eighty-five of the ninety teachers polled believed that "sex hygiene" classes were a good idea. However, many of them did not have the information they needed to teach about reproduction and sex, let alone STIs. But the bigger obstacle, Putnam noted, was not teachers, but administrators and parents. Of the ninety teachers interviewed, "three felt sure they could do it . . . but were forbidden by the principals." Others said that when they had tried to set up classes, they met "trouble with parents." Most of the difficulty with enacting sex education, Putnam predicted, would "lie with adults, not with children."[32]

CHAPTER 2

ELLA FLAGG YOUNG AND THE FIRST SEX ED LECTURES IN AMERICAN PUBLIC SCHOOLS

THE SOCIAL EVIL IN CHICAGO

New York wasn't the only city that was plagued with STIs and "immorality" during the 1910s. At a time when the American Progressive movement was working to reduce corruption, ameliorate poverty, and increase access to upward mobility, the mayor of Chicago, Fred Busse, appointed a vice commission to investigate the extent of sex work and infection. In 1911, the commission published its findings.

The report detailed a city rife with sex work and infection, and was full of data, statistics, and recommendations for how to improve conditions—one of which was sex ed. It explained that the "immoral influences and dangers" of the street could be "counteracted and minimized by proper moral teaching and scientific instruction."[1] The report specifically recommended that "children beyond the age of puberty" could be instructed in sex "in schools under carefully trained and scientifically instructed teachers." It went on to aver that "the teaching of sex hygiene in schools is an important movement which, while not yet past the experimental stage, promises great advances in the promotion of child protection for the future."[2]

In the six years since the ASSMP had been founded, they had promulgated the idea of sex ed widely. The group had continued to meet and to expand their public-facing work and had published three pamphlets: *The*

Young Man's Problem, On Instruction in Physiology and Hygiene of Sex for Teachers, and *On the Relations of Social Disease and Marriage*. By October 1907, Morrow reported that "several thousand copies of these pamphlets [had] been called for."[3]

The ASSMP had also sent speakers to schools and groups, and had tracked developments in legislation, medicine, and education around sex and STIs. And, crucially, by 1911, it had come out strongly, and unanimously, in favor of sex ed in schools. As Maurice A. Bigelow, member of the Teacher's College at Columbia University, put it in an address to the ASSMP that year, "the whole case" for sex ed in schools had "been splendidly presented by eminent writers in the fields of medicine, biology, sociology, and ethics."[4] The less direct approaches initially suggested—like distributing pamphlets, teaching only adult men, and encouraging churchgoing—seemed to be having negligible effects.

The ASSMP had also inspired the creation of a bigger organization. In 1910, the American Federation for Sex Hygiene (AFSH) was formed. An umbrella group of sorts, it was made up of members from the ASSMP as well as other local social hygiene societies. Morrow was made president, and Charles Eliot, who had been the president of Harvard University until 1909, was named honorary president.

So, sex ed was in the air. The Chicago Vice Commission was attentive to it, and they had in their corner someone who could help implement their suggestions: superintendent of Chicago schools Ella Flagg Young.

YOUNG THE REFORMER

Ella Flagg Young was born in 1845 in Buffalo, New York. She trained as a teacher at the Chicago Normal School and taught primary and high school in Chicago. She then served as a principal and assistant superintendent before attending the University of Chicago in 1895. There, she studied under pioneering philosopher of education John Dewey. Dewey was a psychologist and educational reformer with wide-ranging interests. Much of his work centered on democracy, education, and the belief that school is a social institution where children should learn by doing—and Young was no doubt influenced by him. She received her PhD in education in 1900, and in 1909, she was appointed superintendent of Chicago schools—the first female superintendent of any American school system.[5]

In 1912, the chairman of the Chicago Vice Commission, Dean Sumner, found in Young an ally in the fight for sex ed. With her support, in April of that year, the Chicago school board's committee on school management appropriated $2,500 "for the initiation of sex hygiene instruction."[6] This instruction would be given not to the students themselves, but to their parents.

ATTEMPT 1: LECTURES FOR PARENTS

In June 1912, the lectures began, separated by gender—fathers were given a lecture by a male doctor, while mothers heard a lecture by a female physician. One of the lecturers, the physician and birth control advocate Dr. Rachelle Yarros, told the mothers of Chicago public school students about the dangers of STIs, and advised that "innocence and ignorance are not the same thing."[7] Apparently, these lectures proved to be too much for some mothers, who, according to one newspaper, "placed their fingers in their ears when the physicians spoke in plain English concerning the effects of gay revels and midnight hours."[8]

In response, the lecturers promised to "modify their language."[9] But by then, the trends of sex ed were already changing—and experts were suggesting lessons for students themselves. In September 1912, an AFSH special committee that included Dr. Morrow released a report of recommendations.

In it, the authors—Morrow, along with Thomas Balliet and Maurice Bigelow—set out practical advice about providing sex ed for students. "Sex instruction has a purely practical aim," the report began. "Its purpose is to impart such knowledge of sex at each period of the child's life as may be necessary to preserve health, develop right thinking, and control conduct."[10] As such, any course in sex ed should meet children where they were, taking care not to awaken the dangerous sexual instinct that the AFSH special committee believed lived deep within some students. The report urged segregating students by age and gender, and providing only the information considered developmentally appropriate (though, what, exactly, "developmentally appropriate" meant was rarely explained).

Very young children, the committee wrote, should be educated at home by their mothers, who should introduce them to the concepts of growth and reproduction by teaching them about plants and animals. Children ages six through twelve would go on to learn the scientific aspects of plant, bird, and fish reproduction at school. They believed that these lessons were as scientific as they were moral. Watching plant fertilization or chicks hatching from eggs would, for example, the report argued, "impress deeply the mind of the child with the beautiful and marvelous processes of nature by which life is reproduced by life."

At age twelve, the committee argued, students should begin to learn about mammalian fertilization. Their lessons should also introduce what the committee called "sexual morality." These courses would explicitly teach that the family was the main unit of life, that fidelity to a spouse was part of nature, and so on. "Biology and ethics," the committee wrote, "are so closely interrelated that they can be made mutually to reinforce one another." Their moral instructions are familiar even now: "It should be impressed upon every boy that every girl is somebody's daughter and usually somebody's sister," the committee explained as an example of a "sexual law," "and that it is his sacred duty to accord her the same respect and protection which he would exact from another boy toward his own sister." At age sixteen, students could also begin to learn about STIs—namely that they existed, and that "right living" (sex only within marriage) would ensure that they never suffered from them.

For all ages, the committee advised against "detailed descriptions of external human anatomy," and recommended teaching internal anatomy only so far as it would "impress the hygiene bearing of the facts to be taught." The committee was also adamant that these lessons not be taught in a specific sex ed class, but rather be integrated into other classes. The lessons of "sex hygiene," they argued, were everywhere. The anatomical aspects of it should be taught in science class, the moral aspects in ethics class, and so forth. Setting the information apart would do more harm than good, they argued, by making sex seem as if it existed alone in the world, and not as it truly was, tied up with all parts of life.

They also argued that sex ed should be introduced to schools gradually, "only so fast as teachers can be found or trained who are competent to give it, and so fast as public sentiment will support it." But they also warned that schools should not make unreasonable delays. "Even occasional mistakes" in such teaching, they wrote, "will do far less harm than allowing children to continue to gain this knowledge, as many of them now do, from impure sources."

Their report included feedback from other educators and medical professionals, who on the whole seemed optimistic about the project. But those experts still feared that implementing the classes would be difficult. One superintendent of education from Boise, Idaho, wrote that he believed "in sex instruction in schools, but neither parents nor teachers are yet ready for it." The parents of Chicago had proven him correct on this point. But Young remained undaunted, and she continued to advocate for sex ed in Chicago schools. In June 1913, she officially sent to the Chicago Board of Education's school management committee her recommendation that students be given sex hygiene lectures. A firestorm ensued.[11]

ATTEMPT 2: LECTURES FOR STUDENTS

"High school pupils," Young exhorted in June 1913, "need something to improve their morals." She recommended that a series of "personal purity" lectures be given to the students in all twenty-one Chicago high schools, with the option for any parent to excuse their child from the lectures if they wished.[12] The school management committee approved the lectures—a first step before a full vote by the board. But well before the lectures could begin, protests erupted from both the school board and the community. Just a week after it was announced that the school management committee had approved the lectures, a newspaper headline read "No Sex Hygiene Teaching in Chicago Public School [sic]." The article went on to claim that a thousand protests had been lodged—some, novelly, by phone.[13]

Chicago's board of education, then, was at something of a crossroads. American school boards—sometimes called boards of education, sometimes boards of trustees, but all functionally the same—date back to Puritan New England and were designed to be an official body, separate from other school administration, that would oversee public schools. Elected by citizens, the ideally nonpartisan boards were meant to legislate rules, enforce those rules, and choose superintendents to whom day-to-day school operations could be delegated. School boards also have the delicate responsibility of fielding complaints from parents and the community. In this way, the school board is a powerful but somewhat mercurial entity, and depending on the makeup of its members, a board may either back down from its position at the first sign of trouble or hold strong.

In this case, Chicago's board of education was fielding complaints from parents about the planned lectures, but the lectures had also received votes of support from others. Jane Addams, founder of the famous Hull House, wrote a letter backing Young's plan, and A. W. Harris, president of Northwestern University, noted that "frank, scientific and elevating teaching can have only good effects."[14] In July, the lectures were approved 11 to 2 by the board of education. And that fall, on October 27, 1913, about three thousand Chicago students were given their first "personal purity" lecture. Six physicians descended on five public schools, giving lectures to gender-segregated groups.[15] In the following days, the lectures continued apace, and to apparently positive reactions. Principals from around the city reported that only small numbers of students (or their parents) chose not to attend the lectures.[16] "A regular schedule," the *Inter Ocean* newspaper announced in late October, "will be arranged."[17]

In mid-November, Young noted that "parents who at first objected are now on our side, and the only opposition that now exists comes from outside sources and from persons who do not really understand what we are teaching."[18] She proclaimed: "Eventually, I expect to see sex hygiene taught in every city and rural school in the country. . . . It is [as] important for the growing child to know his own body as it is to know arithmetic."

OPPOSITION MOUNTS

But before long, opposition emerged—and with ferocity, especially from Catholics. The Catholic view of sex during this time was not so different from the Protestant one—within marriage, it was regarded as a good thing; outside of marriage, not at all. As Leslie Woodcock Tentler explains in her book *Catholics and Contraception*, "Marital sex . . . was the means that God had chosen to people the earth and swell the hosts of heaven. . . . This . . . endowed marital sex with an aura of holiness."[19] At the same time, however, Tentler continues, "Priests were trained to regard sexuality as external to the moral self and powerfully subversive of it. Sexuality . . . was not integral to identity in any remotely positive way but evidence of our nature's fallenness."[20] It was, therefore, a fine line theologically. In practice, it meant that Catholics were expected, and encouraged, to have sex in marriage that could lead to procreation. "Frequent sex in marriage," Tentler explains, was also believed to deter "spouses from the grave sins of masturbation and adultery."[21]

In general, however, the Catholic church remained—like Protestant churches—silent on the issues of sex other than these blanket proclamations. What they were *not* silent about, however, was their views on who had the authority to speak about what. Catholic clergy were the go-to for Catholic adults when it came to matters of sex—and the home was the proper place for children to learn about sex. In addition, American Catholics largely regarded public schools with suspicion. They felt, not without cause, that the institution was Protestant in nature and therefore hostile to Catholic youth. So, for a public school to implement sex ed, as Chicago's had, could be, and was, perceived as a threat to Catholic authority.

The *New World*, a Catholic newspaper, called sex hygiene "modern fadism" and regarded it as "a very bad step, one that is almost certain to be most injurious to public morals."[22] Reverend Thomas A. O'Malley of Loyola University called "the teaching of sex hygiene in the public schools . . . the greatest crime ever committed against Chicago." In a city that was even then known for organized crime, O'Malley's charge seemed a slight overstatement. But, he continued, "for my part, I would rather see our little ones stark and cold in death. It would at least be a consolation to know that they had died pure and unspotted."[23]

In addition to the Catholic opposition, an anti-science group called the National League for Medical Freedom (NLMF) also condemned the lectures. NLMF argued that the personal purity lectures encroached on the liberties of American children and parents. They derided them as "brutally frank, disgustingly biological and their details nauseating." The NLMF then pointed to the Comstock Law as justification for why the lectures should be discontinued. Obtaining extracts from two personal purity lectures that had been given in October, the NLMF submitted them to Chicago's postmaster, requesting "a ruling regarding their mailability."[24] The Chicago postmaster forwarded them to Washington, where they were flagged as "unmailable" under the Comstock Law.[25] This stratagem lent political credence to the group's outrage toward sex ed. Their journal noted that "it was not surprising that the postal authorities could not approve the extracts from and substance of the lectures because they were not pleasant reading matter."[26] In some ways, however, the NLMF's stunt also backfired because of how blatant the group's machinations were. One of the physicians whose lecture had been extracted commented that it had been edited so much by the NLMF that its "meaning had been considerably changed."[27] The press was likewise not fooled. A *Chicago Tribune* article, commenting on the situation, noted that "the people of the United States are subjected to a censorship of the mails which is declared to be as arbitrary as that which prevails in Russia." The article went on to state that the postal service itself insisted that "it is in sympathy with" the sex hygiene movement, though "the law and previous rulings thereunder compel the action taken."[28]

But the most forceful foe that Young would face came from a seemingly unlikely source: the Chicago Typographical Union No. 16.

TYPOS AND POLITICS

Among Young's many responsibilities as superintendent was the selection of textbooks. In the spring of 1913, before the fights over sex ed would bring Young to national attention, her selection of a certain spelling book had brought her directly into a morass of local politics. One member of the school board, John Harding, a local printer and the organizer of the Chicago Typographical Union No. 16, opposed Young's choice because it was not printed in Chicago. Young accused him of pressuring her to change textbooks.[29] In July 1913, the bitter fight over the spelling books— along with burgeoning concern over the sex ed classes—led Young to briefly resign as superintendent.[30] With the urging of several important women's groups, the board of education refused Young's resignation that summer, 14 to 1, and Young retained her position. The only opposing vote was John Harding.[31]

Then in December, as the sex hygiene lectures were progressing, there was another round of school board plotting and scheming. Young was up for reelection at a regular school board meeting. In a first, secret ballot Young received only ten votes in her favor, out of a possible twenty. Six were cast in favor of the current assistant superintendent, Mr. Shoop, whom John Harding had nominated; and four members of the board abstained from voting.[32] Young needed eleven votes to remain superintendent, and when she saw that she had only ten, she withdrew from the race, saying, according to the *Chicago Tribune*, that "she could not do efficient work without the full confidence of the school board."[33] A second ballot was taken, and, Mrs. Young not being on it, Shoop received the eleven votes.[34]

Teachers, women's groups, and some members of the board were outraged to have lost Young. There was also concern that it was the result of political plotting. The local newspaper the *Day Book* called it a "political coup."[35] The *Chicago Tribune* ran a headline: "Board Ousts Ella F. Young."[36]

Many were concerned that the members of the school board who had been appointed by Chicago mayor Carter H. Harrison II had been central to the "ousting." Although Harrison had appointed those members, he was an ally of Young's—he had supported her when she had been in hot water that summer. Now, Harrison asked the five "ousted" board members to resign, including Harding. They assented, and after this drastic action, there were calls for yet another vote on the superintendent—this time with Young on the ballot again.[37] At the end of December, much to Harding's chagrin, Young was reelected superintendent of the school board. But Harding was not out of strategies.

Less than a week later, the Chicago Typographical Union No. 16 came out swinging against the sex hygiene lectures. Harding, as recording secretary of the union, called Young's teaching practices ludicrous and alleged that she was undermining what the school was meant to do. The union passed a resolution against sex hygiene lectures and established a "vigilance" committee to monitor the school board and "purge the public schools of fads and follies." The resolution stated: "These teachings and lectures are an unwarranted interference with the rights and prerogatives of the parents of the school children."[38]

In response to this, Young noted again that the parents—the ones whose apparent liberties had been infringed upon—seemed to generally approve of the lectures. In November alone, she noted, 21,534 students had attended the lectures and only 230 students, or 1.6 percent of them, had been excused.[39] But on January 8, after four months of instruction, the Chicago school board voted 13 to 8 against continuing the lectures.[40]

Young did not fight the matter further. Chicago public schools, and perhaps American public schools in general, it seemed, were simply not ready to accept sex ed. The Department of Superintendence of the National Education Association signaled as much a month later, resolving that sex hygiene, ideally, should be taught at home. It noted that "the school should be willing and anxious to help the home in this matter as best it can," but ultimately placed the responsibility in the hands of parents.[41]

But Young remained convinced of the value of sex ed, and even characterized her experiment as successful. In June 1914, she addressed the General Federation of Women's Clubs, describing the girls who had attended the sex hygiene lectures as "enlightened [and] with uplifted chins in consciousness of the womanhood that was in them instead of with smirks of ignorance."[42]

Ella Flagg Young's groundbreaking lectures were not the only events of significance in the world of sex ed that year. On March 17, 1913, Prince Albert Morrow died at age sixty-six. His contemporary, E. L. Keyes reflected of him: "The little flame has kindled a great conflagration that is now spreading throughout the length and breadth of our land."[43]

CHAPTER 3

FIT TO FIGHT: SYPHILIS AND WWI

In April 1917—four years after Ella Flagg Young's first personal purity lectures—the United States entered World War I. In the first year of the war, 516,212 men were inducted into duty.[1] By the end of the war, about 2.8 million men had been drafted—and, for many of them, STIs posed a greater risk than enemy fire. In October 1917, Surgeon General William Crawford Gorgas reported that STIs were "the greatest cause of disability in the army. The army loses more days of service from its men due to venereal diseases than from any other cause."[2] In keeping with the norms of the time, experts were quick to blame sex workers. M. J. Exner, an expert on the subject, wrote in 1917 that "it is a matter of history that prostitution follows the army."[3] In the United States, sex workers set up outside of training camps. Abroad, American troops frequently patronized either "clandestine" or regulated sex workers.

In the eyes of the government, every man who contracted gonorrhea or syphilis was not fulfilling his duty, not protecting his country, and was a drain on resources. And so, the government was finally ready to listen to what Morrow and his successors had been trying to tell them for years.

"A VICTORY OVER DISEASE"

In 1917, the American Social Hygiene Association (ASHA)—a merging of the AFSH and the American Vigilance Association, a group dedicated to ending sex work—offered its services and suggestions to the secretary of war, who was happy to accept. In many ways, this government connection was the opportunity that ASHA—and the AFSH and ASSMP before it—had been waiting for. They had spent years developing theories and best practices for preventing STIs, and now they were able to enact them with the full force of the government behind them. William F. Snow, an ophthalmologist turned sex hygiene expert who had been general secretary of ASHA, was made the secretary of the General Medical Board on the newly created Council of National Defense. In this position, he worked to enact ASHA's plans. He was optimistic: the United States, he predicted in 1917, would "demonstrate a victory over disease and moral disaster which will rival its epoch-making record in mastering yellow fever during the war with Spain."[4]

ASHA retained many of the sensibilities of the early ASSMP: It was concerned about both health and morals, and was made up of people sympathetic to both. Increasingly, however, it found itself taking on the role of the old-fashioned moralist as it conversed with groups that had varying priorities.

ASHA's initial recommendations, which were quite extensive, concerned the men at domestic training camps. They proposed four "classes of attack" for reducing rates of STIs, three of which were largely uncontroversial. Class A was about establishing "social measures to diminish sexual temptation." This meant eliminating sex work and alcohol near military camps. The government heeded ASHA's advice on the matter of alcohol, which was discouraged because of the belief that it led to an increased sexual appetite.[5] And with the imprimatur of the federal government, cities and towns near military bases began suppressing and preventing "the keeping or setting up of houses of ill fame, brothels, or bawdy houses." ASHA also created the Commission on Training Camp Activities (CTCA), which provided "counter attractions"—sports, singing, movies, and lectures—for army men so they would not be enticed to engage in vice.

Class B of ASHA's plan centered on the "education of soldiers and civilians in regard to venereal diseases." The Social Hygiene Instruction Division of the CTCA set to work creating syllabi and training lecturers. It pumped out a veritable mass of anti-venereal disease propaganda, including pamphlets, exhibits, and lectures. The army also created some of the first American sex education films, including *Fit to Fight*. The message in all of this material was that extramarital sexual activity was simply not tolerated in the United States military—and since there were no married couples living in the training camps, there would simply be no sex for the enlisted soldier.

Class D of ASHA's plan focused on providing medical care for soldiers infected with STIs. Doctors in military hospitals were to be trained in how to treat STIs, and the correct medicines were to be made available. This included prompt use of a relatively new drug called Salvarsan, an effective arsenical treatment for syphilis that had been developed in 1910 by a German scientist named Paul Ehrlich.[6] As historian Patricia Spain Ward explains, despite some American hesitancies about the drug, the wartime need for treatment led to "the army and navy [being able] to proceed with Salvarsan therapy as soon as they acquired supplies." This was in stark contrast to many civilian facilities, where "patients with syphilis had been systematically excluded from hospitals and dispensaries for many decades."[7] Soldiers were also instructed to report their STIs to the military.

Only Class C of ASHA's plan elicited controversy: "prophylactic measures against venereal diseases." During this time, prophylaxis—referring to prevention or early treatment of STIs—meant a soldier would go to a "prophylactic station" after a sexual encounter. There, he would be supervised as he injected silver salt into his urethra and applied calomel ointment to his penis in an attempt to minimize infection.[8] For many, especially within the military, such measures seemed like an obviously necessary aspect of the campaign against STIs. Military leaders strongly believed that, despite their best efforts, their men would find a way to have sex; they had before, and there was nothing to suggest they wouldn't now.[9] But for those who were committed to the value of abstinence for its own sake—many of whom were in ASHA—prophylaxis seemed like a slippery slope.

How was it consistent, those moralists queried, to on the one hand profess that there was no place for sexual activity in the American military, and on the other to provide medical measures to curb the effects of that activity? The provision of prophylaxis, in their minds, was tantamount to encouraging extramarital sex. As Baltimore social hygienist Edith

Houghton Hooker put it in an April 1918 essay for ASHA's own *Journal of Social Hygiene:* "It is impossible from the point of view of the men to set the stamp of governmental disapproval upon [sexual] incontinence, if, at the same time, the government officially sanctions it."[10]

As something of a compromise, early recommendations advised that soldiers should "be informed of the fact that there are prophylactic measures that reduce the dangers of venereal infection" and that prophylaxis should be readily available in regimental infirmaries. Stations would also be prepared to give soldiers advice and education. "But," the recommendations went on, "any spirit of levity or condoning sexual promiscuity should be discouraged, and obscene stories or objectionable conduct should be rigidly repressed."

AMERICANS ABROAD

This milquetoast—and probably unenforceable—solution may have been okay on the home front, but when American troops were actually sent abroad to fight, rates of STIs rose. This hardly came as a surprise to military experts, who knew that American Expeditionary Forces (AEF), especially in France, would find it difficult to abstain from the government-regulated brothels there, despite official prohibitions against using them. It was, writes Allan Brandt in his book *No Magic Bullet,* "a clash of sexual cultures."[11]

Whereas America was enshrouded in—to use Morrow's words from a decade earlier—a "conspiracy of silence" around sex, France was much more open. France and other countries had accepted sex work as part of their cultures and economies, and worked to make it as healthful as possible, with inspections and medical examinations for all registered sex workers. As Kimberley Reilly wrote, in the *Journal of the Gilded Age and Progressive Era,* "French and British approaches to limiting the spread of venereal disease accepted that soldiers would be sexually active, understood prostitutes and promiscuous women to be the source of this contagion, and attempted to regulate soldiers' contact with such women."[12] The American approach, however, was far more draconian. Troops were supplied with fliers that read, in part, "Do not let booze, a pretty face, a shapely ankle make you forget!! The AEF must not take the European disease to America. You must go home clean!!"[13]

This message was sure to appease ASHA, but American military officers were skeptical of this approach, and internationally, the tactic was derided. As Reilly explains, "During the war . . . Europeans . . . ascribed the motivations of U.S. policymakers to a prudish moralism that was uniquely American."[14]

When the AEF arrived in France, officials invited the American troops to make use of the brothels, which they did—flyers notwithstanding. An article in the journal *Medical History* reports that "disease rates at French base ports climbed quickly above 190 and one journalist recalled seeing American soldiers lined up eight deep at the doorways of one port city brothel."[15] In response, higher-ups simply implemented stricter rules and punishments. Regulations made any locations with brothels strictly off-limits, and further, E. H. Beardsley reports, "any man who contracted venereal disease became liable for court martial and any commander failing to hold his unit's disease rate to a minimum risked losing his command."[16]

What the American military absolutely did not do was provide condoms for its soldiers. This was a notable departure from the policy of all other countries active in the war—except for Britain, which also refrained.[17]

In the end, STIs inflicted casualties on Americans on a huge scale. In 1928, the US government reported that, during the Great War, "venereal diseases, as a class[,] . . . exceeded the total number of men killed and wounded in action by approximately 100,000," and was the fourth-most likely category of disease to cause "permanent disability, requiring discharge from the service" after tuberculosis, valvular heart disease, and mental deficiency.[18]

However, one unequivocal public health success did come out of World War I: the US government was convinced that STIs were a serious issue, and there was now the political will to address it. On January 2, 1918, less than a year before the end of the war, Surgeon General Rupert Blue sent a letter to health officers in each state, noting, "It is evident that the prevention of venereal infections in the military population is largely dependent on the degree with which these infections are prevented in the civil community." Thus, he instructed the "civil health authorities" to take on "the duty of forcefully attacking the venereal problem upon the basis of the control of communicable disease."[19] This was what Morrow had urged from the beginning. Because of this letter, STIs became reportable in twenty-two states and seven cities. Civilian communities increased their public health initiatives: thirty-seven boards of health implemented or planned to implement placards and exhibits to educate their public about sexually transmitted infections, often using exhibits modified from the army.

The government also invested money in the problem via the Chamberlain-Kahn Act, enacted on July 9, 1918. Among other things, the act created the Interdepartmental Hygiene Board, which comprised various military secretaries and surgeons general, as well as the surgeon general of the United States Public Health Service (USPHS). The board was responsible for regulating federal funds provided for social hygiene work. Much of that work would be educational. "Ultimately," a report from the board read, "education and the information which it carries will have a very much larger influence upon the prevention of these diseases . . . than will any other influence."[20]

SEX ED LECTURES ON THE HOME FRONT

During and after the war, there was indeed a growing acceptance of sex ed. A Pennsylvania doctor named Sina Stratton expressed this in August 1918 while addressing the Lancaster County chapter of the Woman's Christian Temperance Union (WCTU). She explained that "the problem of morality is of national size [and] to safeguard the men at the front, we must educate the civil population at home."[21]

Stratton had been lecturing about hygiene since 1913, mainly through the WCTU. Founded in 1874, the group was focused primarily on temperance and prohibition, but was also deeply concerned with labor, prison reform, and suffrage. Much in the way that the ASSMP believed that sex work was the root of all STIs, the WCTU believed that alcohol was the root of many evils. By 1919, Dr. Stratton had become the "superintendent of moral education" for the Pennsylvania WCTU. She traveled the state, lecturing at church groups and public schools.

Around the country, educators were beginning to come to a consensus about the importance of sex ed in public schools. In February 1919, a conference of educators from Maryland, Delaware, Virginia, and the District of Columbia met in Raleigh, North Carolina, to discuss the subject of sex ed in high schools. There, they resolved that "sex education should be included in the high school programs of the United States."[22] The federal government agreed. In November 1919, at the Pennsylvania Educational Congress, the assistant educational director of the USPHS, E. F. Van Buskirk, gave a speech entitled "The Aim and Scope of Sex Education in the High School." [23]

The first, and less desirable, approach to sex ed, Van Buskirk explained, was what he called "emergency" measures: lecturers who gave one-off talks to schools. In such cases, the government could supply slides and films as a stop-gap measure "until such time as the regular teachers themselves can shoulder this responsibility." The preferable approach, Van Buskirk said, was a reliable program of "permanent" sex ed. He echoed Morrow's position that there should be no "specialized course" in the subject, but that the lessons of sex ed should instead be inserted into "biology, general science, domestic science, physiology and hygiene, physical education, sociology, and agriculture." Van Buskirk also emphasized the importance of morality in these lessons. The most important thing of all, he explained, was "to establish certain habits of thought and action which will be in harmony with the ideals and standards of conduct which the experience of mankind had found to be best."

The prospect of including sex ed in schools was made more possible by federal funding through the Chamberlain-Kahn act, which the USPHS had used in part to create fifty pamphlets or "venereal disease bulletins," sorted into six sets. One of those sets, called The Problem of Sex Education in Schools, was geared specifically toward educators and covered topics addressed in the pamphlets *The Place of Sex Education in Biology and General Science* and *The Problem of Sex Education in Schools.*[24] Forty-one states had purchased the complete set of USPHS pamphlets, and 77,298 total requests for pamphlets came from ministers, educators, industries, libraries, and other interested parties.[25] The USPHS also used three films—*How Life Begins* (1916), specifically intended for high school students, and *Fit to Win* and *End of the Road* (both 1919), wartime films geared toward adults—as educational devices. And there was a manual in the works about how high schools should introduce sex ed into their curricula.

Despite Van Buskirk's enthusiasm, there was still much work to be done. In January 1920, the USPHS and the US Bureau of Education sent a questionnaire to 12,025 "accredited and partially accredited high schools" and received 6,488 responses. Within those responses, more than half of the schools reported that they provided no sex ed at all. Of those that did, the majority (1,633) provided the less desirable "emergency sex education" in the form of one-off lectures or film screenings. Only 1,005 schools were following the USPHS' best practices, integrating sex ed "incidentally in the subjects of the regular curriculum."[26] It made sense that in early stages, the "emergency" approach would be the more common one. Dr. Stratton of the WCTU had become one of those outside lecturers herself by this point and, in 1920, was also appointed the "Supervisor of Health Instruction in the Normal schools and public schools" by the Pennsylvania superintendent of public instruction.[27]

Stratton clearly believed in a vision of sex hygiene that joined morals and medicine, just as Van Buskirk had suggested. She believed in the value of giving students basic information, while stressing the value of self-control, which she thought was the "keynote to the well ordered life."[28] She was also committed to promoting the "well born"—essentially, eugenics.

Throughout the 1910s and early '20s, eugenics had become even more popular and well regarded. In the Eugenics Record Office, administrators created biased surveys and reports that were, according to historian Garland E. Allen, "presented to the United States Congress in 1922 and 1923 as evidence that the inferior sub-Alpine, Mediterranean, and Jewish races were genetically inferior to the Nordics, and thus placed a larger burden on society."[29]

Eugenicists, creating this incorrect and biased hierarchy, thus also believed that parenthood should be reserved for those who would not put a burden on society—those who had the so-called strongest genes. As a 1923 essay entitled "Parenthood and Race Culture," from the *Journal of Heredity*, explained, "The emphasis [of eugenics] should be laid . . . on the desirability . . . of increasing the numbers of the fit. . . . It is of . . . importance to breed abundantly from the good stock."[30]

Stratton's work fell directly in line with this way of thinking, with a strong emphasis on parenthood. Stratton argued that schools failed in preparing young people for the most important job they would ever have—the career of parenthood—and that it was a solemn duty to do so. "To appropriate money to take care of sickly children after they come, is like locking the barn after the horse is stolen. We must attack the evil at its source, and train the children in the duties and responsibilities of parenthood," she argued. "It is the right of every child," she went on, "to be well born."[31]

Dr. Stratton's brand of sex ed also had a generalized—and so largely uncontroversial—religious element to it. At the same Pennsylvania educational congress that E. F. Van Buskirk addressed, she stated: "It is the plan of the Creator that in order that life . . . may continue . . . there must be a union of two elements."

DR. STRATTON ARRIVES IN POTTSVILLE

In December 1921, Dr. Stratton gave a sex ed talk to eleven- and twelve-year-old public school students in Pottsville, Pennsylvania.[32] For her, it was a lecture, perhaps like any other. But then came the complaints. According to the *Morning News*, multiple students went home that day and bombarded "their parents with embarrassing questions on matters which they had always regarded as taboo."[33] The parents turned to Pottsville's school board to express their displeasure.

As early as 1915, sex hygiene experts had identified the school board as the place where the fate of sex ed would be decided. That year, Ira S. Wile, a doctor and member of the board of education in New York City, had noted that school boards, which were "essentially lay bodies assuming an educational function," tended to be more conservative than educators attempting to change school curricula, and it was important to keep them in mind when doing so.[34] In the case of Pottsville, the school board responded to the complaints about Dr. Stratton's lecture with quick action in favor of the parents: they put a blanket ban on all lecturers sent by the state, as Stratton had been, unless the superintendent had been told beforehand what materials the lectures would contain.

That was that. Despite sex ed being supported by the federal government, teachers groups, and other advocacy organizations, a few parents were all it took to ban "outside" lecturers from the Pottsville schools. And the state, which employed Stratton, did not defend her. Pennsylvania's head of the Bureau of Health Education, Dr. C. H. Keene, with the air, perhaps, of someone trying to keep their hands clean of a messy situation, stated that the ban was "a matter entirely up to the local school authorities" and was "entirely outside our control."[35] They tepidly noted that "no reports of objections" to Dr. Stratton's lectures had "been received by the division from any parts of the state," but in the end, Dr. Stratton was the only one to defend her work.[36]

She maintained, in her defense, that young people often got the wrong information from their peers, so there was "no harm in learning the story of life in school."[37] And the state continued to employ her—she was not out of a job. By February 1922, she was lecturing again. That month, she traveled to Wellsboro, where the school board noted that "general appreciation of her work has been expressed in the schools."[38]

However, the Pottsville incident highlighted the importance of school boards: they held true power, and could be either trigger-happy or gun-shy, especially when it came to controversial issues. In 1923, the school board in Madison, Wisconsin, for example, banned sex ed outright, noting that "no objection would be raised if parents wished to take their children to lectures on sex subjects, but the members refused to take the responsibility of recommending such lectures."[39]

CHAPTER 4

THOMAS PARRAN AND "THE NEXT GREAT PLAGUE TO GO"

The postwar boom in sex ed—including such emergency lecturers as Dr. Stratton—was being fueled, and financed, mainly by the Interdepartmental Social Hygiene Board, the body that had been established in 1918 by the Chamberlain-Kahn Act to "allocate funding to universities, associations, and States for the control, prevention, and treatment of venereal diseases in response to the alleged war-time escalation of the diseases."[1] The board worked directly with colleges and universities to establish hygiene departments. They also funded scientific research and allocated social hygiene funding for individual states.[2] For this latter effort, many states created social hygiene bureaus to coordinate such work.

But only a few years after the war, in 1922, the federal treasury stopped funding the board, and it was terminated entirely in 1923. Each state, then, was left to make its own choices about how best to continue the work of social hygiene. The various paths they took revealed much about Americans' relationship to sex, punishment, education, and sin.

VIRGINIA'S CHOICE

In Virginia, all social hygiene work was placed under the aegis of the state board of health, the body that created the rules and regulations for the Department of Health. From this shift came a new set of choices. Where would the board put its focus in social hygiene: in education about, care of, or prevention of STIs? It was something of the nature of bureaucracy that choosing to prioritize one meant shortchanging the others.

Nationally, sex work remained the ultimate scapegoat for STIs, so social hygiene efforts often revolved around repressing it through detaining sex workers (a key piece of the Social Hygiene Board's work) and other punitive measures. The First World War had incited many state laws and regulations around sex work. As Michael Imber notes, in a paper published in the *Journal of Educational Administration and History*, in the two years following the 1917 Draft Act, "hundreds of new measures interdicting brothels, prostitutes, pimps, solicitation, frequenting prostitutes, fornications, and adultery, raising the age of consent, creating reform schools for teenage prostitutes, making venereal disease a bar to marriage, and requiring physicians to report venereal disease became law in various states."[3] But, Imber also notes, though the USPHS claimed that by the end of the war "more than 90 per cent of red light districts" had been closed, "many reopened soon after the hostilities ceased."[4]

So, sex work was still a real and present concern in the United States, and in Virginia specifically, even though it had been illegal for a decade by 1926.[5] But addressing it was not a job for the state's Department of Health, the commissioner argued, because the work to be done around sex work was disciplinary, and their department was never "intended to be a punitive agency," and further, they believed that sex work could only be eliminated "through imprisonment."[6] Strike that option. Furthermore, because the Department of Health's work in disease control was defined as "preventative, not curative," they determined they could not operate any clinics. Strike that option too. What, then, was left for a Department of Health's Bureau of Social Hygiene to do? All that was left was education. But that led to more questions, like how such education would take place, through what channels, and by whom.

In 1926, the three-person Virginia Bureau of Social Hygiene (made up of a director, educational director, and stenographer) explained their "chief objective," which was not unlike Ella Flagg Young's early attempt to educate parents. They first wanted to "fit parents and teachers to give such information . . . that will help to save [boys and girls] from some of the tragedies that are caused by ignorance of the real purpose of sex in life."[7] To accomplish this, the state funded "lectures to mothers," sharing lessons that they would in turn, hopefully, teach their children. The lectures were on "the life history of plants, fishes, fowls and animals as well as human life, and the different periods of child life from infancy through adolescence."[8] And as had become standard nationwide, Virginia had purchased government pamphlets with titles like *Keeping Fit*; *Sex Education at Home*; *Sex Education in the School*; *Happy, Healthy Womanhood*; and *Facts About Venereal Diseases*. Those that were relevant to mothers were provided at the lectures.[9]

As for the content of these lectures, historian Allan Brandt explains that, in the relatively short interval between the end of the war and 1926, "the arguments of expediency [around STIs] now held little weight; public health gave way to concerns about public morals." The USPHS even went so far as to withdraw "all its anti-venereal films." One of its most popular ones, *Fit to Fight*, was deemed obscene in New York State. Messaging shifted away from STI prevention to moral concerns about "the family" and the ways in which it was being harmed by "improper" sex. A 1926 report from the Virginia Bureau of Social Hygiene reads: "Some of the most unhappy conditions in the lives of human beings have come from ignorance of the higher and finer ideals of sex."[10] The report cited illegitimacy and divorce as some of those unhappy conditions.

And Virginia was absolutely seeing these so-called problems. In 1924, the state registrar of Vital Statistics recorded that for white Virginians, "out of wedlock" births accounted for "about one out of every forty-four births." For Black Virginians, a much higher "one . . . birth out of seven" was recorded.[11] In the same time frame, the state had seen 28,814 divorces, many of which the report noted were "brought about by sex problems." To fix this, some social hygienists began framing their work as being about training young people for marriage. This was happening not just in Virginia but nationwide. "To lessen the number of divorces and so increase the sum of human happiness," sociologist and professor George Elliott Howard wrote in 1921, "it is needful to lessen the number of marriages which ought never to be formed. To do that, social conditions—the basic causes of such wrong mating—must be improved, chiefly through efficient education for marriage and family life."[12] This was an early seed of what would come to be known as "family life education."

MAURICE BIGELOW AND SOCIAL HYGIENE

And so, "marriage training" became a centerpiece of American sex ed. The importance of preserving the family was also bolstered by the academic subject of anthropology, which had emerged in the 1920s. One of its ideas was the theory that there was a spectrum of civility along which various different cultures could be placed. The "high" cultures were evolved, enlightened, white, educated—and happened to look a lot like the anthropologists who were creating these frameworks in the first place. One of the hallmarks of these "high" cultures was marriage. As sociologist John Cooper erroneously—but popularly for the time— explained, "The return to the monogamous ideal becomes increasingly patent among nearly all peoples who have attained to higher civilized culture."[13] This idea was in accordance with the theory of social evolution, which held that societies and cultures evolve like organisms do. However, the theory assumes the existence of a hierarchy of societies for which there is no actual evidence, and—like eugenics—the theory was steeped in racism and ethnocentrism.

Cooper and his milieu regarded monogamy as "the marital form in closest accord with rational human nature and needs." This lent anthropological support to marriage training as a legitimate and necessary component of sex ed, one that could address rising rates of divorce and other apparent social ills.

And so, by the mid-1920s, every aspect of human relations, it seemed, connected to sex education in some way (or vice versa). In 1924, Maurice Bigelow defined sex ed as

> all educational measures which in any way may help young people to prepare to meet the problems of life that have their center in the sex instinct and inevitably come in some form into the experience of every normal human being. These problems extend . . . from simple little matters of personal sex health to the exceedingly complicated physical and social and psychical problems that concern successful marriage and family relationships.[14]

It was a capacious definition, and Bigelow and others created capacious curricula to match. The federal government supported these projects, too, even if it didn't supply as much funding as it had in the prior decade. In 1922, the government released a publication titled *High Schools and Sex Education: A Manual of Suggestions on Education Related to Sex.* It was a joint effort between the Bureau of Education, Surgeon General Hugh S. Cumming, and social hygienist Benjamin Gruenberg. The project was initially undertaken by E. F. Van Buskirk. The manual set out a framework in which schools would teach social hygiene. In general, the manual suggested that extensive lessons of sex ed be taught in three different ways: through information, interpretation, and inspiration.

The *information* aspect was what people most often thought of when they thought of sex ed: the facts of sex and reproduction, presented most commonly in science classes like botany, zoology, biology, and physiology, or in emergency lectures like Dr. Stratton's.

The *interpretation* of sex was to take place in courses like literature, history, sociology, and psychology. In these classes, students were to learn about "the home as an institution," "illegitimacy," divorce, prostitution, and other sociosexual aspects of life.

The third arm of sex ed, *inspiration*, was the most amorphous and seemed to ask the most of the school as an institution. Inspiration referred to role models—be they real or fictitious, living or dead—who showed students the values of living by "proper" sex standards. Properly deployed, Gruenberg wrote, these role models would show students "chivalry, service, responsibility, fair play, self-direction, social well-being." Also related to this final arm of sex education were extracurricular activities: sports and clubs, which would allow for the genders to interact in appropriate ways.[15]

The manual was well promoted, mentioned in *School Life*, the *Journal of Education*, and the *Eugenics Review*, along with other government publications.[16] The numbers available did show that, nationwide, sex ed was becoming more common in American high schools, whether as a direct result of the manual or independently of it.

"ONE OF THE MOST IMPORTANT STEPS"

It was not surprising, then, that by 1926 in Virginia, the educational director of the Bureau of Social Hygiene, Mrs. Fereba Croxton, considered "the teaching of sex education in the elementary and high schools as one of the most important steps in social hygiene activities." By June 1927, Dr. Ennion Williams had concluded that the work of social hygiene was no longer properly under the purview of the health department. In his report to the governor, he explained that the activities they had been doing, while useful, were "educational rather than health." Consequently, he wrote, he "would be pleased if they were placed with the Department of Education."[17] He proposed that schools would undertake the social hygiene work, and the Department of Health could consult as needed.

In Virginia, as in all states in the nation, sex ed was already being taught in public schools, albeit unevenly. A 1927 survey on the subject, which received replies from 35.7 percent of the state's 339 senior high schools, found that 33 percent taught integrated sex ed, and 14 percent implemented emergency sex ed.[18] About 53 percent of respondents, however, reported no sex ed in their schools.[19] Ideally, Williams's proposal would have led to more—and more effective—sex ed in schools around the state. But when school officials caught wind of the proposed transfer of responsibility, he reflected later, "opposition developed."

Attempting to diffuse the early opposition, Dr. Williams wrote to school officials on every level—superintendents, principals, and college presidents—to try to understand where the hesitancy was coming from. Perhaps there was a simple explanation and a ready solution. Instead, he was met with a surprising response. School administrators, he discovered, were not against sex ed: The surveyed superintendents, he reported, "with few exceptions, considered sex education valuable." What they were opposed to was teaching it in their schools—thirty-one had responded that they were "unequivocally opposed," twenty-nine had "grave doubts or reservations," and "only eight flatly endorsed" the subject.[20] Similar findings were reported from high school principals.

Dr. Williams found this a puzzling conundrum: "Most of them," he wrote of the administrators, "said that sex education was valuable, but a majority . . . did not want the subject in schools."[21]

Dr. Williams brought these findings to the state board of health. Nearly everyone, he explained, seemed to agree that sex education was desirable, and nearly no one wanted to be responsible for implementing it. In the end, the compromise was to ask from Virginia's General Assembly a relatively small sum of money—$2,500—to be spent on literature, approved both by the Department of Health and the Department of Education, which would then be "distributed in conformity with plans approved by these departments."

A few years later, in the *Annual Report of the State Department of Health* for the year ending June 30, 1931, Dr. Roy K. Flannagan lambasted this arrangement, describing the current state of the bureau as "simply an agency for the distribution of approved literature to inquiring individuals and groups." He went even further, calling it the "vestigial remains of a once highly developed functioning bureau combatting venereal disease by all approved methods."[22] And STIs still needed combatting in Virginia. An investigation made by the USPHS in 1927 had found in eighteen Virginia counties, "the combined case rate for gonorrhea and syphilis per thousand of population proved to be 7.07 . . . 8,475 cases of these diseases being under treatment by physicians in these counties on a single day."

Considering those numbers, Dr. Flannagan urged the educational work of the bureau to be "restored as soon as possible, as a preliminary to comprehensive attack on the venereal diseases as soon as the opportunity is propitious." However, by the next year, the Bureau of Social Hygiene had been eliminated entirely, its work later subsumed by the epidemiology department.

SEX ED ACROSS THE NATION

Other states had different approaches to the reality of decreased federal funding for STI control. In 1927, the USPHS, along with the United States Bureau of Education, conducted a survey on the status of sex ed in American high schools as something of a follow-up to a 1920 survey on the same topic. A questionnaire was sent to 16,937 principals, and 5,745 responses were recorded. They found that integrated sex ed had become more widespread: 29 percent of high schools were teaching the subject in an integrated fashion, as opposed to 16 percent in 1920. Correspondingly, emergency sex ed had decreased, with only 16 percent of schools using this option, down from 25 percent in 1920. Biology classes reigned supreme as the place where most sex ed took place, where the authors of the study noted that "reproduction, internal secretions, seminal emissions, venereal diseases, and eugenics and heredity" were often taught.[23] The least commonly taught topics were "the physiology of seminal emissions, menstruation, and internal secretions of sex glands."

The most widely covered sex hygiene topic was "eugenics and heredity," taught in 78 percent of the 1,665 reporting schools. This was followed by reproduction (69 percent), and "social aspects" (51 percent). So, it seemed that "marriage training" aspects of sex ed were the more palatable ones, even as books like *High Schools and Sex Education* urged open conversations about such things as STIs. "In the discussion of infectious disease, gonorrhea and syphilis may be mentioned," the text explained, "by name among the others without prejudice."[24] But these best practices were not routinely being followed.

In part, this may have been due to the overall cultural shift in emphasis from STI control to morals. In 1951, a government publication called *The National Venereal Disease Control Program*, published by the USPHS, explained: "The First World War brought home clearly to the people of the United States that venereal disease was a very present hazard to their well-being," and that, "with the war's end . . . the alarm generated by venereal disease among selectees faded away. 'Back-to-normalcy' was the temper of the times, and venereal disease control measures did not fit into this picture."[25] But there may have been a need to keep that alarm bell sounding.

THOMAS PARRAN'S CALL TO STAMP OUT SYPHILIS

"By the early 1930s," Allan Brandt reported, "the most frequently cited figures suggested that approximately one out of every ten Americans suffered from syphilis."[26] This appeared to be an increase from the 1920s, and a sure indication that STIs were far from under control. The head of the Venereal Disease Division of the United States Public Health Service, Dr. Thomas Parran, knew that something needed to be done. It was much the same problem that Dr. Morrow had faced three decades earlier. But now the experience of the military and the Interdepartmental Social Hygiene Board had shown that it was possible to control STIs, at least to some degree—and treatments, including Salvarsan, were only getting more effective. But the shame and stigma that Morrow had noted during the turn of the century—along with outright ignorance—were still preventing people from seeking treatment. In addition, the course of treatment was still expensive, and physicians themselves still thought of STIs as less worthy of study than other specialties. "Only one in ten cases of syphilis," Allan Brandt noted, "received treatment during the early stages of the disease when a cure was possible."[27]

Parran, who became surgeon general in April 1936, wanted to bring greater attention to STIs, in many ways recreating the work that Morrow had done decades earlier. In July 1936, he wrote an article for a magazine called *Survey Graphic*. The cover of that issue featured a photo of Parran sitting at a desk, his hands folded, his eyes intense, his graying hair contrasting with his dark eyebrows and mustache. The caption read: "Surgeon General Thomas Parran calls on Americans to stamp out SYPHILIS, the next great plague to go."

He wrote clearly and plainly, with neither euphemism nor pleasantry. "Syphilis is a contagious disease," he explained. "It is caused by an organism known as the spirochete, which may attack and destroy any organ or tissue in the body."[28] He made the stakes known: compared to car accidents, tuberculosis, measles, and infantile paralysis, syphilis endangered many more people. But it had a cure, which made the goal of "stamping it out" seem utterly possible. Other countries were already far ahead of the US on this front. In 1935, Parran wrote, the entire country of Sweden had recorded just 431 cases of syphilis. That same year, in the month of April alone, upstate New York had documented "21,984 cases under treatment" and 1,836 new cases diagnosed. Sweden and upstate New York, he noted, had nearly the same exact population. So, why was Sweden so much healthier?

Sweden, for one, did not share America's widespread belief that it was impolite to talk about STIs. America, despite the social hygiene movement that was now more than thirty years old, was still reluctant to give STIs the same public health treatment as other illnesses. Scandinavian countries on the other hand, Parran reported, undertook public health education campaigns about STIs. "In the main square of Copenhagen," he wrote, by way of example, "along with advertisements of department stores, movie houses, parks and other attractions of the city, is posted the list of names, places and hours of all venereal disease clinics."

Parran noted that, in America, the word *syphilis* was "omitted by command of the broadcasting company" during some radio talks, with no such standards for other maladies. In addition, state guidelines—including sex ed guidelines—precluded "free discussion" of STIs. This kind of restriction made it "very difficult to teach people to avoid syphilis, to look out for early symptoms, and to get treatment when such symptoms are observed."

This polite silence had another major drawback—a financial one. "Philanthropists," Parran wrote, "have been afraid to donate funds for research in syphilis, though such funds have been readily available for almost every other cause under the sun from leprosy to whooping cough. By the same token, legislators have been loath to appropriate for it." And indeed, both leprosy and whooping cough were handled by public health authorities in the United States with none of the squeamishness seen around STIs. The public health campaign around STIs had ended with the war—and silence was again the ethos of the day.

So much of all this silence was still built on the longstanding belief that contracting an STI represented a moral failing, and simply did not happen to "nice" or "good" people. Parran, like Morrow thirty years earlier, now stressed that there were many *innocent* "victims" of syphilis, including a large number of congenital cases. He urged Americans to "free our minds of the medieval concept that syphilis is the just reward of sin [and to] deal with it and discuss it as we would any other highly communicable disease."

Even as Parran echoed Morrow on this point, in other important ways he also struck out on a new path. Whereas Morrow's work had presented moral and medical solutions as complementary, Parran saw the two as related but distinct. Yes, syphilis was transmitted through sex. Yes, that sex was often regarded as "immoral"—but Parran thought that exclusively recommending abstinence was simply not practical. He viewed the problem as a doctor, not a moralist. Parran argued that Americans must test widely and relentlessly for syphilis. Then should come treatment, contract tracing—"examine for syphilis [in] the family and all other contacts of the syphilis patient," then preventing congenital syphilis by blood tests "before marriage and early in each pregnancy"—and last, of course, education. "The facts about it," he wrote of syphilis, "must be known to all the people. . . . Our children will hold us criminally careless and incompetent if, with the means at hand, we fail to end this scourge within our generation."

It was a groundbreaking article. It placed the responsibility for eliminating STIs in the hands of medical professionals rather than social hygienists. It also reached audiences that Morrow had never been able to access. His essay ran first in *Survey Graphic* and then in the popular magazine *Reader's Digest*, which had some five hundred thousand subscribers—a far different scope and reach than Morrow's 1904 *Social Diseases and Marriage*. In October 1936, Parran was on the cover of *Time* magazine.[29] And in August 1937, Parran breached the last publishing taboo: women's journals. The *Ladies, Home Journal* finally allowed venereal disease coverage when it published an article cowritten by Parran and microbiologist Paul de Kruif entitled "We Can End This Sorrow." This was news in itself.

THE NATIONAL VENEREAL DISEASE CONTROL ACT

In December 1936, for the first time since immediately following World War I, state boards of health received federal funding for STI control. Two years later, in May 1938, President Franklin Roosevelt signed the National Venereal Disease Control Act into law. It allocated $15 million over a three-year period for venereal disease "prevention, treatment, and control . . . for the purpose of making studies, investigations, and demonstrations to develop more effective measures of preventions, treatment, and control of the venereal diseases."[30]

It was a surprisingly popular piece of legislation. Even the American Medical Association supported it while simultaneously battling proposals for national health insurance (citing fears of encroaching socialized medicine). "Only organized religious groups raised any significant objections to the bill," Allan Brandt wrote.[31] ASHA—despite never having been strictly a religious group—felt a strong measure of ambivalence about the bill. As times continued to change, ASHA remained almost stodgy in its unwavering emphasis on abstinence.

As a result of the act, people began getting tested and seeking treatment more frequently. Individual states also created more guidelines meant to curb infection. "By the end of 1938," Brandt explained, "twenty-six states had enacted provisions prohibiting the marriage of infected individuals."[32] These states required couples to undergo blood tests for syphilis before marrying. Although in retrospect, the tests were little more than ritual, the requirement itself suggested a new seriousness in the fight against STIs. Other states also began to require pregnant people to take blood tests, leading to an impressive drop in infant mortality rates.

Parran's work also put significant pressure on sex ed experts, who found themselves having to address some of the concerns he had raised. Parents were in a tizzy, both to learn that STIs were such a problem, and also to realize that their children might be taught about them.

SEX EDUCATION OR SOCIAL HYGIENE?

On October 20, 1938, Maurice A. Bigelow, who by then was serving as the chairman of the National Education Committee of ASHA, addressed some of these concerns via the New York City radio station WNYC. In many ways, it was the speech of someone hoping to quell an anxious audience: we can picture among his listeners a worried mother, a father with a furrowed brow. He spoke to the aftershocks of Parran's great public health initiatives. "The national health drive against the venereal diseases," Bigelow explained, "leads many parents and teachers to ask how much stressing of these diseases is proposed or in progress in American schools."[33] He was quick to assure his audience that "the venereal diseases are not going to be overstressed in the regular programs of high school and general colleges. . . . The topics of greatest interest in the sex education programs are centered in normal life relations of men and women."

Bigelow believed that this type of sex ed—which focused on "normal life relations"—would still prevent syphilis. After all, abstinence before marriage was the best way to avoid STIs, and obviated the need for the obscener lessons of so-called venereal disease education. For this reason, he urged the use of the term *social hygiene* rather than *sex education*, which was becoming more popular and seemed to connote an emphasis on STIs. In this moment, Biglow effectively drew the line between medicine and morals more boldly than ever before—for those who knew where to look.

While Parran believed that medicine would rule the day when it came to disease prevention and that attempting to change morals wasn't particularly worthwhile, Bigelow and the social hygienists of ASHA doubled down on morals as the best prophylaxis. But Bigelow was not unsympathetic to Parran's project overall, and he even believed it could be valuable for the work of social hygiene. "If and when the national anti-venereal drive is decidedly successful," he wrote, "then it may be possible to popularize the fact that social hygiene means social health in all relations of the sexes and that it includes many problems of permanent significance which have no possible connection with the venereal disease."[34] But this nuance was lost on the popular media, as evidenced by headlines like the one in the *Press and Sun-Bulletin* out of Binghamton, New York, which read "Sex Education Courses Opposed by Dr. Bigelow."[35]

Despite their differences in approach, Parran and Bigelow shared one important omission: prophylaxis. As Allan Brandt put it, "Despite the emphasis on science and medicine that Parran's efforts engendered, chemical prophylaxis was seldom advocated. . . . Public health officials refused to encourage the use of condoms. . . . Even washing with soap and water after intercourse . . . never received the sanction of public health officials in their fight against venereal disease."[36]

In 1920, latex had been invented and was quickly used to make condoms. It was more stretchy than regular rubber and safer to manufacture. Joshua Gamson writes in the *Journal of the History of Sexuality* that following its introduction there was "a second revolution" in condoms (the first being after the vulcanization of rubber was discovered). "Sales increased enormously, and prices dropped. By the mid-1930s, [there were] fifteen major condom manufacturers . . . producing one and half million a day."[37]

But the Comstock Act was still standing, as were many of the "little Comstock" laws that states had enacted. These regulations meant that it was still illegal to mail condoms, and in several states, condoms were illegal to purchase or use. But by the 1930s, a series of court cases had clarified some important exceptions that made the laws far less potent.

In 1916, Margaret Sanger—the birth control activist who would go on to found Planned Parenthood—had brought forward a test case on the subject. That year, she and her sister opened a birth control clinic in the Brownsville neighborhood of Brooklyn, New York. There, they provided information about birth control and sex to those who asked for it, in flagrant disregard of New York's laws. Sanger was arrested, put on trial, and imprisoned.

Although she was found guilty by the lower court and the court of appeals, the judge in the latter case made an important clarification. Judge Frederick Crane reaffirmed that physicians could prescribe contraceptives—including condoms—to treat "disease," and he defined disease capaciously enough to include pregnancy. As Maria T. Vullo wrote in the Historical Society of the New York Court's periodical, this decision "enabled physicians to prescribe contraception for general health reasons."[38]

In the years after the Crane decision, Sanger continued her work. The singular birth control clinic that she had founded was more formally organized into the American Birth Control League (ABCL) in 1921. A guiding principle of the league was the desire that all children should be, as Sanger wrote, "conceived in love . . . born of the mother's conscious desire . . . and only begotten under conditions which render possible the heritage of health."[39] To attain those lofty goals, the ABCL organized birth control clinics, coordinated research on the subject, and educated the public on the importance of birth control.

Then, in 1936—the same year that Parran's article was published—Sanger was the force behind another test case, this one a challenge to the 1930 Tariff Act. As a newsletter from the Margaret Sanger Papers Project explains, the Tariff Act was "a direct descendent of the Comstock law, which prohibited the importation of contraceptives and contraceptive information."[40] To make the situation right for the case, Sanger arranged for a shipment of pessaries—diaphragms—from Japan to be shipped to a doctor who worked at the Birth Control Clinical Research Bureau that Sanger had established. The package was seized by US Customs because its contents impeded conception. However, Sanger and her lawyer, Morris Ernst, argued that because diaphragms could be used for a health purpose, not just to prevent pregnancy, the Tariff Act did not pertain to physicians.[41] In somewhat of a surprise to Sanger, she was victorious. The government appealed, and in the fall of 1936, just as Parran-mania was taking over, the case went to the US Circuit Court of Appeals. In December, the judge upheld the lower court's decision.

In effect, the decision, as the Margaret Sanger Papers Project newsletter tells us, "opened up the ports and mails to contraceptive trade and generally made it legal and acceptable for doctors to dispense birth control to married women."[42] Except in states where such laws were still taken seriously—Connecticut and Massachusetts most notably—"law officials and the courts treated the anti–birth control measures as antiquated and irrelevant" following this ruling.[43]

And so, Parran could have felt empowered to suggest to his readers that they ask their physicians about condoms as syphilis-prevention tools—an action that was now certainly legal. But he did not, and it is not entirely clear why. Allan Brandt noted that Parran's Catholicism may have "perhaps already pushed his morality to the breaking point through his campaign against venereal disease; on the issue of prophylaxis, he simply could go no further."[44] But it was not just Parran and his Catholicism that stayed mum on the subject of condoms, despite their legal status. In 1940, ASHA and USPHS put out a joint statement that downplayed any type of prophylaxis besides abstinence: "The prevention of syphilis and gonorrhea by chemical or mechanical means is supplementary to and not a substitute for the prophylaxis of these diseases by educational measures which employ ethical and religious motives," it read. "Educational, religious, sociologic and legal activities which tend to prevent exposure to infection are of great importance."[45]

CHAPTER 5

ELLSWORTH BUCK'S DRIVE TO EDUCATE NEW YORK CITY

In August 1938, Ellsworth Buck, the chair of the Committee on Buildings and Sites of the New York City Board of Education, became concerned about the new science syllabus that had been approved for the junior high schools. He wrote to the chair of the committee on instructional affairs, Johanna Lindlof, requesting that the syllabus "be referred back to the Board of Superintendents . . . primarily because of the section on Reproduction which . . . covers insects, flowers and birds but makes no mention whatever of mammals."[1]

Lindlof forwarded Buck's concerns to the superintendent of schools, Harold Campbell, so that the board of superintendents, which made decisions about curricula, could reexamine the syllabus. In November, the board of superintendents wrote back to Buck. They explained that the multiple committees originally involved in the curriculum's creation had actually "considered at great length" whether or not to include mammalian reproduction in their curriculum, and had ultimately decided to omit it, since "certain difficulties . . . might come in teaching the subject."[2] But after receiving Buck's letter, the board of superintendents had dutifully reconsidered. In October, they'd heard from the Committee on the Revision of Course of Study in Science, along with a number of science teachers from across the city. Some were in favor of the inclusion of mammalian reproduction, citing the idea that "a matter-of-fact discussion of the subject by a mature adult would have a good effect on the pupils." They also considered reports from the General Science

Committee and the General Committee on the Revision of Course of Study. But, they told Buck, they would not be changing their original stance. Most students, after all, would go on to take biology in senior high school—where mammalian reproduction was covered. By then, the thinking was, the students would be mature enough to handle the topic, and the teachers were more prepared to teach it.

The full board of education—comprised of seven people, including Buck—then took a roll call vote to approve the junior high school science curriculum as it stood. Five members voted in favor of it. Two voted against it. One was Buck himself, who explained that he didn't "believe the syllabus [did] an honest job."³ The other was Lindlof, the chairperson of the board.

"The children in our schools at the age of 13 are old enough," Lindlof said, "since they are studying the process of reproduction in the lower animals, to know the process of reproduction as far as mammals are concerned." Then she added, perhaps saying what no one else would: "There is absolutely no question of sex hygiene in this proposal." And then she went on further: "I think our children will be better children, cleaner children, better physically, morally and spiritually by facing the facts of life and knowing the truth about human beings." Without realizing it, Lindlof had stumbled on what many experts thought the very point of sex education *was*—to learn about human reproduction and, in so doing, improve themselves morally. But although Lindlof and Buck were outvoted and the syllabus passed, Buck wasn't done.

AN UNLIKELY CHAMPION OF SEX ED

Ellsworth Brewer Buck was born in Chicago, graduated from Dartmouth in 1914, and then trained at MIT. He moved to Staten Island in 1919, where he was the chairman of the board of the chewing gum company L. A. Dreyfus Co. He did not strike the profile of a sex ed pioneer. But the mammalian reproduction issue niggled at him. After the vote, he announced he was going to launch an investigation into the current state of sex ed in New York City. He had his secretary, Eugene R. Canudo, conduct "a thorough study of facts, figures and opinions" on the issue. In January 1939, Buck shared Mr. Canudo's report, *The Case for Rational Sex Instruction in New York City Schools*, with the board of education. The report, and the vast public health and social shortcomings that it documented, wouldn't have been surprising to the various doctors and social workers of New York City. But for the school board members, who had perhaps never thought about the challenges that sex posed to young people, it may have been eye-opening.

The report cited New York City's welfare commissioner, who had recorded "57 children born out of wedlock to girls 16 years or under" in 1938. It went on to explain that "three of these girls were 13 when their babies were born; one was 14; 18 were 15; and 35 were 16 years of age."[4] This was just the tip of the iceberg.

The report went on: The deputy police commissioner noted that Juvenile Aid Bureau statistics were underreported, but even the official numbers were shocking. Between May and October 1938, the New York Police Department had found four rape victims between the ages of thirteen and fifteen, and one under the age of thirteen. They had also documented thirty-eight "victims of sex offenses" aged eighteen and under. Three boys and three girls, ages sixteen through eighteen, had been found in "houses of prostitution." And just like STIs were underreported, these statistics almost certainly were too—meaning that the city was rife with young people being sexually victimized. And the old problem of STIs was found among youth, too. From January to September 1938, the New York City Health Department had identified 27,612 cases of syphilis and 9,724 of gonorrhea in people ages one through twenty-four.[5]

Canudo's report also cited a 1935 sociology book called *Girls on City Streets* by Rosamund and Jacob Goldberg, which focused on girls between the ages of eleven and sixteen who were working in the sex trades. The authors reported that these girls—victims, really—were "ignorant of the real meaning and consequences of certain actions and circumstances" and found "themselves involved in tragic situations which could easily have been avoided." If these girls, the Goldbergs argued, had been armed with information about what was actually being asked of them—sex acts that were, perhaps, referred to euphemistically, or even in plain terms, but without an explanation of the risks involved—they could have avoided finding themselves "on the street."

In all, it was a grim picture, medically and socially: gonorrhea and syphilis were affecting young people in particular, and the American family appeared to remain in deep peril, as evidenced by the rates of "illegitimate" children. And so, as had already become a pattern, those who were concerned about these facts thought about what could be done—and landed on sex ed. Canudo argued eloquently that school was the best venue for sex ed.

SCHOOLS: THE BEST PLACES TO DO THE WORK
"The school is the only agency which reaches all the children, regardless of color, creed or background under similar circumstances," Canudo wrote. "Its policies are uniformly determinable and may thus be made to represent the best thought of all the people. It is adaptable to new conditions and, by a re-education of its personnel, can prepare itself to meet new needs."[6]

Students themselves seemed eager for this education. A National Education Association (NEA) committee had, Canudo reported, asked twenty thousand high school students "to list the personal health problems they desired to have answered," and "a very large proportion of both boys and girls showed interest in problems dealing with sex." Further, a study among college seniors "recently found that, given the opportunity to report upon and criticize the instruction received in physiology and hygiene in high school and in college, these seniors complained of omission of matters concerning sex."

When it came to suggestions for how to implement such sex education, Canudo's report wasn't particularly innovative—and it didn't have to be. It simply outlined the information, interpretation, and inspiration method that had already been set forward by Benjamin Gruenberg in 1922. The report also recommended that the school's established courses in biology, physical education, and home economics be modified to include lessons on sex hygiene. In social studies and English classes, the stories of what happened when sex went wrong, or right, could provide a strong interpretive framework for students.

The report was strongly worded and had a clear point of view. It also showed that Buck's views had become stronger. Whereas a few months earlier he had asked merely for the inclusion of mammalian reproduction in junior high science classes, now he was coming out swinging for sex ed throughout New York's junior and senior high schools. He promised the board, "I shall ask the Committee on Instructional Affairs to give further consideration to this question at its next meeting." Still, Buck's cause might have remained confined to the board of education if the press hadn't caught wind of it.

MAKING HEADLINES

On January 31, 1939, the *Daily News* ran the headline "96 Unwed Mothers Under 16 Here in '38." Using Buck's report itself, along with the facts and figures it had cited, the article commented on the bleakness of the situation. It also reported that Buck had plans to "demand sex education in the city's junior and senior high schools at a meeting of the board's instructional affairs committee Thursday."[7] This turned a meeting of the instructional affairs committee of New York City's board of education into a newsworthy event. At the meeting, Buck gained a small success: the instructional affairs committee passed a resolution suggesting that the board of superintendents study Buck's report. But opposing voices soon mobilized.

The Teachers Alliance, a conservative interest group, sent a thirty-eight-page letter to the board of education, the superintendent, and the associate superintendent calling Buck's plan "reactionary in that it confuses mere information with character."[8] They also insisted that sex ed should be given only in the home by parents.

Another familiar opponent entered the fray: Catholics. *The Tablet,* a Catholic newspaper published by the Diocese of Brooklyn, ran an editorial ("from the managing editor's desk") in March claiming that "a school system which deprives the parent of the privilege and the responsibility of giving his child sex instruction is guilty of educational totalitarianism."[9] The editorial held that establishing sex ed would be a "clear infringement of religious rights of students and parents," because each religion has "definite viewpoints with regard to sex instruction." Parents, it went on, have the "natural right to dictate what their children should learn at school" and "they should be consulted as to the type of instruction their children are to receive."[10]

Even traditional sex ed advocates were wary of Buck's plan. The executive director of ASHA, Walter Clarke, suggested that a sex ed program be rolled out slowly, over the course of three years, and only in "selected public schools" on a trial basis.[11]

But Buck also found some full-throated support. Parent associations, which were organized by school, were a venue through which any proposal could gain popularity or be killed. They were—and are—yet another important voice for school boards to take into consideration when making decisions. The Parent Association of what was then Public School 103, located on Fourteenth Avenue in Brooklyn, adopted a resolution in March 1939 in favor of Buck's plan.[12] In the same month, the Parents Association at Seth Low Junior High School 96, also in Brooklyn, wrote a letter of support to Buck himself, saying, "We hope therefore that you will be successful in your campaign to extend education to a field in which the children are vitally interested and which affects their happiness in life."[13]

In May 1939, the controversy around Buck's proposal went national when he published Canudo's report with his commentary in an eminent magazine called the *American Mercury*. At this time, the magazine did not yet have the conservative and antisemitic slant that it would unfortunately take on in the 1940s. In the article, Buck drew a parallel between the controversy around sex ed and the controversy that had plagued the teaching of evolution since the Scopes Monkey Trial of 1925.

The trial had centered on a 1925 law in Tennessee that had outlawed teaching human evolution in state-funded schools. The ACLU, which was opposed to the law, manufactured a trial to challenge the law. John Scopes, a high school science teacher, had agreed to take part in the trial. In the end, he was found guilty of breaking the law.

The *American Mercury* had been particularly attentive to the trial, with its publisher H. L. Mencken firmly on the side of science. As such, Buck's commentary was particularly appropriate: "If the Tennesseans, by fiat of a group of legislators, are compelled to inform their students that men are made out of ribs, most educators in the remainder of the country are hardly better off: they are still not permitted to deny that babies are made out of cabbages."

He wasn't being foolish in his hopes for sex ed, he continued. "It would also be absurd to declare that the introduction of a course in mammalian biology in the junior high schools would instantly be followed by a drop in the illegitimacy rate, and the disease and rape rates that move with it. But it certainly would seem that the removal of the veils of mystery with which the subject of sex has been surrounded would do something to cut down on the 2,400 annual cases of child venereal disease in New York, or the 1,800 cases of unmarried motherhood under the age of fifteen in the country."[14]

The *American Mercury* brought more attention to Buck's fight, and in June, Superintendent Campbell appointed a joint committee on social hygiene to study the possibility of a full and ambitious sex ed program in New York public schools. The eight-person committee included three associate superintendents, four members of the board of education—including Buck and Johanna Lindlof—and one high school principal.[15]

This led to more opposition from *The Tablet*, which took to interrogating the motivations behind sex education and implying the worst: "What is behind this relentless urging? Is it an honest concern about the moral problems arising from sex ignorance? Is it a healthy interest in the welfare of the school children or is it just a morbid interest in sex?"[16] *The Tablet* also stirred up a Red Scare around sex ed: "Its inspiration is pure paganism, active atheism or irreligious communism. . . . Is this repeated pressure for sex education in New York City schools another manifestation of a drive against Christianity and Christian purity?"

But the social hygiene committee was undaunted. As they got to work, yet another notable American magazine took up the issue. In October 1939, *Forum and Century*, known for its format of presenting pro-and-con viewpoints on an issue, spotlighted sex ed. On the pro side was Buck: "It is only a matter of time before aroused public opinion will compel the introduction," he exhorted, "in every public-school curriculum in the country, of material which will enlighten children of high-school and junior-high-school age on the so-called 'facts of life.'"[17]

Taking the opposing view were two leaders of the Teachers Alliance of New York City, George J. Lent and Francis S. Moseley. They claimed that the "pedagogical difficulties" of teaching sex ed were so insurmountable that implementing it was simply not feasible. They also invoked another favorite myth of the anti–sex ed crowd: that sex ed was not actually concerned with character but with "hygiene," "not with ethical ideals but prophylaxis." What they had overlooked, however, was that Canudo and Buck's report *had* accounted for character training. The report held, for instance, that home economics classes could "impress the girls with the importance of so conducting themselves as to insure [sic] the best influence upon the thoughts and actions of members of the other sex with whom they come into contact in the course of daily and social life."

But this was apparently not interesting to Moseley and Lent, and the charge that sex ed was amoral was a particularly potent argument even as the social hygiene establishment had made it clear that when push came to shove, they chose morality over medicine.

In 1932, the *Report of the Subcommittee on Social Hygiene in Schools*, from a group that had convened at the White House Conference on Child Health and Protection, spoke directly to this question. "While sex education was first planned to solve health problems," the committee wrote, "the ultimate sex education must attempt to guide sexual conduct by moral principles."[18] And so, "sex ed"—as defined by the social hygienists who laid a great and rightful claim to it—was certainly not just fact-giving prophylaxis lessons.

Perhaps responding to this mounting press and controversy, New York's joint committee on social hygiene was dismantled in November, less than six months after it was assembled. The *Daily News* reported that school executives had instead delegated the work to the "curriculum committee of the Board of Superintendents." Eventually, that board decided to move responsibility from schools to the Department of Health.[19] It would be decades before New York City would officially require public school students to take sex ed.

CHAPTER 6

WORLD WAR II

B y late 1940, it was clear that the United States was going to enter World War II. The army, navy, and USPHS—recalling the high rates of STIs during the First World War—decided that they needed to prepare for another spike in the coming years, in both military and civilian settings. And so, they contracted ASHA again. The organization approached the situation in much the same way they had previously. ASHA's executive director, Walter Clarke, explained in November 1940 that their plan was "based on the familiar four-fold social hygiene program"—those "classes of attack" that ASHA had articulated during the First World War: "social measures to diminish sexual temptation," which included restricting soldiers' access to alcohol and sex workers; educating soldiers and civilians about STIs; providing medical care for enlistees who had contracted STIs; and (the one that had been the point of much controversy) providing prophylaxis for the soldiers. Despite the increasingly legal status of condoms, Clarke's 1940 report referenced only prophylactic stations and "early disinfection" by way of prophylactics.

Clarke noted that all of these measures would be "pointed up to meet the present emergency, that is, with the emphasis on health protection at a time when health is of paramount importance." He was confident: "Experience has shown that the plan works. The word is 'Forward!'"[1]

FORWARD ON HEALTH PROTECTION

Like during the First World War, the military provided pamphlets, films, and lectures to educate enlistees about the dangers of infections and dissuade them from having sex. Also like during the First World War, ASHA believed that these measures alone would be enough, while military higher-ups were far more skeptical. They had seen firsthand that the prophylactic stations were what had reduced rates of STIs in the past—not the lectures and pamphlets. As Major Gaylor W. Anderson of the Division of Venereal Disease Control for the War Department explained, "It is unlikely that we can ever take the man who has been promiscuous before and convert him after he comes into the Army to a life of continence. No matter what program of lectures and moral teaching will be made available it will be futile."[2] As such, in something of a break from ASHA, the army decided to provide what Allan Brandt called a "major program to ensure the provision of prophylaxis, both condoms and chemical treatments, to the troops."[3] This program included "hundreds of stations . . . for chemical treatments after intercourse, as well as providing condoms *en masse*. . . . As many as fifty million condoms were sold or freely distributed each month during the war."[4]

ASHA was not pleased. At their 1942 business meeting, they discussed the dissonance between providing prophylaxis while also providing instruction to avoid sex in the first place. Board of directors member Alphonse M. Switala wrote, "Prophylactic stations may depress diseases incidence [but] they will not make him more mindful of his essential dignity as a man; they will not make him more capable of self-mastery worthy of the citizen of heaven."[5] He urged looking toward a "larger truth" in which the patient's "illness is preventable and curable not by physical therapeutics and prophylaxis alone but to a vastly greater extent by moral therapeutics and moral prophylaxis." He believed this to be true of not only the military population but also of civilians.

And civilians were becoming a group of special concern among social hygienists, as more data came to light about whom military men were having sex. At the beginning of the war, conventional wisdom still held that sex workers were the main transmitter of STIs.

"DELINQUENT" WOMEN AND A NEW MORAL PANIC

In 1942, however, a syphilis expert reported that in terms of infections, "the old time prostitute in a house or the formal prostitute on the street is sinking into second place. The new type is the young girl in her late teens and early twenties."[6] And this young woman was not a sex worker—she was just a normal person. A "rough analysis" of cases from nine naval districts found these women—known as "pick-ups," as opposed to sex workers—accounted for 64 percent of sexual contacts that occurred.[7] The army also reported an increase ("in some areas as much as 70 per cent") of sexual contacts with women who were "promiscuous or delinquent" but not sex workers.[8] This greatly disrupted the decades-old belief that STIs were contracted almost entirely from sex workers and was an important moment of recognition that vectors of disease can come from anywhere. However, rather than humanizing the problem, this new insight instead cast these young women as morally corrupt and a problem to be solved.

In early 1943, an ASHA committee embarked on a study to "determine, insofar as possible, the extent and seriousness of sexual promiscuity among girls."[9] Who were they? Where did they come from? Was there some common element in their background? The committee traveled to communities around the country, conducted case studies on "sexually delinquent girls," and found, or manufactured, a number of factors that seemed to unite them, including "grave maladjustment of the girl in the home and often in school, low standards of sex morals and sometimes criminality in the parents . . . and often low intelligence in the girl herself. Jealousy of parents or of siblings appears as a factor surprisingly often."[10]

This quick pathologizing of sexual activity was not surprising, and further investigation by ASHA into these "delinquents" led to a new moral panic. Some experts, like psychiatrist Winfred Overholser, argued that the girls who displayed "sex delinquency" were seeking attention. He posited that "if the child feels that he is wanted at home, if the atmosphere of the home is one of calm and affection, the child will feel reasonably secure and there will be less call for aggressive behavior for the purpose of attracting attention."[11] This was yet another reason, ASHA and other experts believed, that morality-focused sex ed was necessary. It could affirm the value of the family, espouse "good morals," and guide young women and men to the path of moral righteousness.

A CALL FOR COMPULSORY SEX ED

By the 1940s, however, ASHA was no longer the sole interested party when it came to sex ed in the United States, so they could no longer dictate the character of sex ed on a large scale. As the area of study became more well-known, others wondered if sex ed could be applicable to them too—and they were far more concerned with STIs than with moral righteousness.

Even before the issue of "delinquent girls" became known, at least one school district was concerned about how the war was affecting their students when it came to sex. In September 1942, the Los Angeles Tenth District's PTA wrote to the district's board of education, calling for a compulsory sex ed course. "Our boys," the group wrote, "are totally unprepared for the advanced information given them in the service camps, often causing severe emotional shock. . . . We also feel that our young girls are in need of added information for their protection."[12] Despite this urging, Los Angeles's Tenth District did not make sex ed compulsory.

In 1943, the NEA joined the call, adding syphilis and gonorrhea to their list of diseases about which it was appropriate for high schoolers to learn. In the same year, Maurice Bigelow would note the "thousands of alarmed parents who are now demanding immediate lectures and motion pictures on venereal diseases in order to protect their boys and girls against possible infection."[13]

ETHICS OR HEALTH?

ASHA, unsurprisingly, did not meet this call to disseminate STI information wholeheartedly. Maurice Bigelow argued that giving "health information" alone was not "guaranteed to prevent venereal infection." He, and ASHA, reaffirmed that education that put "ethical attitudes and standards" front and center was still the most prudent approach.[14]

In 1944, ASHA president Ray Wilbur, along with the chief of the San Francisco Department of Public Health Venereal Disease Division, Richard A. Koch, gave an address explaining this at the National Postwar Conference on Venereal Disease Control, held in Saint Louis, Missouri. What America needed, they proclaimed, was a set of "social standards that will create cultural obstacles to promiscuity, and consequently, to exposure to venereal disease."[15] ASHA urged community and multiagency cooperation to promote these "social standards," including a "coordinated health education program in the public schools" and community centers. "If the results of promiscuity," they explained, "are to be controlled only by medical treatment, we will fail." If, however, *all* interested parties—the social hygiene experts, the doctors, "the ministers, the sociologists, the educators, the peace officers, the prosecutors, and the jurists"—banded together "to fight against promiscuity and venereal diseases," then, they predicted, "we cannot fail."

Not everyone was convinced. Dr. J. E. Heller, the chief medical director of the Venereal Disease Division of the USPHS, while conceding at the same 1944 conference that "prevention through personal prophylaxis, higher moral standards, prostitute repression, and education are all essential," these efforts "are and always will remain secondary to treatment."[16]

And at this time, treatment was becoming more effective than ever. In 1943, an American doctor at the Venereal Disease Research Lab in Staten Island, New York, found that penicillin—an antibiotic that had been discovered in 1928—was a nearly miraculous cure for syphilis.[17] In March 1944, Pfizer began mass producing the "miracle drug" at a repurposed ice plant in Brooklyn, New York. With this medication now at hand, it made sense that Heller was skeptical of Koch and Wilbur's proposal. "If you believe that official health agencies should actively participate in education for morality," he queried of their hope for a highly coordinated control effort, "is it possible that this would establish a dangerous precedent, possibly leading toward governmental interference with religious and familial life?" The lines between morals, medicine, family, religion, and government were beginning to show.

SEX ED IN WASHINGTON, DC

In the spring of 1943, the public senior high schools in Washington, DC, began teaching a newly revised and approved health course. The course included one section about "human reproduction."[18] It offered the already-familiar meld of medicine and morals. Students were taught about the reproductive organs; the basics of reproduction, including conception and the development of the embryo and fetus; and STIs. Then they moved on to the "reasons for relations between the sexes," which included:

1. "Desire for progeny (married)
2. "Natural and instinctive attraction
3. "Sex union as the culmination of a perfect bond of love and understanding."

The course also included information about the "desirability of restraint of reproduction"—a clear argument for abstinence. Young people were learning that they shouldn't act on instinct, and that the ability to choose not to have sex was a gift of human intelligence. Abstinence, the curriculum explained, would lead to a "happy and more perfect union in marriage," "protection from disease and undesired conception," "satisfaction resulting from knowledge that man has not been dishonorable or taken advantage," and "higher respect for self and partners."[19]

It was a curriculum that ASHA would have approved of. But in April 1943—after the courses were already underway—school board member and physician James Gannon called the syllabus "shocking" and wanted the whole thing thrown out. Its lessons on abstinence and restraint were properly taught, he thought, by "doctors and ministers."[20]

Initially, Gannon was the sole objector to the course. The president of Washington, DC's PTA defended the course, arguing that "doctors and ministers for the most part haven't enough time" to teach students these lessons. The chairman of the Committee on Marriage and the Home for the Washington Federation of Churches added that "the statistics indicated the majority of children in Washington are identified with no particular church and have no inclination to seek out a minister specifically for sex guidance."[21] And the district's director of physical education, Hardy L. Pearce, told the *Washington Post* that the course had received "no record of complaint" and had been endorsed by the Association of School Administrators."[22]

But the wheels of outrage had been set in motion. An unsigned editorial in the *Washington Post* on May 1, 1943, claimed that the curriculum seemed "unnecessarily elaborate." It also queried, "without disparagement, whether high school teachers have themselves the knowledge to enter into so many ramifications of what, after all, is not the simplest of subjects."[23] Dr. Gannon's complaint seemed to be having an effect, despite the experts who had spoken against him. In May, the city's board of education agreed to a "more simple outline" for the course. This version, severely shortened, mentioned "clean living" and "community health," and the "obligations of parenthood," but the lessons on the reproductive organs, abstinence, and "disorders of reproductive system" had been excised.[24]

Gannon reported that he was happy with this. The *Post* also reported that Gannon "hoped when the course is being given, some mention of venereal disease will be made, specifically its dangers and effects, in view of the large increase of cases in Washington."[25] However, Gannon's own advocacy had already stripped the course of most of the key contextual information around STIs—any mention of them would have been incoherent.

Around the same time, new data from a special committee of the Washington, DC, Board of Education—set up to investigate "problems of wartime and postwar child delinquency in the Nation's capital"— became available.[26] During the 1942–43 school year, the committee's investigation found, eighty-eight students within the district, all between the ages of thirteen and fifteen, had been "excused" from public school "because they were found to be pregnant." Another forty-five had been told to stay home to care for their "illegitimate infants." And pregnancy, of course, was not the only measure of so-called delinquency. In July 1943, twenty-one venereal-disease clinics had admitted more than one hundred "teen age children for treatment, twenty under 15 years of age and eighty-six between 16 and 19." The committee's leader, Dr. J. A. Murphy, the chief physician of Washington Public Schools, called for increased and earlier sex ed, noting: "If sex weren't a synonym for sin but were approached naturally, it would be helpful."[27]

This pronouncement came six months after Gannon had decimated the district's revised health course. Rather than take Murphy's advice, the district dropped the course entirely less than a year later. Dr. Gannon reported that, going forward, "teachers will merely answer questions as these arise, and furnish in the regular courses, such as biology, such moderate information as is constructive, non-controversial and helpful." And so another effort at sex ed—even in truncated form—was dashed.[28]

CHAPTER 7

THE BIRTH AND BOYCOTT
OF THE SEX ED FILM

As the 1940s progressed, the American public was becoming more amenable to the idea of sex ed. In June 1943, a Gallup poll inquired about the rise in proposals to teach sex ed in high schools due to "the increase of sex delinquency in wartime, particularly among school girls." Sixty-eight percent of Americans reported that they approved of such proposals. Sixteen percent disapproved, and sixteen percent had no opinion.[1]

At the same time, more and more experts were calling for sex ed. In December 1943, child guidance experts attested to the need for "improved and increased sex education" to a Senate subcommittee.[2] In June 1944, the American Medical Association urged "its membership to cooperate in backing a two-year course in biology in all high schools" citing the fact that "the medical profession . . . cannot be indifferent to wide-spread public ignorance of biological facts and principles."[3] In the same year, the Federal Councils of Churches, the United States Junior Chamber of Congress, the National PTA, and the National Educational Association all called for sex ed in some form or another.[4]

But these calls were not met by equally enthusiastic implementation, in part due to the difficulty in finding properly trained teachers. Enter the E. C. Brown Trust, founded in 1939 when the eponymous physician and founder of the Oregon Social Hygiene Society left a large portion of his estate to promote "social hygiene on behalf of the youth of Oregon . . .

a reverence for the married state, and . . . the prevention of sexual abuse especially venereal disease."[5]

The trust operated out of the University of Oregon. It had been instrumental in the passage of a 1945 state law that mandated health courses—with content about sex—in all Oregon public schools. By the late 1940s, it was interested in creating a film that teachers could screen in sex ed classes. By dint of good fortune, a psychologist named Lester Beck was also at the university at the time.

HUMAN GROWTH

During the Second World War, Beck had worked in the Army Pictorial Service, where he had evaluated films and other training aids. He also used films in his teaching, and was known on campus for his interest in what academics characterize as "provocative topics, including hypnosis, parapsychic powers, human development, and 'love and marriage' (a euphemism for adult sexuality)."[6] Beck was hired by the E. C. Brown Trust to write the script for the film and supervise its production. The result of the collaboration was a nineteen-minute film called *Human Growth*, narrated by actor Eddie Albert, who would later to be known for his roles in *Roman Holiday* and *Green Acres*.

When the film crackles on, a red screen appears and the words "UNDERSTANDING OUR SELVES" appear in big letters, followed by "Human Growth." We see a boy, maybe twelve, sitting on the floor of his living room, reading a book about "Tennessee Indian people" as his parents look on. His sister, a year or two younger, walks into the room. "He's reading about . . . adolescents like him," she says. The family discusses the book, in which the son learns that the children of that Indigenous group didn't wear clothes until they reached "sexual maturity." "That's an interesting point, George," the dad says. "In fact, it fits in very well with a film Josie"—his sister—"told us about." The next scene takes us into Josie's classroom. The teacher says, "The film we're about to see shows the earliest phases of growth, as well as the changes that occur during childhood and adolescence. This motion picture was selected to give you an understanding of the way the cycle of human growth is repeated, over and over, from generation to generation." She reads out a list of questions, which the students copy down diligently. They are ready to learn. So are we.

A student starts the film-within-the-film, and "Human Growth" again flashes on the screen. A ten-minute cartoon follows, presenting without fanfare, the external changes that bodies undergo during puberty: boys and girls grow taller, gain weight; girls grow breasts, the boys' shoulders broaden. Then the film turns inward—showing glands, hormones, then testes and ovaries. "Hormones cause hair growth and voice changes," Albert tells us, "often making young people feel more manly and womanly." Then we are introduced to cartoon sperm cells and a cartoon ovum. "It is from the union of sperm and ovum, of father and mother, that life begins." A cartoon diagram of the male reproductive system shows testes producing sperm cells: "This happens during mating, and sometimes during sleep. It is the normal function of the body." Then we move to a diagram of the uterus, fallopian tubes, and vagina. Menstruation is explained.

Then comes "mating." Albert tells us that when young people "have completed their education, have a steady job, want to get married, and are ready to accept the responsibility of having and raising children, [they] will reproduce." There is a proper order to things, we are learning. The film explains that "the sperm cells of the father, during mating, pass from the penis into the vagina of the mother." An explanation of *how* the sperm is passed into the vagina is markedly absent. Fertilization, pregnancy, and birth are described. "Growth continues," Albert says, "and this baby will become a full-grown boy or girl, and eventually a father or mother, thus continuing the cycle of human growth." The film-within-the-film ends, and we return to our classroom. The teacher leads a conversation; she answers students' questions. Then she addresses the viewers directly, encouraging us to ask our own questions of our teachers.

The film was completed in the fall of 1947 after Beck "pretested" it, "Hollywood-like style," with a slideshow, to various groups around the state of Oregon—PTAs, churches, and other civic organizations. After its official completion, Beck showed it to another group and found that of the seven thousand total parents and teachers who had been shown the film in its finished version, the "responses were overwhelmingly favorable."

Despite the positive early reception, however, the University of Oregon was reluctant to distribute the film on a large scale, reportedly "nervous that the film would be too controversial if it were improperly exhibited," and hoping instead for a soft launch of just a few film prints for distribution to begin with.[7]

This plan was foiled, however, when Beck invited journalists from *Life* magazine to observe the film being screened to a group of seventh graders. The magazine covered the film and its screening in a five-page feature in May 1948. "The subject of sex has always been a stepchild of U.S. education," began the article, "partly because some parents object to its inclusion in the school curriculum but mostly because it is such a difficult and delicate subject to teach." But *Human Growth*, the piece went on, was "epoch-making," "a hit," and "successful." Other press was quick to cover the film too.[8]

Then came the orders from schools across the nation. In 1948 and 1949 alone, newspapers reported the film was screened in fourteen cities, from Reno, Nevada,[9] to Mamaroneck, New York.[10] By October 1949, the Associated Press reported that *Human Growth* was available in all states except Rhode Island, and the E. C. Brown Trust estimated that over 460,000 people had seen it.[11] It was screened by PTAs, by doctors, by parents, and by students themselves, in classrooms and community spaces nationwide—often to great acclaim.

A NATIONAL DISCOURSE

It seemed that, just maybe, sex ed was here to stay. An *Indianapolis Star* article from October 1948 proclaimed that "the national clamor of action on the problem of child sex education has snowballed near the size of a public movement."[12] A June 1949 spread in the *Pittsburg Post-Gazette* read: "Among the nation's top educators it is no longer a question of 'should sex education be given in public schools?' But of what and how the children should be taught about this most basic of subjects."[13]

In April 1948, the New Jersey State Board of Education officially suggested integrating sex ed into appropriate classes in its public schools.[14] In June, three Michigan state departments (health, public instruction, and mental health) jointly released guidelines for sex ed in schools, citing increasing cases of syphilis, gonorrhea, illegitimate children, and divorce.[15] And when Dr. Earl McGrath was sworn in as US Commissioner of Education in March 1949, he also announced his support of sex ed in schools.[16] The students themselves continued to express favor too. A survey in February 1948 found that 92 percent of Florida high school students (and 75 percent of their parents) wanted "preparation for marriage in their curriculum."[17] A national Purdue Opinion Poll found 82 percent of high schoolers surveyed believed that "instruction in sex problems" should be taught in high school.[18]

Opponents to sex ed still existed, of course. Many people voiced concerns about teacher ability, student character, and other practicalities.[19] Seventy-eight percent of those polled in Iowa, for example, in 1948 believed that sex ed was best handled by parents.[20] Others believed that sex ed did more harm than good: in June 1948, a police psychologist in Los Angeles said that "in the past few years we have had freer and freer discussion of sex among children, yet we have seen juvenile delinquency mount and mount."[21]

But most commonly, people who opposed sex ed cited reasons rooted in politics and religion. In March 1951, California state senator Hugh M. Burns, chairman of the California House Un-American Activities Committee, claimed, according to the *San Bernardino County Sun*, that "Communists are using sex education in schools as a means of attaining their objectives" of breaking "down the family unit."[22] Catholics, in general, also remained staunchly against sex ed, and the popularity of *Human Growth* galvanized their opposition. In March 1949, the New York State Catholic Welfare Committee released a statement after two films—*Human Growth* and *Human Reproduction*, the latter made by the educational publisher McGraw-Hill in 1947—were added to the state health department's film library, available for distribution on request.[23] The committee claimed that if a public school were to screen either of these films, the results could be injurious (that they had been out for years already was apparently not relevant).

They warned that "classroom presentation of this subject" violates "principles of sex instruction, offends Christian modesty and is liable to leave grave consequences in its wake."[24]

It was a potent message, and it began to spread in Catholic communities around the state. In April 1949, the official newspaper of the Rochester Diocese, the *Catholic Courier Journal*, ran a front-page editorial by Monsignor William Hart called "Protect All Children." "Catholic protest," Hart wrote, "against this public school experiment in sex education is very much in order. Catholics are just as much opposed to endangering the morals of public school pupils as they are to endangering the morals of parochial school pupils."[25]

In October, the New York State Catholic Welfare Committee took further action. They wrote to the state commissioner of health, Dr. Herman Hilleboe, stating that sex ed in New York public schools was "at variance with traditional Christian teaching, and asked for the two films to be removed from the state library.[26]

Dr. Hilleboe responded that the films would remain—Catholic protest or not. But he also offered them the possibility of a religious exemption. "If Catholic groups wish to have Catholic children excluded from school showings of the film," he wrote, "the Department of Health will be glad to defer to the Department of Education for decision on this matter. The Department of Health has great respect for all religions." Hilleboe went on to explain that the department was not going to "usurp any parental rights . . . but it does propose to use its scientific knowledge to help parents who seek our assistance in bringing health information to their children."[27]

Hilleboe's November letter did not quell the tide of Catholic disapproval, however. On December 4, during High Mass, the auxiliary bishop of New York, the Reverend Joseph F. Flannelly "cautioned Catholic parents against allowing their children to see" the film *Human Growth*.[28] Then, according to one paper, Flannelly led the congregation in a recitation of the Legion of Decency Pledge, in which the congregants pledged to "condemn and stay away from indecent and immoral pictures."[29]

Then came action in Minnesota. That same month, Archbishop John Gregory Murray, the *Minneapolis Star* reported, ordered Catholic children not to attend sex ed classes. Murray, the paper reported, explained that "under church law any formal discussion of the subject of sex has to be confined to the relationships between parents and their children, physicians and patients, priests and members of their congregations." In a pastoral letter that was read in "most of the 283 churches" in the archdiocese, which included Minneapolis, Murray wrote that parents had a "conscientious duty as well as . . . constitutional rights to withdraw their children from any school that professes to give instruction in sex."[30]

It was a stirring letter, and it garnered media attention from local newspapers. But Murray had, perhaps, overstated the situation. The assistant superintendent of Minneapolis public schools explained that while *Human Growth* and *Human Reproduction* had been screened in "some junior and senior high schools" in the city, there was no "general plan of instruction in sex education now in effect."[31] This incident, in addition to highlighting the fervor sex ed could bring to communities, also showed just how hard it was to define "sex education." For Murray, the fact that the films had been shown in Minneapolis schools at all indicated that the district was teaching sex ed. But the superintendent didn't see it that way—after all, there was no course called "sex education."

Regardless, Catholics marched on. In October 1950, the National Council of Catholic Women resolved that children should receive information about sex exclusively from parents, and that "sex education which consists merely in biological information is more harmful than helpful."[32] In November, the Catholic bishops of the United States denounced the subject at their annual meeting.[33] The fact that American sex educators, including the creators of *Human Growth*, had included ethical considerations in their presentations of the material was not acknowledged. In September 1951, Pope Pius XII went so far as to "[criticize] efforts to increase sex instruction in schools."[34]

It is worth remembering that, for all the controversy around the film, *Human Growth* did not explain or reference the act of intercourse at all. It also never mentioned STIs, contraception, or the idea that one might want to avoid becoming pregnant. To the modern eye it is quaintly old-fashioned and downright sexist, conforming to the status quo of the period. It assumed sex happened only within marriage—and only between a man and a woman.

Despite the bland sex ed that was being prioritized in public schools, national rates of STIs were decreasing. In March 1950, the medical director of the Division of Venereal Disease for USPHS, W. H. Aufranc, reported that the "attack rate of syphilis has decreased consistently for the last three and one-half years." He cited three reasons for this decrease: "improved case-finding technics, improved diagnostic aids and, last but not least, the widespread use of penicillin in the treatment of syphilis." Aufranc was optimistic about this downward trend. "If judicious expenditure of funds, effective use of trained personnel, and careful employment of facilities are continued," he predicted, "syphilis will eventually be controlled to the same extent as smallpox, typhoid fever and diphtheria."[35]

In particular, thanks to penicillin's spectacular efficacy, the sense was stronger than ever that medicine alone could, and would, curb the STI crisis. That prospect tacitly challenged the value of "moral prophylaxis" and the insistence of abstinence as the best disease-control policy. The value—and extent—of abstinence was dealt another blow in mid-century America in the form of a book called *Sexual Behavior in the Human Male*.

THE KINSEY REPORT

In the 1930s, Alfred Kinsey was a zoology professor who found himself teaching a marriage course at Indiana University. At first, his colleague Wardell Pomeroy recalled, Kinsey "knew no more about human sexual behavior than the ordinary zoology professor," but when he discovered the complete dearth of hard data about human sexual habits, his curiosity was piqued.[36]

Kinsey, Pomeroy went on, "found that actually we knew more about the sex life of our farm animals and our laboratory animals than we knew about the human animal. He was frankly amazed and shocked that so little research had been done at the time." In Kinsey's work as a zoologist, he'd had to amass hundreds of thousands of gall wasp specimens in order to produce stable statistical curves from which he could make generalizations about their mating practices. The available data on human sexual behavior did not come even close to that level.[37] From a scientific point of view, it was impossible to generalize about the nature of human sexuality—and yet people were happy to do so and to extrapolate standards and norms from there.

So, Kinsey decided to build a body of knowledge that was more scientific. In 1947, he founded the Institute for Sex Research, which was affiliated with Indiana University but was a nonprofit backed significantly by the Rockefeller Foundation. Kinsey was the director, and he had a research team for support.[38] His first landmark work, published in 1947, was a book called *Sexual Behavior in the Human Male*, now often referred to as the Kinsey Report. It was an instant sensation. As *Life* noted in 1948, the fact that this highly scientific book was so popular among lay readers was in itself noteworthy. "Not only as a marathon best-seller but more as a phenomenal source of talk and controversy," Francis Sill Wickware wrote, the Kinsey Report "within a few months virtually has attained the status of a new American institution."[39]

The controversy it garnered was from all corners. His peers, for one, had valid criticisms of his methodology. The book relied on interviews and surveys of 5,300 men, and Kinsey's sampling procedures (all the men were white, many from prison populations) and possible self-selection bias, among other things, were not above reproach.[40] But more popularly, the findings contained within it rattled Americans, especially those who had believed they'd understood the basic nature of American sexual activity.

The report, flawed though it may have been, suggested that the common story that sexual life began only after marriage was not a lived reality. It revealed that many of the men had had "homosexual experiences" and masturbated. And, crucially, it found that at least 60 percent of them had had "coital experience before marriage."

Kinsey, ever the zoologist, noted that from a biological and anthropological standpoint, this was not surprising. "In all other anthropoids," he wrote, sex "begins as soon as the animal is physically capable and psychically oriented toward socio-sexual contacts." In other words, he went on, it was "not surprising to find that most human males do have intercourse prior to marriage."[41]

Nonetheless, many Americans were shocked. American society insisted that people dated, married, and had sex—in that order. But Kinsey's work suggested otherwise. And moreover, it suggested that it was not always harmful to have sex before marriage. "It is sometimes asserted," *Sexual Behavior in the Human Male* reads, "that all persons who have pre-marital intercourse subsequently regret the experience . . . but a very high proportion of the thousands of . . . males whom we have questioned on this point indicated that they did not regret having had such experience."[42] Further, the evidence seemed to suggest that for *some* people, premarital sex may have even led to better "marital adjustment" in the long run. Kinsey and his team, however, were careful to note that a successful marriage was the result of a number of factors.

For some, Kinsey's reporting was tantamount to an argument against premarital sex itself. In August 1953, a Baptist minister in Springfield, Missouri, exhorted that the Kinsey Report "strikes at the Bible and at God's law concerning the sanctity of marriage."[43] Other unhappy readers saw red: a 1953 letter to the editor of Wilmington, Delaware's *News Journal* stated that "all this propaganda on sex by Kinsey and his few backers, encouraging the people to violate the Bible, sounds very much to me like the work of the Communists."[44]

The social hygiene community was more cautious in expressing their concern. In February 1950, at ASHA's thirty-seventh annual meeting, a panel discussion was held in response to the Kinsey Report. The panel, called "Sexual Behavior: How Shall We Define and Motivate What Is Acceptable?" comprised a Yale anthropologist named George Murdock, a Protestant clergyman, a Catholic clergyman, and a professor of philosophy.[45]

The proceedings began by affirming the panelists' common ground: a shared belief in "the family as the basic social unit." That common ground was quickly lost, however, when Murdock led with his social scientific view of sexual activity. He began innocuously enough by affirming the value of the family. "There is no society known to history or anthropology," he said, "that lacks the family." Marriage, he argued further, was the universal "legitimate way of founding a family." But what was *not* shared among every society was America's dogma of premarital chastity. And, Murdock said, in societies that were more permissive of premarital sex, the institution of marriage was still strong. Sexual chastity, therefore, he argued, was not a *useful* sexual taboo like the incest taboo. His bombshell line was simple and clear: "Nothing in man's social experience indicates that premarital chastity has any scientific value." Murdock argued that Americans should reexamine their belief in the fact that premarital sex was the ultimate sin.

Murdock urged his audience to "accept the evidence of the social and psychological sciences and to arrive at the ethical judgment that socially controlled premarital experimentation in the interests of marital happiness and family stability is preferable to the alternative mélange of perversion, vice, sexual neurosis, and excessive divorce." If churches led in the dismantling of this taboo, all the better, Murdock argued. Then, young people "might flock to the churches that now repel them, and religion might even be restored to that position of central social significance which it enjoys in most societies but has lost in our own."

Unsurprisingly, his fellow panelists did not greet his ideas with strong support. The Catholic clergyman on the panel, the Reverend William J. Gibbons, conceded that while "help may be derived" from the social sciences, they could never effectively point society to the correct way of living. That privilege was reserved for God and the church alone. The functions of the family, Gibbons went on, "have a deeper origin than social utility; they are in accord with the divine plan of society." The two men, in essence, held worldviews that overlapped very little.

DIVERSIFYING OPINIONS

As mid-century dawned, it was becoming clear that American society had no monolithic authority to whom they could appeal for answers, especially when it came to sex. At the turn of the twentieth century, when Morrow had been writing, the medical, religious, and legal views on sex had all been pretty much the same: remain abstinent before marriage. But that trifold unity was beginning to crumble. Medically, abstinence was no longer the only way to remain safe: now there were condoms and antibiotics. Legally, while adultery and other relevant laws were still on the books in many states, federal funding for STI control such as condoms tacitly acknowledged the reality of American sexual lives. Yet, churches—and religious adherents—remained stalwart in their calls for abstinence.

Time magazine and *The Survey* both reported on Murdock's statements at the ASHA panel.[46] Syndicated columnist George Sokolsky argued that "It is always dangerous . . . to let the moral barriers down at all. They seem always to fall down altogether. . . . That is what is so wrong with Professor Murdock's thinking."[47] Catholic outlets were also quick to register their disapproval. *America: The National Catholic Weekly* ran an editorial called "Sex Anarchy" that excoriated Murdock, claiming, "The day may not be so far off when the American people will angrily understand that prophets of sexual lawlessness are the natural allies of human cruelty. . . . The sweet, flowery path of sexual 'liberation' leads straight to sexual promiscuity, destruction of family life, and in the end to the gas chamber and concentration camp."[48]

Other experts, however, seemed to be reaching the same conclusions as Murdock, in some way or another. "We are in the midst of a tremendous change in our customary attitudes toward sex," said Lester A. Kirkendall, a professor of family life at Oregon State University, in October 1950.[49] Kirkendall had studied under the great social hygiene and family-life expert Maurice Bigelow, who had shaped so much of sex ed in the 1930s and prior. When Bigelow retired, he passed the torch to Kirkendall. "For centuries," he continued, "many people have clung to the idea that any expression of sex, especially during the premarital period, was sinful." But this was changing. People were beginning to think of sex as something different, and Kirkendall saw a need for a new morality around it altogether: "We should neither be afraid of sex nor laud it just because it is sex. Our problem is to recognize it as a normal phase of living and approach it in an understanding manner." Sex was not scary and separate—it was normal and integral to a full and whole life.[50] Kirkendall offered examples of questions he might receive from thoughtful students in the modern world: "If a couple love each other, and use contraceptive measures, isn't it all right for them to have intercourse?" "Why should we deny sex desire, when it is natural?" "Why is prostitution wrong?" Teachers had to be prepared to answer these questions with honesty and openness. "Platitudes and pious evasions will be rejected by youth," Kirkendall explained. "They want to understand why certain standards exist, and, if they are observed, what may be gained from following them."

This idea suggested a huge departure from traditional sex ed. Instead of using sex ed to uphold the value of marriage, strengthen the family unit, and create the best parents, Kirkendall was suggesting that it be used to answer students' questions about their own lives.

In January 1952, the *Monroe News-Star* out of Louisiana published a piece called "Two Schools of Sexology," which outlined this schism. The article argued that, in the US, "there are two principal schools of sex-education counselors," which "split wide apart on two points: namely the sanctity of marriage and the question of normality and abnormality. The first school upholds the sanctity of marriage and differentiates between normal and abnormal practices. The second school," the article read, with perhaps some measure of hyperbole, "holds that nothing is sacred and nothing is abnormal."[51] Although the article did not mention Kirkendall by name, in many ways he represented, fairly or not, the second school. What had always been an uneasy partnership between medical and moral views of sex ed was now nearing an outright feud; but both parties felt equally entitled to a seat at the table when it came to determining sex ed's future.

CHAPTER 8

SEX ED AND FAMILY LIFE EDUCATION IN THE 1950s

Low rates of STIs in the earliest years of the 1950s had been promising, but in 1953, rates of syphilis increased "in 15 states and the
District of Columbia, gonorrhea in 17 states and the District," ASHA's
Journal of Social Hygiene reported. Despite this, the federal government
announced that it was preparing, in 1954, to "slash funds for VD control
more than 76%," from about $9.8 million in 1953 to $2.3 million in 1955.[1]

In response to this dramatic decrease in funding, ASHA, along with
the Association of State and Territorial Health Officers (ASTHO) and
the American Venereal Disease Association (AVDA) released a joint
statement voicing their vehement opposition. "Now is no time," they
wrote, "to cut our VD program so drastically." To the government budget, the line item may have seemed negligible, but ASHA, ASTHO, and
AVDA—all of which were strong advocates for federal funding for STI
control—knew that "complete control of venereal disease [was] far from
imminent," and cutting the budget was "dangerous in the extreme." This
was the first *Joint Statement on the Venereal Disease Problem and Programs
in the United States*, subsequently published annually.[2]

The statement signaled an overall shift in ASHA's focus: historically
a proponent of wide-ranging educational initiatives, the organization
now pivoted to advocating for better federal funding of STI control.
In May 1954, Philip R. Mather, president of the group, explained that
ASHA's new job was to "help our public health services to sustain their

fight to the finish against VD in the face of disproportionately deep budget cuts. We must use all the skill we can muster to establish public understanding of the simple fact that complete VD control has not yet been achieved, indeed, is not even imminent."[3] Later that year, ASHA discontinued its *Journal of Social Hygiene*, which had been published continuously since 1922.

Meanwhile, rates of infection continued to rise. In 1956, national rates (as opposed to the state-specific rates observed in 1953) increased for the time since 1948.[4] And the data suggested that infections were rising among American teenagers. In June 1956, the USPHS reported that "200,000 teenagers are now getting syphilis and gonorrhea every year." In 1959, reports found that "the greatest increase in venereal disease cases . . . was in the 10 to 14 year junior high school age group."[5]

These high rates of infections in young people garnered significant media coverage. In 1960, journalist Joan Beck, famed for her trailblazing column, You and Your Child, wrote a series of articles on the subject for the *Chicago Sunday Tribune Magazine*. The first was called "The Shocking Facts About Teen-Age Sex: Tawdry Movies and Magazines, Timid Parents and Schools Are Keeping Our Youngsters in Ignorance—and Jeopardy." Beck reached the same conclusion that so many others had before her: "Our young people," she wrote, "need more and better education about sex and marriage. What they're getting today at home and in school is far too little and much too late."[6]

And, so, the early 1960s saw an onslaught of new calls for increased sex ed in light of these high rates of STIs—but such calls rarely interrogated what exactly "sex ed" *was*. There had been so many ideas and motivations behind the concept for so long that it had become a muddle of biological facts, lessons about parenthood and dating, and occasionally information about how to balance a budget or recognize the symptoms of syphilis.

OBSTACLES TO EDUCATION ON STIs

When health officials called for sex ed classes, they might not have been picturing courses about grocery shopping or how to get along with the opposite sex on a date—but that is what many of these courses were. There were myriad reasons why actual information about sex and its risks was not being taught. Some schools were concerned about community backlash. Others were attempting to reduce the increased scrutiny that teachers found themselves under in the 1950s as the latest Red Scare progressed. In June 1953, an NEA study found that teachers were "reluctant to consider controversial questions in the classroom," including "religious education, sex education, Communism, socialized medicine, local politics, race relations, UNESCO, and the United Nations."[7]

And even a sex ed class that contained thorough biological information about puberty and reproduction was likely to be silent on STIs—the problem of the hour—entirely. The prospect of teaching about them was contentious even among sex ed experts and proponents themselves. In 1954, a health-education professor, Elena M. Sliepcevich, had warned in the *Journal of Social Hygiene* that "education about venereal disease does not give an individual the same insurance as vaccination against smallpox," and noted that "there are complex social and moral implications which must be taken into consideration."[8]

Indeed, the 1960 Joint Statement on Venereal Diseases noted that "a reluctance among parents, teachers, school administrators, and health workers to support and participate in educational efforts" was among the "major blocks to VD control."[9] (Of course, ASHA did not mention that perhaps their earlier efforts to distance themselves from "venereal disease education"—such as Maurice Bigelow's 1938 radio address, in which he assured his listeners that sex ed was *not* venereal disease education—may have had something to do with this reluctance.)

But educators did not entirely ignore STIs during this time. A 1957 survey had found that there was "'some degree of teaching' about VD in all forty-eight states."* But that education was far from uniform. Eleven states reported "only incidental teaching." Twenty indicated that STIs were discussed in health courses. Fourteen states integrated "VD into their physical education classes; thirteen in their biological courses; nine in home and family living; eight in home economics; and eight in social studies."[10]

And, so, perhaps it was not surprising that a 1960 study of six hundred teenagers seeking care from social hygiene clinics for a possible STI found that only "14% had gained any of their information from School

---

* Alaska would become a state in January 1959, Hawai'i in August of the same year.

instruction." Beyond that, the study found that "only 10% had a good knowledge of the venereal diseases" and "only 42% had ever read or heard anything about venereal disease."[11]

The data seemed to suggest that young people were not getting the information they needed, even if they had completed sex ed, in part because sex ed and venereal-disease education had been conceived of as two distinct subjects. On the other hand, in some schools, any discussion of STIs seemed to turn any class into sex ed. In June 1961 in Virginia, where STI rates were rising, an official from the department of health was quoted as saying, "You can't teach venereal disease without teaching sex education, and you can't do that in Virginia."[12] The distinctions that the social hygiene community had created were not holding up to real-world use—something made harder by state laws and guidelines that made specific provisions around teaching about sex.

CONTROVERSY GROWS

As cities and states tried to determine the difference between sex ed and STI education and what was acceptable and what wasn't, citizens were also taking note. Although the classes had always brought controversy, by the late 1950s and early 1960s the tenor of that controversy had deepened into something more reactive. Some sex ed experts saw the protests as healthy and productive. In November 1957, Nolan C. Kearney, the assistant superintendent of the public schools in Saint Paul, Minnesota, and a member of an ASHA project, stated, "Public education is dependent upon public support and direction. As we improve our knowledge of classroom learning, we adopt new methods, new procedures. . . . We try out new approaches. . . . This process provided opportunities for criticism by many citizens."[13] However, Kearney also noted that some of the criticism "is sincere and some is not. Some will result in the improvement of education and some will not. Some of it is obviously destructive, bitter, and designed for selfish and unpredictable purposes." Kearney was not alone in noticing this pattern.

Sex ed had already acquired several monikers by the mid-century—*sex hygiene, social hygiene, personal purity*. Another was *family life education*, or *FLE*, which was something of a sibling to *sex education*: growing alongside it, often understood in relation to it, and forced to define itself in relation to it. The term had come into use as early as the early 1940s. Family life courses were usually given at the high school or middle school level, and they dealt with families in general, the qualities of a good marriage, and how to run a household, often containing only a small unit on sex. Sometimes FLE didn't contain any sex ed at all. But through the 1950s, students, parents, and the media had begun to conflate the two entirely—some assumed that *family life* was merely a gentler term for *sex ed*.

FLE, however, had a long and distinct history, and professionals of its own. Many of them were deeply interested in and concerned about sex and sex ed, and they found themselves answering for sex ed, since—whether they claimed the term or not—they often did some amount of teaching of the subject. One of those people was Judson Landis, an FLE expert and textbook writer, who explained in 1951 that "strong community resistance to sex education should be respected," but that it was "often necessary to differentiate between real community resistance and the voices of a few cranks in the community."[14]

But the "cranks" had real consequences for sex ed. Their complaints, Kearney explained, tended to "make administrators hesitant to initiate or enlarge programs that may be misunderstood. Imagine critics charging that free love is being advocated, that children are being taught to transgress 'safely,' that teachers and children engage together in 'dirty talk' in school, that sex is presented as clean and beautiful, and so on ad nauseam. Programs," he warned, "must be most carefully presented."[15]

But even with careful presentation, uproar over sex ed was alive and well. Nationwide, fervor against any type of course that contained any information about sex—whether it was called venereal disease education, FLE, or sex education—was growing, sometimes in response to what can only be described as very modest proposals.

BATTLES IN MONTANA AND KANSAS
In February 1962 in Missoula, Montana, for example, there was a two-and-a-half-hour discussion at a school board meeting over a relatively uncontroversial proposal. The Missoula Family Life Council, part of the Missoula Ministerial Alliance, was requesting the use of the county high school building for a voluntary course in family life education, which would cover aspects of sex. The Missoula Family Life Council reported

that Missoula, like so many towns and cities in the United States, was seeing "increasing problems of pregnancies in girls in their early and middle teens, teen-age marriages and high divorce rates," according to the *Missoulian* newspaper, and this course aimed to address some of these problems.[16]

The proposed course would require parental permission and be taught by experts in "religious and psychological problems, sociology of dating, engagement and marriage, financial responsibilities of marriage, and physiology and anatomy." But the chairman of the school board, along with one other member, opposed the project. The latter member "opposed the proposal on moral grounds," but would "favor a course approved by the State Department of Public Instruction."[17]

Only one school trustee (the district's term for school board member) was fully in favor of the project, because of "the problem that exists." The others were not outright against it but were hesitant to give their support. One thought the matter was "a responsibility of the churches" (presumably without any help, however minor, from the schools), and two said they would be more comfortable if the course was taught as part of the school's official curriculum.

"Most" of the approximately twenty-five parents present at the meeting, *The Missoulian* reported, "objected to having the course in school." All the experts who were slated to be part of the voluntary, non-school course were supportive. After the long meeting, the board members tabled the discussion.

When classes and books weren't the target of protest, teachers were. In March 1961, in Great Bend, Kansas, high school teacher Nadine Stallard was fired for "poor judgment in presenting sex education material in a Family Living course" to fifty high school seniors. The material was described as "too detailed and in poor taste." Stallard had been employed by the school system for four years, where she was also a psychologist and counselor.[18] There was no indication that she had been teaching anything that departed significantly from what was being taught in thousands of other FLE courses nationwide.

As soon as her firing was made public, there was outcry. Sixty-four students and forty-five adults signed a petition asking the board to reconsider Stallard's termination. "Statements by students," one paper reported, "in the Family Living course indicated a majority feel the course is worthwhile."[19] Stallard herself noted that "in hiring her to teach the course, the board was indicating it wanted the course taught according to accepted current standards." But the board members maintained that "the material is much too detailed and in poor taste for students of high school age," and she was not reinstated.

So, by mid-century, sex ed was in a state of chaos. ASHA, once among the biggest advocates for the subject, had moved on to other work. The once-collaborative medical and moral stakeholders in the project had turned into icier colleagues, if not to outright rivals. Teachers were afraid to talk about sex. State, local, and school rules made it difficult to know what was acceptable and what was not. Nobody knew what was *right*. It was a time of disjuncture, and the school systems, teachers, and students were all feeling it—as rates of STIs and teen pregnancy continued to rise.

CHAPTER 9

THE FIRST NORTH AMERICAN CONFERENCE ON CHURCH AND FAMILY

S ome people of faith were not willing to stand by and watch the moral and medical camps of the sex ed community go their separate ways. There was too much at stake: Divorce rates, teen pregnancy, abortions, and sexually transmitted infections were all rising. Young people, some believed, were dating too early. There was no one source for them to consult on the issues of sex, sexuality, and dating.

And so, in the spring of 1961, 532 of these concerned people of faith gathered at the Baptist Assembly Ground in Green Lake, Wisconsin, for the inaugural North American Conference on Church and Family (NACCF), where they hoped to provide some clarity on the reality of sex and determine just what should be done about the problems associated with it.

The conference was a joint endeavor between the National Council of the Churches of Christ in the USA (NCC) and its Canadian counterpart, the Canadian Council of Churches. The NCC had formed in 1950 as a merger of the Federal Council of Churches (FCC) and affiliated groups. Still active today, it is an ecumenical organization with a socially oriented outlook.

Conference attendees, one of the cochairmen reported, came from "twenty-eight certifying denominations and several other unofficial representatives—Mormon, Southern Baptists, Unitarian, Roman Catholic, and Jewish faiths."[1] The idea for the conference had been born out of the council's family life department, led by John Charles Wynn and co-chaired by married couple Evelyn and Sylvanus Duvall, who also wrote family life textbooks.

The "call to the conference," which had been sent to churches within the NCC and its Canadian counterpart, listed twelve issues: early marriage, mixed marriage ("cultural, religious, and racial"), divorce and remarriage, "teen-age sex attitudes and behavior," pregnant brides, illegitimacy, masturbation, homosexuality, adultery, family limitation, abortion, and voluntary sterilization. By the end of the conference, organizers hoped they would have articulated "the fundamental nature of marriage and family life," developed "a Christian ethic of sexual behavior," and provided "clarification regarding the moral aspects of the newer developments in family planning." It was a bold vision, one on par with Dr. Prince Morrow's ASSMP at the turn of the century.

PRE-CONFERENCE READINGS

To aid in this lofty goal, each delegate was sent an impressive collection of twelve essays before the conference itself, to read in preparation. As the introduction to the collection explained, these articles addressed "some of the most pressing issues around sex, with the most up to date research . . . written by twelve of the most serious researchers of the day."[2] The essays were not softened or sanitized for this churchly audience. The experts were truly at the tops of their fields and pulled no punches. Facts were laid bare, diagnoses were offered, and when necessary, pleas were made.

The assigned essays contained a deluge of information. Delegates would have learned that "in the American culture, about one out of every six brides is pregnant at the time of the wedding"[3] and that of homosexuals, "to this group belong many of our most useful and able citizens in all walks of life—including members of the clergy"[4] (a fact that would have been shocking to a great number of people in 1961). The delegates would have read an article by the director of information and education of Planned Parenthood about the current contraception methods recommended by doctors, and how wealthy women were more likely to receive contraception than poor women. They would have read a piece by Alan F. Guttmacher, the chief of the department of obstetrics and gynecology at Mount Sinai Hospital in New York City, who explained that abortion laws in the United States worked "badly!" and "chaotically!" with "little uniformity and consistency."

At the time, there were no federal statutes about abortion, but each state's policy was, Guttmacher explained, "about the same," modeled on an English law originally penned in 1803. Most states outlawed abortion outright, some with exceptions for "therapeutic abortion" if the life of the mother was at risk. Guttmacher forcefully argued that "modern physicians cannot practice good, total medical care under the restrictive prohibition of terminating pregnancy solely to save a life." Abortion was of interest to the conference but was not yet the political lightning rod it would become in the decade to follow.

SPEAKERS AND WORKSHOPS AT THE CONFERENCE

At the conference, delegates listened to twelve speakers (one per topic), split into twenty-five workgroups, and grappled with the very real and raw information presented, all under the aegis of progressive Christianity.

David Mace—who, along with his wife, Vera, directed the American Association of Marriage Counselors—was the conference's worship co-ordinator. He opened the conference with an affirmation that sex was part of God's creation: "The Bible says plainly that God made us sexual beings. There was no mistake. The hand of the Creator did not slip. He could have made us in any way he chose. It was his clear, deliberate purpose to make us man and woman, male and female. Sex is deeply rooted in divine purpose."[5] This was a liberal Christian viewpoint of sex—one that did not decry it as an impure act that was necessary only to make children, but rather affirmed it as part of the human experience.

As John Charles Wynn explained during his address at the conference, Protestant churchgoers were owed specific standards around sex, rather than the platitudes they typically received. Protestant churches, Wynn said, tended to be happy to "speak up concerning matters of piety and propriety—and to maintain a discreet silence about specific matters of personal and interpersonal nature that puzzle people most." When it came to the real and specific questions related to sex— "artificial insemination, sterilization, illegitimacy"—the Protestant literature was typically mum.[6] This conference was a direct rebuke to that.

The speakers brought their immense knowledge and background to the task. Wardell Pomeroy, the psychologist who worked closely with Dr. Kinsey at the Institute of Sex Research, spoke about masturbation, which had long been decried by religious people, as well as some doctors, as psychologically—and sometimes physically—unhealthy and abnormal. Pomeroy urged the delegates to rethink not only their received beliefs on masturbation, but also the broader assumption that there was any kind of "normal" when it came to sex. He asked: "When you talk about deviant sexual behavior, you have to ask, 'what does it deviate from?'" This question had, frankly, not been asked before, at least not in mainstream circles. Traditional Christian values would describe "normal" sex as heterosexual intercourse within a married couple. But this was not a scientific definition—it was a moral standard.

So, Pomeroy had begun working toward a scientific definition of "normal" sex. He picked five criteria—statistical, phylogenetic, moral, legal, and social. An act could be "normal" in one category but "abnormal" in another. He used masturbation as his test case, explaining that *statistically*, it was "normal"—that is to say, 50 percent or more of people did it. Phylogenetically, too, masturbation was normal among mammals. In fact, many "normal" mammalian behaviors were regarded as abnormal when practiced by humans. Other mammals, Pomeroy explained, had nonmarital coitus, homosexual relations, and engaged in "mouth-genital contact."

As to the other criteria, he defined morality, tellingly, as being "what is considered right or wrong by the church." Legality was, of course, whether something was permitted by law. The "social" criterion was a particularly interesting one. Pomeroy had constructed it with help from the Group for the Advancement of Psychiatry. It asked whether the action had outcomes that impacted society. Some sexual activities—like masturbation, consensual extramarital intercourse, homosexual coitus, or "mouth-genital contact"—were "not immediately harmful to another individual." Other sexual acts, however, were—rape and child molestation being the most obvious.

Pomeroy's proposed criteria for normality were paradigm shifting: they named the origins of beliefs that previously had been unspoken attitudes or unspoken references to the Christian moral code. Overall,

Pomeroy discouraged use of the terms *normal* and *abnormal*. He told the delegates: "If you find that you must use these terms, let me caution you to define the criterion under which you are calling a particular bit of behavior 'normal' or 'abnormal.' I think it might clear up your thinking."

MARY CALDERONE, PREACHER OF SEX ED

When it came to the future of sex ed, the most important conference speaker was someone who had not even contributed to the assigned collection of essays: Dr. Mary Calderone, the medical director of Planned Parenthood. Her talk was titled "Moral Aspects of Family Planning." She urged churches to educate their young people about sex, and as she broached the topic of STIs and teen pregnancies, she nearly took on the tone of a preacher herself: "A considerable proportion of premarital experiences with the inevitable results of venereal disease and out-of-wedlock pregnancies must be occurring among church-going and Sunday-school-belonging young people."

She continued: "How do you reconcile the fact that sexual energy *is* a driving force centered in a certain part of your body that makes you feel as if you would explode if you don't realize it with the fact that, on the one hand, our culture stimulates that sexual energy with all sorts of stimuli assailing the five senses and, on the other hand, holds up the stop sign with moral codes and economic necessity, saying in effect, 'No and no and no again?' . . . If we are not to be destroyed by this unleashed energy, we must learn to use it constructively, and learning implies education. Who is to do that educating? Again let us face the fact that parents can't—they don't know how and they are emotionally unable to. The schools won't. The reasons for this are many but the facts are there, they won't."

So she issued the churches a challenge: "If marriage is truly to be a sacred undertaking, then it is surely within the bounds of religious teaching for a portion of every year's curriculum to be given up to a churchly discussion of the place of sex in modern life. . . . It is not enough to say 'You shouldn't.' We have to know *why*, in the face of birth control that will become more and more freely available, other controls that are more and more non-existent, and adult contacts with young people that may become less and less."

It was a powerful plea, a sermon, perhaps—well reasoned and well argued. But it didn't sit well with everyone. Dr. Harold Haas, the executive secretary of the Board of Social Missions of the United Lutheran Church, said to Dr. Calderone: "Your very enthusing has us jazzed up . . . and this creates a problem for me." He went on, close to indicting her: "I get the impression that you may be saying that the mission of the church is to supplement the mission of the PPFA [Planned Parenthood]."

THE IMPACT OF NACCF

When the conference adjourned, Calderone's plea had not been adopted wholeheartedly. The delegates' recommendation for sex ed was only that churches should "cooperate with school and other community agencies in programs of sex education."

But more broadly, the conference did seem to lead to some changes in how Protestants thought about sex. Perhaps the conference's clearest impact were the publications that resulted from it: the conference readings were made available in book form under the title *Sex Ways in Fact and Faith*, published by Association Press in 1961. The conference proceedings in full were also published as *Foundations for Christian Family Policy* in the same year by the NCC.

Individual churches made progress as well. In October 1961, *Parade*, a Sunday newspaper magazine, published a two-page article by journalist Ed Keister with the headline, "Is the church changing its mind on sex?" Keister asserted that "organized religion for nearly 20 centuries has taken a puritanical view of sex. But today that attitude is changing dramatically." He noted that "the progress of the sex revolution . . . has been uneven, with some denominations moving further and faster than others. The Methodists, for example, have pioneered in work with engaged couples. Lutherans have made the teenage bride a matter of special concern. But almost all have taken at least preliminary steps toward bringing sex education into the church."[7]

The next year, in 1962, the Family Life Committee of the Michigan Congregational Conference reported that they had "been making a serious study of the book *Foundations for Christian Family Policy*, with a view to helping the churches develop sound and forward-looking family life programs."[8] In October 1963, the Unitarian Church in Arlington, Virginia, had launched a sex ed class for children, citing a need to provide information that wasn't available elsewhere: "the Arlington Public Schools offer no sex education, even banning from their libraries all books on the subject, and have rebuffed every effort to place the subject in the curriculum."[9] In the same year, a study group at the Southern Baptist Church's Conference on Family Life recommended that they "include a stronger emphasis on sex education in Sunday school."[10]

But probably the biggest effect of the NACCF on sex ed was the springboard it provided for what would be the most important sex ed advocacy group in the United States.

CHAPTER 10

THE BIRTH OF SIECUS

CALDERONE AT PLANNED PARENTHOOD

By 1941, Margaret Sanger's ABCL had ballooned into 222 birth control clinics, and in 1942 it took on the name Planned Parenthood Federation of America, or Planned Parenthood for short. Through the 1940s, it had expanded its scope considerably through programs and affiliate groups. In 1953, Mary Calderone, at age forty-nine, became Planned Parenthood's first medical director.

As medical director, Calderone's job was, as she put it years later, to lead the group "on a sound medical and public-health basis." During the 1950s, Planned Parenthood was in a moment of change. As Calderone's most recent biographer, Ellen More, explains, the group's leadership was "determined to become identified not with the ideology of feminist agency and the language of 'birth control'"—as had been the case under Margaret Sanger—"but with the . . . 'rational' idea of 'family planning.'"[1] Under Calderone's leadership, Planned Parenthood began undertaking clinical trials for new types of diaphragms and spermicides, and the group would later also work with the FDA to help evaluate oral contraception. She also served as liaison between Planned Parenthood and two major medical organizations: the American Public Health Association (APHA) and the American Medical Association (AMA). As More put it, during this time Calderone was seeking "stronger and clearer endorsements of family planning as essential to public health and sound medical practice." To make her case, she "presented contraception as preventive medicine against the 'diseases' of abortion and teenage pregnancy."[2]

And her efforts led to real change. In 1959, due in great part to Calderone's hard work, the APHA released an official resolution in regard to the "population problem," calling for "full freedom . . . for the selection and use of such methods for the regulation of family size."[3] In making such a resolution, Ellen More explains, APHA became "the first large professional organization to [endorse] family planning as part of ordinary medical care."[4]

The next year, 1960, the FDA approved the oral contraceptive known as Enovid, entwining medicine and family planning even further. Once approved, it became known simply as "the Pill," an extremely popular form of birth control—although it was not legal in all states for all people; the Comstock Law and some "little Comstock" laws still stood. State laws around abortion were often similarly restrictive. While at Planned Parenthood, Calderone spoke about the injustice of "illegal abortions." She knew that Americans had always sought, received, and performed abortions, and she attended to that fact openly and honestly. Her own views on the subject tended toward the pragmatic rather than the radical. "I am not for abortion," she wrote in 1959, "but trained in public health. I am for preventing any need for abortion, and I also am for facing the problem of illegal abortion which is with us."[5] She thought primarily of abortion as a "preventable disease" and decried the hurdles to obtaining contraception that had made unplanned pregnancies—and therefore abortions—so widespread. In 1959, she gave an address to the Maternal and Child Health Section of the APHA—later published in the *American Journal of Public Health*—in which she spoke passionately about the inhumanity of the abortion law in the United States: how whether or not something was a "therapeutic" abortion—which is to say, legal because it was for a reason deemed appropriate—was often left up to a doctor who might be easily swayed by a well-to-do family or the right amount of money.

The problem of illegal abortion, then, was to Calderone "far broader in scope than just the question of a woman who does not want a particular pregnancy." To address some of the structural inequities inherent in the current state of abortion in the United States, she suggested increasing access to healthcare, including "the means of regulating parenthood," but also urged "continued and realistic sex education." In her work at Planned Parenthood over the years, one of the things that Calderone saw most clearly—and which stayed with her most profoundly—was that Americans simply did not have the information that they needed when it came to sexual health. As she reflected in 1971, years after leaving the organization, "Many individuals . . . wrote letters to me about sexual problems that had nothing to do with planned parenthoods. These people simply had no other place to write to."[6]

FINDING ALLIES

Calderone had all of this in mind when she attended the NACCF in 1961 and gave her impassioned speech urging Protestant churches to teach sex ed. While the delegates' responses to her talk had been mixed, some agreed with her and were in a position to do something about it. One of those people was Lester Kirkendall, the family life professor who had spoken so eloquently about the mid-century cultural changes around sex. Kirkendall, like Calderone, had encountered many people who needed information on sex and had nowhere to turn. Between his war service and his arrival at Oregon State University, he had taught psychology to American GIs in Florence, Italy. One of his classes was Psychology of Marriage, which at its height enrolled more than eight hundred people. He found that many of his students were seeking guidance not on marriage, but on sex: "'Is premarital intercourse right or wrong, and why?' 'Will having sexual intercourse strengthen a relationship?' 'If two persons agree to engage in sexual relations, what then makes it wrong?'"[7]

Kirkendall had developed a somewhat radical ethic: He did not see sex within marriage as inherently good, nor sex outside of marriage as inherently bad. Rather, he explained, he was concerned with "the quality of relationships." Had everyone involved in a given sexual encounter felt respected? Were they mature enough to understand the consequences of the encounter? "Once we become genuinely concerned," he explained in his NACCF address, "with the creation of relationships which have in them trust, integrity, respect, and a broad, reaching-out interest in others, we have to think differently about sexual expressions."[8]

So, at the NACCF, Kirkendall and Calderone found allies in each other. They shared similarities in subject interest and approach—but most of all in the belief that there needed to be some great new push toward sex ed in the United States.

In the late 1950s Kirkendall had traveled to Sweden, where he'd visited the RSFU—the Swedish Association for Sexuality Education. He had also visited Denmark and the Netherlands, which had similar organizations—all geared to providing information about sex for its own sake. At NACCF, he shared these experiences with Dr. Calderone, and they decided together, as he put it, "that the United States need[ed] such an organization also."

A NEW ORGANIZATION

According to Wallace Fulton, the president of the National Council on Family Relations (NCFR), by April 1963 Calderone had "come to the conclusion that there is need for a new, independent organization which would deal with the informational and education aspects of human sexuality."[9] Fulton, who had convened a meeting of sex ed and FLE experts for a panel, noted that among his peers, "there was a fairly widespread agreement th[a]t such an organization might indeed be a worthwhile undertaking."

The next year, in June 1964, Calderone left her position at Planned Parenthood to become the executive director of her newly founded Sex Information and Education Council of the United States (SIECUS.) The independent nonprofit's stated purpose, in full, was

> To establish man's sexuality as a health entity: to identify the special characteristics that distinguish it from, yet relate it to, human reproduction; to dignify it by openness of approach, study and scientific research designed to lead towards its understanding and its freedom from exploration; to give leadership to professionals and to society, to the end that human beings may be added towards responsible use of their sexual faculty and towards assimilation of sex into their individual life patterns as a creative and re-creative force.

SIECUS clearly viewed sex differently than any of the public sexual health advocacy organizations that had preceded it. For SIECUS, sex was not only part of "family life," it was part of *health*. It was not only *reproduction*, it was a "creative force." It needed be addressed with *dignity* and with *science*, not with—perhaps the implication was—shame and religion. The group's founding documents went on to explain that the great scientific and social changes in the world had also led to changes in and around sex. SIECUS pledged to provide an "objective, responsible and positive approach to sex" where there hadn't been one before.[10]

The original board of directors consisted of Fulton (who was also the president), William Genné (who had been integral to the NACCF), Clark Vincent, Kirkendall, and Calderone. SIECUS declared its "broad, interdisciplinary approach," its wish to cooperate with existing groups and educational efforts, and its desire to "expand the scope of sex education to all age levels and groups," not just children and young people. They saw themselves as an "organization's organization"—they hoped to serve as a "clearing house" for information about sex, to help codify studies and materials, to "plan, obtain support for, carry out or sponsor, and publish, such research and programs . . . toward the stated purposes of the organization," and to "provide a continuing forum whose scientific atmosphere will make it possible to consider and discuss, with dispassionate objectivity, all aspects of human sexual behavior."

In some very important ways, then, SIECUS shared a lot with the ASSMP, formed sixty years earlier. Although they were separated by massive advances in medicine and society, both had been founded by doctors who had seen that *something was not right* with the way that Americans thought about sex, that education was key to addressing this, and that open communication was invaluable to the process. SIECUS also, like the ASSMP, saw the importance of religion in the conversation about sex. As Calderone had made clear in her address to the NACCF, she believed that churches could be a vector for sex ed. Both the ASSMP and SIECUS were ambitious, idealistic, and clearheaded. But where the ASSMP had assumed so many things—that moral truths were obvious, that chastity was good, that there was a "normal" type of sexuality to point to and strive for—SIECUS was marked with a very 1960s belief that everything was open for discussion.

In President Fulton's inaugural article for the *SIECUS Newsletter*, he wrote that the group expected "to work closely with established, family-centered, interdisciplinary organizations." He may have been thinking of groups like ASHA, but also churches and groups like the NCFR, which cared deeply about "family life" and family life education. The promise to coordinate showed an understanding of the larger context that SIECUS was part of—but in other ways, SIECUS positioned itself as radical and new.

Calderone herself seemed to betray some ignorance of the long history of sex ed in the United States. In May 1964 she addressed the National PTA, noting, "Although we do know a good deal about reproductive education, as yet we have little idea of what sex education should be," and in January 1965, she explained that her goals for SIECUS included "probably studies to determine . . . what sex education really is."[11]

The group positioned itself as up for any challenge—and in the mid-1960s, there were many challenges that sex ed could address. In addition to the persistent social woes of STIs and teen pregnancy, a new concern—overpopulation—had also entered the fray.

THE OVERPOPULATION PANIC

By 1960, the world's population had hit three billion—an impressive number. But more remarkable, and troubling, than the number itself was the rate at which the population had grown. "The increase," one academic tells us, "from 2 billion to 3 billion took about 35 years, whereas the increase from 1 billion to 2 billion took about 125 years and the addition of the first billion took from the beginning of the human race until about 1800."[12] Scientists were concerned: who was to say that the rate of growth wouldn't continue to climb? Thanks to technological and medical advances, death rates had dropped, while birth rates remained high. How would the planet support so many people? These were big, important questions. To answer them, centers were formed, studies were funded, and articles and books were written.

The biggest fears centered on food production, depletion of nonrenewable resources, and poverty levels—especially in growing nations.[13] The United States took a deep interest in the issue. In 1961, the State Department appointed a population officer, and the US also funded international projects meant to slow the feared population boom.[14] Both domestically and abroad, limiting family size was identified as an obvious way to curb population growth, and it was this more than anything that pushed groups like the APHA to endorse family planning as healthcare. It also breathed new life into arguments about sex ed.

Biology professor Irwin Slesnick argued in an article for the journal the *American Biology Teacher* in 1964 that young people should be taught about the problems of overpopulation in schools, which necessarily included lessons on limiting family size. Students should be instructed in "contraceptive materials and practices," he argued, that allowed "couples to plan with reliability, when to have a family, and how large the family will be."[15] As schools were already dubious of teaching the simple facts of reproduction, this was going to be a hard sell—but Slesnick believed it was of paramount importance. "The majority of young adults," he said, "become sexually mature, poorly informed of the facts of sex and reproduction, and ignorant of the social and individual implications of their role in maintaining the human species."[16]

The overpopulation issue did not immediately seed sex ed classes in every American school, but it was a crucial factor in one of the AMA's most significant policy changes. In 1964, the AMA revised its position on contraception, formally dropping its once "neutral" position to one of support. Now, the group urged, doctors should "accept a major responsibility in matters related to human reproduction as they affect the total population and the individual family."[17] And in the same year, the AMA announced its support for school-based sex ed due to rising rates of STIs. "Unless education authorities create and improve programs concerning health and sex instruction in our schools," said Dr. Robert Kaplan, a consultant in health and fitness for the AMA, "the number of cases of venereal disease will continue to increase."[18]

MODERNIZING SEX ED—AND MANAGING EXPECTATIONS

When it came to sex, the world was truly shifting and changing, and schools themselves were noticing that their established sex ed and FLE curricula were not addressing the problems at hand. In 1963, the longtime director of health services for the public schools of San Diego, California, said, "Sex education in our schools really isn't very educational," and noted that the classes tended to end up being "as innocuous as possible. The most graphic description of impregnation in one widely used school movie, for instance, goes something like 'And so the male eggs meet [the] female egg.' . . . This doesn't satisfy today's teenagers."[19]

And so, it was not so surprising, perhaps, that SIECUS found quick public acceptance of its mission. In June 1965, Calderone reported: "In the 4 months that followed the first modest, public announcement of the existence of SIECUS, we received over a thousand requests from schools, colleges, public health and education departments, obstetricians, psychiatrists, pediatricians, general practitioners and many other professionals, asking for assistance in setting up sex education programs."[20] SIECUS also garnered quick financial support, receiving a grant in its first year from the Commonwealth Fund, a private foundation dedicated to funding healthcare initiatives.[21]

Some seasoned experts within the family life field, however, regarded SIECUS with some measure of hesitation, in part because it brought so much attention to sex ed where it had languished in near obscurity for decades. Curtis E. Avery, director of the E. C. Brown Trust—the organization that had produced the landmark film *Human Growth*—wrote in 1964 that, while the subject had once fought "for recognition and acceptance," now the subject "is forced to defend itself against the over-expectations of many people."[22] There was a popular sense that one sex ed class could directly reduce rates of teen pregnancy and STIs—a prescription as surefire as a dose of penicillin. This was not realistic. But Avery believed that sex ed was still valuable. "If sex education does no more than dispel sexual ignorance," he explained, "it is justified but not on the grounds of prevention of premarital intercourse, pregnancy and VD."[23]

But Avery's warnings were not heeded, especially as rates of sexually transmitted infections continued to climb. In 1965, the *13th Joint Statement on Venereal Disease* announced the seventh consecutive year rise of infectious syphilis.[24] In September of the same year, the AMA called on "all state and local medical societies . . . schools, hospitals, and federal, state and local health agencies to join the campaign to acquaint the public with the nature of venereal disease."[25]

And even though organizations like ASHA and the E. C. Brown Trust had been promoting sex ed for decades, SIECUS's novelty and relatively high profile made it the go-to authority during this time of perceived need. Just a month after the AMA campaign was announced, SIECUS released their first study guide, "intended," the pamphlet explained, "primarily for discussion leaders and for individuals interested in intensive, self-motivated study." The title was *Sex Education*, and the author was Lester Kirkendall. In it, Kirkendall outlined his basic views of sex ed, what he thought of as weaknesses in existing programs, and his recommended objectives and ranges for programs.

In many ways, what he laid out was not so dissimilar from early conceptions of sex ed, which made sense given Kirkendall's close professional relationship with Maurice Bigelow. "Sex education," the guide affirmed, "must be broadly conceived, concerning itself with the biological, psychological and social factors which affect personality and interpersonal relationships." Where it had a more decidedly 1965 flavor was in the addition of phrases like "reality-orientated," as well as its stated commitment to dealing with "actual sexual patterns." The guide also promoted an approach that would help young people form their own values: "values by which to live, and standards by which to make important decisions." This was a profound departure from early models of sex ed.

Morrow, Bigelow, and even people like Curtis Avery had written with the assumption that there was just one correct way to have sex: within marriage. But as the data had aways shown, people were having sex "in non-marital situations"—and now extramarital sex had fewer medical and legal ramifications than it had in the past. Kirkendall and SIECUS, by extension, wanted sex education to reflect that. So, he argued that sex ed should be about the formation of specific values: "respect of the basic worth, equality, and dignity of each human being; the right of each individual to self-determination; recognition of the need for cooperative effort for the common good; and faith in the free play of critical intelligence."[26] This too was a departure from the established understanding of sex ed.

CENTERING THE SCHOOLS

Whereas the standard line among longtime sex ed experts like ASHA, the E. C. Brown Trust, and other social hygienists was that sex ed was best taught at home, with the school and church providing support, Kirkendall gave a full-throated endorsement of school-based sex ed—not as the second-best option, but as the best moral and pedagogical choice. While Dr. Calderone had called the churches the best site for sex ed in 1961, by 1967 SIECUS was prioritizing the schools. Young people, Kirkendall argued, should not receive only their parents' perspectives on sex—this wouldn't adequately prepare the child for the "cosmos that has become as complex and varied as is today's world." Instead, young people should be exposed to a range of ideas early on. "Education," Kirkendall wrote, "is obtained by interchange and the free interplay of ideas." Ideally, sex ed classes would give young people the opportunity for such interplay.

But the current state of sex ed, he went on, was not conducive to that type of real learning. Standard sex ed lessons, he said, were typically "imposed" rather than introduced in such a way to allow students to exchange ideas. In part, this was because sex was such a difficult topic to teach. Teachers might resort to a "didactic approach," he explained, "when questions of standards, personal behavior, and a development of moral values arise." This didactic, perhaps even prescriptive mode of teaching, Kirkendall explained, "may provide a feeling of security for the adult," but it did not offer the opportunity for real learning, nor for communication between the generations.

The guide also presented another radical departure from sex ed and FLE norms when it stated that young people themselves were "sexual beings with sexual needs," and needed to be taught about the "immense possibilities for human fulfillment that human sexuality offers." This acknowledgment had often been missing in family-life education, which discussed sex only in the context of a married future.

These were bold and innovative ideas, but SIECUS was a bold and innovative group. There was real optimism about the organization, from without and within. In April 1965, at a Vassar Club meeting, Calderone said she did "not anticipate the kind of opposition such as faced Margaret Sanger for many years in her crusade for birth control."[27] In 1967, SIECUS noted with pride the strides it had made. It was proud of the "flood of inquiries" they were receiving and the "heavy demand" for their publications.[28] It continued to receive funding from the Commonwealth Fund and had also received monies from the Public Welfare Foundation and the Ford Foundation.

The United States government had indicated its support of SIECUS in 1966 when the Department of Education had, according to a *SIECUS Newsletter*, "provided almost all the necessary funds for a SIECUS Working Conference" that December.[29] The government also provided federal funding for specific programs that brought sex ed to schools, including "Aid to Schools in Low Income Areas," "Supplementary Educational Center and Services for Elementary and Secondary Schools," "Community Service and Continuing education programs," "Vocational and Technical Education," and others.[30]

Sex ed was taking hold in a very real, very modern way, and all seemed to be going swimmingly for SIECUS and for the subject. "During our first three years," Calderone reflected later, "our only frustration was lack of funds to do what we wanted to do as quickly as we knew it needed to be done."[31] But, soon, SIECUS would have a very new set of obstacles.

CHAPTER 11

THE RELIGIOUS RIGHT COMES FOR SIECUS

AS BOYS GROW IN ANAHEIM

In August 1962—one year after the NACCF, and two years before SIECUS was officially founded—Mr. and Mrs. Brownie of Anaheim, California, parents of four, attended a school board meeting to register their displeasure with a film called *As Boys Grow.*[1] The film, from 1957, was routinely shown to boys in the school district and centered on a coach with his track team, comprised of young teenagers. The coach explains, without fanfare or humor, the realities of puberty, reproductive systems, and masturbation, as well as the dangers of premarital pregnancy.

The film, Mrs. Brownie charged, made no mention of "right or wrong . . . of marriage, love or religion." A group of her allies at the meeting agreed—they wanted the film banned in the district.[2]

Superintendent Paul Cook stood behind the film. It would continue to be screened in the schools, he said, but every parent had the right to excuse their own children from watching it.[3] This concession was not enough for the couple, who returned to another school board meeting with an escalated request: now, they not only called for the film to be banned, but they also, recalled school nurse Sally Williams, "requested that all reference to sex be deleted from the entire school curriculum, including biology."[4] The board rejected their request, although they did concede to stop screening *As Boys Grow* in schools, at least temporarily.[5]

In response, the Brownies took to their local newspaper, the Long Beach *Press-Telegram*. In a letter to the editor they wrote that they "cannot and will not ever believe that the majority of parents of the students in the Anaheim Union High School District would for one moment go along with this trash."[6]

Superintendent Cook and the school district's board of trustees took the Brownies' claim seriously. Did the parents and students of Anaheim truly not want sex ed? As Cook recalled, he and the board "recognized that the district either had to bow to this demand or solicit the opinion of parents and patrons on their attitudes on sex instruction in our public secondary schools." That October, he formed an advisory committee to investigate the question.[7]

THE ANAHEIM CURRICULUM

The committee members represented a wide range of interests and motivations. The chairman, the Reverend Harry F. Stief, represented the Anaheim Ministerial Association. Other committee members included representatives from the Buena Park Boys Club, the Orange County Probation Department,[8] the Orange County Medical Association, and the Anaheim Police Department.[9] The group hired an independent company to survey Anaheim-area adults about sex ed. The results were clear: the Brownies were wrong. "Ninety-two percent of the adults," it was reported, "in the Anaheim Union High School District felt that we must give adequate instruction in sex education at both the junior and senior high school levels."[10] The takeaway was obvious: Anaheim should have sex ed.

The committee recommended the creation of a "standard sex education program" for all schools in the district. Although *As Boys Grow* had been screened in Anaheim public schools, Paul Cook later explained that in 1962, when the Brownies protested, only two schools in the district were instructing students in sex, "at a minimal level."[11] The committee encouraged, then, the use of standardized "classroom texts, reference materials and visual aids." Other recommendations included specially trained and qualified teachers ("whenever possible they should be married"), classes separated by gender through junior high, and parental notice of the curriculum via letter at the beginning of the year, "stating that parents may withdraw children from the course if they wish." The notification would also inform parents and guardians that they were "welcome to examine course materials and visit classes."[12]

"Moral issues," the committee noted, would be "emphasized and stressed," and the topic of STIs would be included. The creation of the curriculum fell to Sally Williams, the school nurse who had been at the latter board meeting that the Brownies had attended.[13]

The result was a curriculum—published first internally in 1967, with in-depth lesson plans and scope and sequencing for seventh through twelfth grades—that was clearly influenced by the changing views of the time but also deeply entrenched in the tradition of the subject. It had the hallmarks of modernity, at least on the surface—it seemed to listen directly to Lester Kirkendall's statement that a good sex ed class would not "impose" a lesson but would instead be based on a free interchange of ideas. As one version of the curriculum guide explained, the class aimed to help "the student to determine his solutions to problems in the light of his own goals and philosophy within the context of the community's goals and values."[14] This moral relativism appeared to be leaps and bounds ahead of the early twentieth-century pamphlets that had spelled out a Judeo-Christian morality with no room for any other options.

But when it came to suggestions for behavior, Anaheim's sex ed curriculum relied on traditional rhetoric. One suggested text, *On Becoming a Woman*, advised teenage girls, "Your restless body and mind lead you to question everything you hear and read and learn and see; to question politics and religion and your parents and sex. And you find that most of your skepticism leads only to a new appreciation of accepted standards."[15] On the issue of birth control, the district's curriculum guide noted that "student questions about birth control and contraceptives are to be answered within the concept of family planning." In other words, questions about how an unmarried student (presumably most of the students in these classes) might procure or use contraception would not be answered.

But the curriculum did openly discuss topics that had once been taboo, such as homosexuality. It moved away from the longstanding view of homosexuality as a "perversion." However, it was still far from embracing the idea. In the ninth-grade section, the curriculum noted that a person who'd had "a few homosexual experiences" was not necessarily a "homosexual," and that homosexuality was "relatively widespread in our society, although it is not approved, condoned, or encouraged for males or females of any age."[16]

GAINING MOMENTUM

Whatever internal textual tensions were present in the curriculum, the courses were a success. The school district held a pilot program in 1965, one year after SIECUS had formed. By 1966, the course was, according to Vi Ehinger of the *Los Angeles Times*, "so well accepted that it will go into its expanded version in grades 7 through 12 this September."[17] By 1967, Superintendent Cook was decidedly proud of what he had created. In November, he called the class "an unqualified success. . . . I could not have asked for better response from the students, the teachers and the parents."[18]

The positive feedback kept coming. In November 1967, the *Los Angeles Times* reported that the course was "being copied around the world. . . . The district is receiving requests from churches and schools in England, Japan, East Africa, Italy and many school districts throughout the United States to supply information on the course."[19]

Like SIECUS, the Anaheim program was responding to a major need, and it seemed to offer concrete solutions to very real problems. Rates of STIs were continuing to rise, especially among young people, through the mid-1960s. ASHA reported that in 1966 "the rate of infectious syphilis among teenagers (15–19) was 22.5 per 100,000 population, more than twice the national rate of 10.9 for all age groups. Gonorrhea among teen-agers reached a rate of 424.9 per 100,000 in the same year, compared with a national rate of 178.6 for all age groups."[20]

Anaheim's curriculum soon became strongly associated with SIECUS—despite the fact that there had been no formal links between the two when the curriculum was created. But both gained popularity around the same time, and the Anaheim program did share many aspects of SIECUS's approach, especially when it came to ostensibly allowing young people to come to their own conclusions.

The Anaheim program and SIECUS did become formally connected in the later 1960s. Sally Williams was a SIECUS board member by 1967.[21] And in 1968, the publisher Harcourt, Brace, and World published

Anaheim's curriculum in book form as *Family Life and Sex Education: Curriculum and Instruction*. The authors were Sally Williams and Esther D. Schulz, SIECUS's associate director for educational services. Mary Calderone wrote the introduction. In it, she was clear that the original Anaheim curriculum had been created independently of her organization. It had been formulated, she explained, "well before SIECUS was established," and "SIECUS . . . can claim no credit for it."[22]

SIECUS also popularized ideas that seemed born of Cook's experience in Anaheim, especially the idea of creating a committee tasked with assessing the needs of sex ed in a community and, if a need was shown, proposing next steps for implementing such a program. In 1967, the *SIECUS Newsletter* published an article written by Mary Calderone and Frances Breed that explained this concept, entitled "Community Responsibility for Sex Education."

Community support was essential to sex ed, they wrote, and anyone who was interested in advocating for it in their community should step forward. Once there was enough interest in bringing sex ed to a given locale, a committee should be formed that included all kinds of people: "representatives of the clergy, medical and para-medical professions, school board and administration, teachers, parents and social agencies."[23] The committee should then hold "small meetings" or workshops for the public, "allowing time for public awareness and support to grow; make sure that the school administration is aware that the Committee's active support does not mean active interference!"

Then, the committee might suggest a specific plan or curriculum and present it to the school board. If opposition arose, it would be welcome as an opportunity for dialogue. A practicing Quaker, Mary Calderone often attributed her organizing approach to her religious background. In Quakerism, each person is believed to have inward access to God, and there is a high value placed on communal discernment—a belief that a higher truth can be revealed when a group is working toward a specific goal or action. "Whenever opposition is expressed," Breed and Calderone wrote, "opportunity should be made for it to be heard and answered. Those who start from a negative point of view, once the facts are properly presented, may become involved in the program and may become its strong advocates."[24] They believed each community would create the committee it needed, which in turn would create the sex ed course that the community needed.

This model gained steam in 1966 and 1967. In those years alone, more than a dozen sex ed committees were formed across the country, from Austin, Texas,[25] to Fremont, California,[26] to Lehigh County, Pennsylvania.[27] These committees were all different, of varying sizes and approaches and paces of work, but all indicated that there was sustained interest in the project of sex ed across the country. A nationwide movement seemed to be gaining momentum.

But, by September 1968, the shining example of Anaheim's model curriculum and committee-based approach would seem almost like a relic of a different 1960s preserved in amber.

A NEW RIGHT IN ORANGE COUNTY AND BEYOND

In the six years between 1962 and 1968—as Anaheim-style sex ed was developed, implemented, praised, and endorsed by SIECUS—America at large saw a staggering amount of social change. The Supreme Court banned recitation of prayer in public schools. Conservative Republican Barry Goldwater lost his 1964 bid for the presidency, causing a spike of action from the John Birch Society (JBS), an ultraconservative activist group founded by Robert Welch. Malcolm X was assassinated. Bloody Sunday took place in Selma, Alabama, during which civil rights protesters were attacked, and in the same month, the first United States troops landed on the shores of Vietnam. Communism became, yet again in the United States, a bugaboo for conservatives, who condemned anyone with real or perceived ties to the ideology. The Voting Rights Act passed, which banned racial discrimination in voting; and Medicare and Medicaid were established. The Black Panther Party was formed. Ronald Reagan was elected governor of California. Race riots began and spread. Martin Luther King Jr. was assassinated. The Civil Rights Act of 1968 was signed.

The country was remaking itself. Activists were challenging America to make good on its promises of life, liberty, and the pursuit of happiness for more than just the white Protestant hegemony. And a sector of white Americans, who saw this movement as a direct threat to their rights, fought back. And they had a number of outlets through which to do so—including, importantly, the JBS.

One of the places that the JBS thrived in the 1960s was Orange County, California—home to Anaheim. Orange County was an extremely important location in the United States during this time. The area had become wealthy during the 1950s, when defense contracts had brought a huge amount of money to the county. The boom in military-industrial jobs in turn attracted many migrants—mostly white—from the Southern and Midwestern Bible Belt. These changing demographics led to an increase in population, and an increase in conservative Protestant churches.[28]

The JBS was originally conceived of as a group opposed to communism and socialism, but by the mid-1960s had revealed itself to be far more than that. By 1965, the group had become vocal in its opposition to civil rights, calling the "Negro rights movement . . . part of the Communist-led revolutionary movement against capitalism."[29] The JBS, which was originally based in Massachusetts but had local chapters around the country, found real support in Orange County, from ordinary citizens to (reportedly) bigwigs like Walter Knott of Knott's Berry Farm. But there was also something darker, and bigger, brewing in sunny Orange County: a new strain of American ideology variously called the *new right*, *religious right*, *radical right*, or *far right* by outsiders and the press.* Academic Lisa McGirr, in her book *Suburban Warriors*, describes the movement as originating "in booming suburban enclaves, nowhere more powerfully than in Orange County, California."[30]

The religious right explicitly melded right-wing politics with Christian theology. Its members were mainly white and overwhelmingly held racist views. Their strain of Christianity prioritized personal salvation over social gospel and, as McGirr puts it, "opposed what they perceived to be a decline in religiosity, morality, individual responsibility, and family authority." This same conservatism "championed virulent anticommunism, celebrated laissez-faire capitalism, evoked staunch nationalism, and supported the use of the state to uphold law and order."[31]

These believers turned to what they called "'traditional morality'—a belief in moral absolutes, and a God-centered vision of the nation." This worldview had no ambiguity: there was only good and evil, God and the

---

* I choose to use the term *religious right*, as I believe it to be the most descriptive and least value laden of the monikers—but each term denotes essentially the same group.

devil, America and communism. And in that grand schema, sex ed fell squarely in the company of evil, Satan, and the Reds. The subject matter undermined parental authority, endorsed atheism, condoned premarital sex, and did all this through the public school system—itself a symbol of ever-expanding governmental overreach.

Throughout the summer of 1968, opposition to sex ed became an "it" issue of the Right. Ultraconservative activists were quick to demonize both Anaheim's program and SIECUS, strengthening the public association between the two in the process. In June 1968, right-wing commentator Frank Capell wrote a column entitled "A Look at Sex Education" in his newsletter, the *Herald of Freedom*. He, like so many others, was obsessed with the dangers of communism, and he warned his readers that "sex and communism are involved in the personnel of a fairly new organization": SIECUS.[32]

GORDON DRAKE

Other religious right organizations took the message further, creating pamphlets and whole books. Among the most famous and inciting was Gordon Drake's *Is the Schoolhouse the Proper Place for Raw Sex?*, which was published in 1968 by an Oklahoma-based evangelical conservative group founded in 1950 called the Christian Crusade. The Christian Crusade was led by Billy James Hargis, who was among the first great American radio preachers.

Although American Protestantism had long contained major schisms, by the 1960s, fundamentalism was making an important resurgence in the religious life in the country, deepening the divide between denominations. Christian fundamentalists like Hargis and Drake, who believed in the literal word of the Bible, moved into what some scholars now call a "separatist phase," withdrawing from other Christian groups that disagreed with them and distancing themselves from them vocally. To Drake, the Bible was very clear on sex: "God speaks out plainly and repeatedly against all adultery, fornication, prostitution, and such perversions as homosexuality." Sex ed programs like SIECUS's and Anaheim's were, in his mind, direct affronts to God's desires.

The Christian Crusade ran an impressive direct-mail empire, and Drake's book was sent to many conservative Christian homes. The book laid out a case against sex ed in general and SIECUS in particular. It was written in a raw and religious tone that elevated the issue to one of utmost importance. And he quickly identified an Enemy #1.

"Dr. Mary Calderone," the book begins, "has a burning mission. To alert and convert the youth of America to a new sexuality." Calderone, he explained, was "telling young people about their right to enjoy premarital intercourse—if they so desire it. . . . The thrust of SIECUS is to get the most sex information to the child as early as possible."[33] This was an overstatement—if not a warping—of Calderone and SIECUS's position, but Drake's book was not about truth. It was propaganda. And it was wildly effective.

Some of Drake's claims were old standbys: sex ed was "intruding into a private family and church responsibility," and the courses provided "no attempt to build character; [and] merely spell[ed] out the options available in the sensual grab bag of sexual delights." But Drake more pointedly censured SIECUS and "new" sex ed, citing specific "objectionable" materials that he attributed to SIECUS. A set of slides called *How Babies Are Made* was, according to Drake, "an animalistic viewpoint of sex which is shocking and completely inappropriate for children three to eight years of age—the age group for which they were designed." The slides, which were later published as a book, used paper cutouts to show how flowers, chickens, dogs, and, finally, human beings produce new life.

SIECUS was not, in fact, in the business of creating original materials or curricula (the exception was a filmstrip called *Sex Education, USA*, made for PTAs and other interested groups). They did endorse, consult on, and recommend materials, including *How Babies Are Made*. But Drake accused SIECUS of being a well-orchestrated, devious, and underhanded machine trying to infiltrate all public schools. He cited SIECUS's ties to the US Office of Education and recent arrangements with publishing houses as evidence of this.

Drake's book promulgated myths that would be cited as anti-sex-ed gospel at school board meetings and in letters to the editor for years to come. One of the most long-lasting was the claim that in some schools, "the male and female sex organs are fashioned by little children" out of clay. He cited an article from *McCall's* magazine, which in turn cited a 1967 piece from *Time* magazine entitled "On Teaching Children About

Sex."[34] The *Time* article reported that "in the classroom, teachers . . . especially in the elementary grades . . . commonly assign children to model the male and female genitals in clay or make drawings of them and their workings. Some instructors use plastic manikins from which the exterior genitals can be removed to reveal the apparatus within."[35]

It is true that anatomical models were used in sex ed classes during this time. However, the anecdote about modeling genitals in clay seems to have been manufactured. The activity was certainly not part of any reputable curriculum.

Drake's book ended with a strong call to action: he urged parents to form opposition groups before sex ed had even been put into their local public schools. These groups would "engage in an active education program of their own enlisting the understanding and support of service organizations, ministers, educators, school board members, elected officials, and the news media."

Some such groups already existed, he explained, and the more that popped up, the better. "In a local PTA," he wrote, "it takes only one person who is fearless and sure of his stand and who commands respect, to crystalize the views of the majority of silent—but thinking members. It takes one person with intelligent and persuasive gifts as a speaker, or a letter writer, to enunciate the unspoken feelings of the majority of well-meaning Americans. . . . IT TAKES YOU!"

PHOEBE COURTNEY, JACK HYLES, AND MOTOREDE

Drake's book was the first in what became a small boom of conservative Christian screeds against sex ed in the late 1960s. In 1969, a well-known member of the religious right, Phoebe Courtney, published *The Sex Education Racket: An Exposé*.

Courtney's "exposé" rehashed most of Drake's talking points, and then went a step further. Courtney quoted known anti-sex-ed doctors to argue that sex ed was psychologically harmful. Among these supposed experts were Melvin Anchell, a doctor and psychoanalyst, and Rhoda Lorand, a psychologist. In their arguments, both Anchell and Lorand pointed to the Freudian concept of the "latency period," which held that children between the ages of about seven and twelve had no interest in sex. Sex ed, the argument went, was an interruption of this normal period of one's life, and, as Lorand wrote, "it is a mistake to interfere with the latency period, when the major portion of sexual energy and curiosity is normally redirected into learning academic subjects and physical skills."[36] Anchell, who went on to testify frequently on the dangers of sex ed, often for a fee, maintained the same basic argument. The concept of such a "latency period," however, was widely regarded as inaccurate. A Penn State psychologist, Dr. Carlfred Broderick, reported in 1969 that there was "no latency period where sex was not of interest."[37]

But the right-wing publications kept coming, and the arguments therein kept escalating. In 1969, Indiana pastor Jack Hyles released a pamphlet called *Sex Education Program in Our Public Schools; What Is Behind It?* His argument against the courses covered many of the same points as Courtney's and Drake's, but from an even more decidedly evangelistic, Bible-based point of view. After telling his readers that SIECUS's board members and associates "should have their pictures in post offices across America with the word WANTED underneath them," he urged them to "check on your child. Stand up, be different. . . . Well, you say, 'I am afraid little Johnny will be embarrassed.' It wasn't easy on Shadrach, Meshach, and Abednego, you know. Daniel was not the most popular boy in the Senior class. . . . What's wrong with Christians' believing something, living by it, standing by it, dying for it!"[38]

Around the same time that these pamphlets were being published, in 1969, the JBS, which had started to lose some steam, now created an offshoot called MOTOREDE—short for "Movement to Restore Decency"—which focused exclusively on fighting sex ed. MOTOREDE chapters were founded across the nation, including in Westchester County, New York;[39] South Bay, California;[40] and Wisconsin.[41]

And so, by the late 1960s, people who wanted to protest against sex ed no longer had to rely on just their own communities and instincts. Now they could read detailed plans written by religious leaders, political pundits, and psychologists on how best to thwart sex ed. Now they could join groups that had been founded for that exact purpose. Now they were part of a national movement. SIECUS watched as all this was happening and saw clearly what they were up against. In April 1969, Calderone stated that SIECUS and sex ed were being subjected to "a party line of . . . lies, skillfully constructed half-truths and quotes out of context—to lend a semblance of credibility and sober documentation."[42] She described the "small town newspapers, radio and TV stations, and a few big cities, swallowing this party line, and parroting verbatim across the country the fabrications fed to them as truth. . . . We see organized intimidation, using well-known propaganda techniques, of honest citizens at meetings of local boards of education."

And indeed, from 1968 to the early 1970s, school boards, local newspapers, and state legislatures across the country lit up with sex ed dramas, the plot changing slightly but the broad outlines nearly always the same.

LOCAL SKIRMISHES, MOMS, AND LAWSUITS

In hamlets, medium-sized cities, and veritable metropolises, events took on almost eerie similarity: Boards of education would hold meetings. Attendance would be low, as it normally was. The board would announce reasonable plans to implement sex ed. A committee might be appointed. Months later, the local newspaper would report that sex ed was ready to be introduced into the schools. The curriculum plans were announced. The board was ready to approve them. Then, the drama ensued. Pickets, protests. School boards at a crossroads.

In the spring of 1968, the San Luis Coastal Unified School District in California proposed a "Health and Family Living" program,[43] which the press often referred to as a "sex ed" program. When opposition to the proposed courses arose, the board attempted a compromise: it would pull the most objectionable materials (including *How Babies are Made*), and also establish a twenty-seven-person committee to attempt to develop a sex education curriculum that worked for everyone.[44] However, this committee was created only *after* opposition had formed—a timing that was not in keeping with SIECUS best practices. Because battle lines had already been drawn, the school board itself requested that two of the committee members be specifically pro–sex ed and two opposed.[45]

The fight was not confined only to the school board. In the fall of 1968, sex ed opponents began running advertisements in the local paper that were designed to look like op-eds, expounding on the dangers of sex ed.[46] They included testimonies from parents who claimed their children had been adversely affected by sex ed, and at one point featured an open letter from anti–sex ed activist and psychoanalyst Melvin Anchell. In the same year, four parents filed a lawsuit against the school district for its sex ed program, calling the courses "a blanket indictment by the defendants of the ability of parents and homes in this district to instruct their children."[47]

The sex ed drama in Tustin, California was particularly interesting due to the city's proximity to Anaheim (just ten miles away). As early as January 1968, there had been rumblings in Tustin about adopting a version of Anaheim's curriculum. In March, a small group of parents officially proposed to the Tustin Elementary School District board of trustees the addition of a "family life and sex education curriculum."[48] At the same meeting, however, opponents of sex ed recited a litany of complaints. The board responded with what the *Tustin News* called a "90-day truce," and the announcement that it would form two committees: one board committee and one citizens' committee.

The truce gave each side more time to gather evidence in its favor. And Tustin's anti–sex ed activists didn't have to look far. Anaheim's sex ed course was already becoming a useful rhetorical counterpoint for conservatives—it was a symbol of everything wrong with liberal America. They believed that it told kids they could do whatever they wanted if it felt good, that homosexuality wasn't a sin, and that parents didn't have all the answers. Anaheim residents who opposed the courses were especially effective at sharing these messages. One Anaheim mother claimed that the course was "turning away from Christian dogmas as laid down by the Ten Commandments."[49] An alliance of anti–sex ed parents began to form across Orange County.

In May 1968, some of these parents formed a group called MOMS: Mothers Organized for Moral Stability. The *Pasadena Independent* reported that the group charged that the increasing number of sex ed courses in the area was "directly attributable" to SIECUS.[50] MOMS president Katherine Allen spoke to what Sharon Hoagland of the *Tustin News* called a "standing-room only crowd" about the dangers of "SIECUS style" sex education.[51] MOMS grounded their position in parental rights and

Christian morals. "We insist," Allen exclaimed, "that we be allowed to rear our children as we choose. If we make mistakes let them be our own mistakes—not the schools[']!"[52] Gordon Drake's book, published later that year, mentioned MOMS by name as an example of how to fight sex ed.

In 1967, the New Jersey State Board of Education "directed" school districts to create sex ed programs, prompting a flurry of actions that led to discontent statewide.[53] When public school officials in Parsippany, New Jersey, announced in April 1968 that they were, according to the *Herald-News*, "investigating [a] SIECUS program" for the district, the opposition was prepared—despite the fact that SIECUS did not create any of its own curricula. Parsippany resident Edith Winters immediately warned the board of education about SIECUS's evil ways. "It is immoral," she claimed.[54]

Mrs. Winter then started a petition trying to get sex ed officially banned before it had a chance to begin.[55] In the same month, two other Parsippany women with similar sympathies started their own group called PAUSE—Parents Against Undemocratic Sex Education.[56] Mrs. Winter quickly became involved in their efforts. In November 1968, Gordon Drake traveled to New Jersey to address the group.[57]

In July 1969, the Paterson, New Jersey *News* published a primer on the situation in Parsippany. As the paper reported, in that city, "a fight between the Board of Education and PAUSE raged briefly with each threatening to take the other to court" after the circulation of flyers with images of "animals copulating," purportedly showing the kind of pornographic content that the proposed sex ed class would contain. Both the board of education and PAUSE accused the other of circulating the flyers.[58] The Paterson *News* also published the entire proposed curriculum guide, attempting to elucidate just what all the fuss was over.[59]

Florida, which was home to several MOTOREDE chapters, also saw the formation of local anti–sex ed groups. One was called Citizens Committee for Moral Education, based out of Orange County, Florida (not to be confused with Orange County, California), and active in the latter half of 1969.[60] Their outrage about sex ed led to a school board meeting that lasted a staggering 13.5 hours in September 1969, beginning at 8 a.m. and ending at 9:30 p.m.[61] The next month, the chairman of the county school board received an anonymous package that contained, according to the *Miami Herald*, "a selection of pornographic photographs and a note: 'I thought you might want this for your sex education course.'"[62]

In November 1969, a group filed a lawsuit against the Orange County, Florida, school board.[63] Donations were collected to fund the suit, and were sent in by individuals as well as groups, including the Citizens Committee for Moral Education and several area churches.

Louisiana outdid them all when it came to anti-SIECUS and anti–sex ed bills. In May 1969, state representative Fredric G. Hayes of Lafayette introduced a bill that would ban sex ed "below the ninth-grade level or to mixed classes of boys and girls." The bill was classified as a "fiscal matter" because, reported the Shreveport *Times*, it "would block the use of state funds for the purchase of supplies or instructional materials on sex education below the ninth grade."[64] The bill claimed that *anything* that SIECUS endorsed was automatically "sex ed."[65]

Despite strong endorsements of sex ed during the House Public Education Committee's hearings on the subject, from important groups like the League of Women Voters and the Louisiana School Boards Association; and despite persuasive testimony from Dr. Robert Doud, the director of the family life and sex education program in New Orleans Parish public schools (parish being roughly the equivalent to county in other states), the bill passed in Louisiana's House of Representatives, 94 to 4.[66] It was then sent to the state senate.

One of the many reasons for such "generally confused debate" was the potential impact of the bill, which was altogether unclear. Dr. Doud was particularly concerned about the way the bill was written, noting that since its definition of sex ed included not only human reproduction but also that of "animal, fish, reptile, or other living creatures," regular old biology classes could be disrupted as well.[67]

Other opponents of the bill were concerned about academic freedom: James Roberson, the president of the Louisiana School Boards

Association, noted that he didn't "believe that we need the Legislature to write bills pertaining to school curriculum."[68]

OUTCOMES

How did these various skirmishes end? Even though the contours of the protests were similar across different locations and even years, the outcomes were often very different, because the communities themselves were so unique. In December 1968, the California locales learned that the state government would be getting involved in sex ed. Jack Magee reported in the San Luis Obispo *Tribune* that the state board of education intended to determine whether specific material "put out by" SIECUS violated "state statutes or board policy." This, again, despite the fact that SIECUS did not create its own materials. Even among high-ranking officials, this particular point was often lost. In April 1969, after a five-hour hearing, the state board of education issued an official resolution, which would function as a guideline for school districts across the state. James Bow of the Associated Press called the resolution "a compromise between groups urging full instruction in human reproduction for small children and others seeking abolition of sex education."[69]

The resolution held that "family life and sex education" should be taught in schools—but that human reproduction would not be taught until fifth grade, and parents could withdraw their children from the course. The board also resolved that SIECUS's "program" was "not appropriate for California schools," a clear concession to those who opposed sex ed.[70]

But the state board of education wasn't the only governing body interested in sex ed in California schools. In February 1969, state senator John Schmitz of Tustin, an avowed Bircher, "introduced a bill to prohibit compulsory sex education in the elementary and secondary schools of California."[71] Under his bill, public schools wouldn't be able to require students to take any class that "described, illustrated or discussed . . . the human reproductive organs, and their functions and processes." Classes that contained such subject material would only be available to "children whose parents request them in writing." Schmitz also introduced a senate resolution asking for an investigation of "current public school sex education programs" and called for a "resolution requesting school boards throughout the State to refrain from implementing any new programs of sex education" until said investigation was complete.[72]

In March, Schmitz filed three separate pieces of legislation on the subject of sex ed. The first was a bill that would make compulsory sex ed unlawful in the state; the second was a senate resolution "calling for," as California's City News Service reported, "a full investigation by a legislative committee on the objections and charges made against current public school sex ed programs." The third was a joint resolution, which asked school boards to "refrain from implementing any new programs on sex education or family life education" until his proposed investigation was complete.[73]

In April, the Senate Education Committee listened to four hours of testimony on the subject, and officially recommended a "freeze" on any new sex education and family life courses in any California public schools until an investigation was completed.[74] At the same time, the committee also decided to wait to vote on Schmitz's bill to ban compulsory sex ed in the state.[75]

Later that month, the committee made changes to Schmitz's main bill, which had originally required parents to give their children written permission to attend any class "where human reproductive organs and their functions and processes are described, illustrated or discussed." The committee amended the bill to instead allow parents to opt their children out of the classes. This opt-out option, AP education writer James Bow noted, put the bill in line with the state board of education's guidelines released earlier in the year.

In May, Schmitz's measures were on the senate floor. The first, his bill to require parents to be able to opt out of the course, passed 30 to 6. His second, a senate resolution that would officially ban any new sex education courses in public schools, also passed, 23 to 11.[76] In June, the California State Assembly Education Subcommittee on Instruction and Teacher Relations recommended the passage of Schmitz's bill. At the end of the month, the assembly passed the measure 55 to 15.[77] In August, Governor Ronald Reagan signed the bill into law.[78]

While all this was happening, California school districts were left to handle their own sex ed skirmishes as they occurred. In San Luis Obispo, where a group of families introduced a lawsuit against the district over sex ed classes in September 1968, the district fought back, first asking for the case to be dismissed. Their request was denied, and the trial marched slowly on. But in February 1969, as Schmitz was filing his measures against sex ed statewide, San Luis Obispo's citizens' committee returned with their findings.[79]

The committee had reviewed the course of study originally proposed by school administration and, finding nothing too objectionable in it, officially recommended it for San Luis Obispo district schools.[80] In March, parents who had filed the lawsuit against the district unsuccessfully filed an injunction in hopes that the course would not proceed, but it was denied.[81] Sex ed came to town. In San Luis Obispo, the fight for sex ed was successful.

In Tustin, the fight dragged on in a different way. There, the committee model that Dr. Calderone was so optimistic about devolved into spectacle. In August 1968, the chairman of the citizens' committee, Paul Ruffner, resigned after the school board changed the number and nature of the committee meetings. As the *Tustin News* reported, originally there were to be three private meetings in which the committee was to select "the criteria for the proposed family life and sex education class curriculum which would then be presented to the board for its approval."[82] Now, Ruffner and the rest of the committee were being asked to not limit the number of meetings and to allow public participation in them. The new venue for the meetings seated three hundred people. Ruffner explained he believed it was "barely possible that something could come out of" the meetings under those circumstances.[83]

But after such heightened emotions and drama, Tustin's story, as the *Tustin News* put it "died . . . quietly in committee session."[84] Sidestepping the issue altogether, the committee in Tustin recommended that the school district "maintain the current health course" and instead focus on strengthening "the narcotics instruction," citing the fact that the latter was a bigger problem for area teens.[85]

It was not only in California that legal mechanisms were wielded to pause sex ed. In New Jersey in March 1969, Republican assemblyman John H. Ewing introduced a resolution calling for a legislative probe into the sex ed programs.[86] In May, Republican assemblyman Francis Coury introduced a resolution that would "prohibit the introduction of sex education programs until completion of a legislative investigation."[87] In July, the two resolutions passed.[88]

The sex ed probe took place that summer, and a public hearing was announced for August. The right wing employed the same stratagems on this higher level as they had locally: they rallied their witnesses, claimed that sex ed was an intrusion on the rights of the home and God, and decried SIECUS and its members as immoral. Edith Winter, fresh off an unsuccessful bid for the Parsippany school board, found her summer busy; PAUSE was particularly adamant about getting witnesses to testify against sex ed, calling for "clergymen, doctors, and lawyers" to line up against the subject, according to the *Herald-News*.[89] In the end, the nine-hour session was only able to accommodate 20 of the 105 speakers who wished to testify. The *Asbury Park Press* estimated that 250 people came to watch.[90]

Witnesses in support of sex ed included the president of the New Jersey Medical Society, the director of obstetrics and gynecology at Hunterdon Medical Center, and a member of the American Academy of Pediatrics, along with the state Federation of District Boards of Education and the state Association of School Administrators.

The nine-hour hearing approached spectacle-like heights. The *Daily Register*, of Red Bank, New Jersey, reported that "opponents of the sex education programs, most of them trim, well-dressed young matrons," ignored "repeated warnings against public demonstration [and] jeered [the] state Commission of Education . . . and other supporters of the programs."[91] A joint legislative committee charged with taking stock of the sex ed situation in the state continued hearing testimony, with a second hearing in September.[92] There, one witness, a spokesman for the National States Rights Party, spoke for ten minutes, calling sex ed a "satanic attack upon the morality of the white Christian youth of America" and saying that the courses were inspired by the Talmud.[93] The hearings finally concluded in December.[94]

Then, the Joint Education Committee set to work reviewing the testimony and preparing its recommendations. In the meantime, some school districts—like Parsippany—were actively in the process of launching sex ed programs. In Parsippany, no recommendation against implementing any new programs—regardless of who it came from—was going to stop the process. So, after more than a year of planning and protest, in October 1969 Parsippany officially adopted a sex ed course following the results of their citizens' committee. In keeping with the overall chaos of implementing sex ed writ large, Herb Gage for the Passaic *Herald-News* reported that when the vote finally came, "no one knew it was passed since the whole audience had broken up . . . and was not paying attention to board actions."[95]

It wasn't until April 1970 that the Joint Education Committee, which was cochaired by Assemblyman Ewing, released its recommendations.[96] The recommendations were staunchly anti–sex ed: they included limiting sex education, requiring parents to "opt-in" their children, and "a ban on materials distributed by . . . SIECUS."[97] Ewing stated that while no legislative action was planned to enforce these recommendations, "new laws might be necessary if the committee's proposals were ignored by the state board of education and local school boards."[98]

The responses to these recommendations from state and local school officials were vehemently negative, suggesting that Ewing might have to make good on his threat. A spokesperson for the state education commissioner said that the "state board has never banned anything and would be very reluctant to do so. There is a question of educational freedom."[99]

In Louisiana, once the senate received the anti–sex ed bill, they established a study committee for the bill, with plans to report back the next year.[100] In the meantime, the full state legislature passed a resolution to "ban sex education in all grades of elementary and secondary schools" until the committee reported back.[101] Unlike in New Jersey, where the resolution to "freeze" sex ed programs was essentially a recommendation, in Louisiana there was slightly more bite. Here, the resolution was clear that no state, federal, or local funds could be used for "materials, textbooks, visual aids, [or] other supplies used in the conduct of courses of study in sex education."[102]

THE END IN ANAHEIM

There was a larger narrative unfolding about who would have the power when it came to sex ed, and it was taking place back where it had all started: Anaheim. To many, Anaheim's school district seemed to have birthed the first modern sex ed class. Its link—both perceived and real—to

SIECUS had cemented its cultural importance, and its early popularity had seemed to indicate nothing but upward movement for the overall project of sex ed—a success story for Paul Cook, for SIECUS, and for sex ed on a national scale. But the reality was more complicated. In many ways, the full program hadn't even gotten the chance to begin. Before even one year of the classes could take place, the anti–sex ed movement came for it.

Like many other communities around the nation, Anaheim had an anti–sex ed group of its own. By January 1969, the Citizens Committee of California (CCC) was calling upon the school board, the *Los Angeles Times* reported, to "fire Supt. Paul Cook and Mrs. Sally Williams, coordinator of the district's family life-sex education program."[103] The leader of the CCC, James Townsend, openly admitted that the group's tactics were aggressive: "We decided to wear them down by every means at our disposal . . . public education, attending the board meetings, publicity, anything that would draw attention."[104]

When a school board election came up in April 1969, the CCC knew it was a golden opportunity for their cause.[105] They were able to capture two of the three open seats on the board, seating them with what the *Los Angeles Times* called "avowed foes" of the sex ed program. The new board quickly got to work undoing all of Cook's and Williams's accomplishments—even as both were still employed by the district. By September, the *San Francisco Examiner* reported that "Anaheim Sex Foes Claim Victory," as they had reduced Cook's sex ed program to a shadow of its former self. Instead of having forty-five board-approved textbooks, now they only had four. Instead of forty films at their disposal, now there were just two.[106]

The CCC called the new version of sex ed "an absolute victory for our side" but also cautioned: "We are not satisfied. . . . We want the whole program eliminated."[107] By October 1969, Paul Cook had officially resigned, and Sally Williams had gone back to her former position as school nurse.[108]

The new, pared-down sex ed program opened for enrollment in February 1970, with a marked drop in enrollees. Paul Cook's original curriculum had been taught to 28,000 of the district's 35,000 students, but this new version only enrolled 6,663 students.[109] In part this was due to new guidelines around the course—it could no longer be taken in lieu of physical education, and was only offered to three grades as opposed to six—but it was still a marked difference.[110] The content of the course had been significantly modified as well. It no longer included such topics as "premarital and extramarital sex relationships, dating, necking and petting, menstruation and body functions, body changes during adolescence, marriage counseling and venereal disease."[111]

In March 1970, Williams called the new program "a farce," noting that "the course is supposed to help students to make decisions. Now they're being told what the decision is supposed to be."[112]

CHAPTER 12

THE NEW BATTLES OF THE 1970s

The 1960s should have been a golden era of sex ed. Sex ed had consistently polled well among the public. Administrators and teachers were increasingly supportive, and it had been endorsed by many experts. Anaheim's curriculum had emerged as a shining model of a "new" type of sex ed, published and available for anyone who wanted to use it. But instead, by the end of 1970, it was as if a tornado had ripped through the sex ed landscape of the United States. In some places, entire sex ed programs had been dismantled through the power of pickets, protests, petitions, or school board elections. Other programs had survived only by chance. Still other communities had made preparations for a storm that never came to their particular area. But now there seemed to be a brief moment of calm. In October of that year, Harriet Pilpel, general counsel for SIECUS, wrote in the organization's newsletter, "We can look ahead with confidence to the work of the next few years." This attitude seemed to be shared by the media. The *Palo Alto Times* reported in 1971 that "sex education, once an issue that enlivened many a dull school board meeting, now rarely raises parental ire."[1]

This moment brought a chance to reflect. What had often been lost in all this torment, in the marathon board meetings and protests, was what the true nature of this "new" sex ed really was. The religious right had its familiar talking points, which claimed that SIECUS and "Anaheim-style" courses were turning their children away from God and family and toward immorality and sex—but even the most cursory content analysis revealed that this was simply not the case. What experts found was that for all the sense of newness around "Anaheim-style" sex ed courses, the actual course content was very staid.

THE NEW OLD SEX ED

In 1972, a doctoral candidate named Louis Maslinoff published a study of forty-seven sex ed curriculum guides from public schools in an attempt to determine what sex ed looked like in America. Was it, as the JBS claimed, teaching young people to abandon God and the authority of their families, turn to hedonism, and have sex before marriage? His study found that "standard values"—that is, the stereotypical values of the American nuclear family, which included abstinence before marriage—were "built into the curriculum manuals."[2]

Moreover, Maslinoff discovered, these materials also routinely excluded what seemed like very obvious topics. "It would appear," he wrote, "that there are some notable omissions in sex education problems: reasonably honest information about copulation, admission of the pleasurable feelings accompanying the sex drive, acceptance of the reality of pluralistic standards among different groups of people," among others.[3]

In elementary schools, Maslinoff reported, "value statements urge . . . self-restraint in dating relationships." In higher grades, he went on, while there may have been a recognition of "the sex drive with concomitant emotional feelings which are considered normal, and in some instances even desirable," the *values* that were "associated with [that] drive generally counsel restraint or sublimating activities."[4]

The Right believed, or at least espoused, that these courses were built on a foundation of situational ethics or the "new morality," in which every person could make their own choices rather than submitting to religious imperatives. Maslinoff reported that this fear was unfounded. While independent decision-making got some isolated encouragement, he explained, it wasn't in the context of male-female relationships. "Stress is given to ego-identity and the appreciation of one's body."[5]

The next year, in 1973, Maslinoff published a similar article that focused on the content of sex ed films. There, too, he found a similar pattern of elision. Overall, Maslinoff concluded, "there is a general avoidance of the coital relationship and the male's function in the reproductive act."[6] Of the film *Human Growth*, which was still being recommended and used in public schools, Maslinoff noted that "while the film shows the sperm in the vagina, it fails to relate it directly to the penis."[7]

THE IMPACT OF SEX ED

All of this content analysis of sex ed led to another core question about the overall project: Was sex ed successful? If so—or if not—by what measures? As people like Curtis Avery of the E. C. Brown Trust had pointed out in the mid-1960s, people liked the idea of using sex ed as a public health tool. This had only become more true in the intervening years, and if this idea held water, there should be quantifiable health outcomes associated with the courses. An article for the March 1973 *SIECUS Report*, prepared by Frederick Bidgood, explained that "the effects of any experimental educational program fall into three broad categories: changes in knowledge, in attitudes or values, and in behavior."[8] Of the first category, which was, the article explained, "the easiest to measure [and] the most familiar to school personnel," sex ed was effective: students in sex ed courses routinely gained information from their classes—something that was not entirely remarkable, but worth noting as a matter of data.[9]

It was the other two categories that were more interesting: Did sex ed classes affect students' attitudes and values? Did they affect their behavior? These were the questions that connected to health outcomes. And their answers were harder to determine. As Bidgood's article explained, "Changes in sexual attitudes or values, while given frequent lip service [are] difficult to substantiate."[10] Studies from the early 1970s on this subject seemed to have come to conflicting conclusions: one from 1970 found that "gains in knowledge . . . do not, *per se*, produce significant changes in sexual attitude," while a separate study from the next year found that "students can gain significantly in self-image and self-acceptance" after taking a course.

Changes in behavior, perhaps the highest-stakes potential outcome of a sex ed course, were also, Bidgood explained, "difficult to measure." Multiple studies had found, however, that sex ed led to "increased ease, openness, and satisfaction in parent-child communication and interaction about sex."[11] Of course, this was not necessarily the kind of change in behavior that one hoped would be reported, especially when looking at sex ed as a public health measure. Instead, the expectation might be that young people who had taken a sex ed class would report that they were deciding not to have sex, or were using condoms or other forms of birth control. But the absence of this kind of conclusion, Bidgood noted, may have been due to a lack of data around it. "No major studies," he explained, "have been conducted to show any direct correlation between sex education programs and V.D. or unwed pregnancy rates."[12] But he did note that "there are some indications that" sex ed programs "can act to increase the rate of *reporting* V.D."[13]

So, the question of sex ed outcomes was still open. That did not stop people and organizations from hoping, and claiming, that sex ed would reduce rates of STIs and teen pregnancy. The 1970 White House Conference on Children stated that, in order to help reduce teen pregnancies, it was essential to include "in school curricula . . . instruction in the social and psychologic aspects of human reproduction and the importance and means of achieving responsible parenthood."[14]

In California, rates of STIs were staggering, and the idea that school-based sex ed could be a tool against their spread set the stage for yet another multiyear legislative battle. The numbers were indeed grim: in 1970 in Los Angeles County, "gonorrhea among 15 to 19-year-olds [had] increased 150% over the past five years and syphilis, 134%."[15] And these, of course, were only reported and recorded cases. The actual numbers were, in all probability, much higher.

But current law in California—as spearheaded by Senator Schmitz—empowered the state government to strip teachers of their credentials if they failed to notify parents of an upcoming sex ed unit or failed to provide class materials for parental inspection. And while this may have sounded reasonable enough on paper, as the Long Beach *Press-Telegram* pointed out, "the law in effect bars teachers from tailoring courses to pupils' need by requiring them to decide in advance exactly what materials will be used."[16] The *Los Angeles Times* noted that many teachers played it safe and avoided the subject altogether.[17] Other educational infrastructure didn't help. A state report prepared in 1971 found that "none of the state's seventh and eighth grade textbooks even mentioned VD."[18]

MARCH FONG IN CALIFORNIA

In early 1971, Democratic assemblywoman March Fong from Oakland saw these rising rates of gonorrhea and syphilis and decided to do something about it. "We have hidden from our responsibility to talk to young people frankly and openly about VD," she stated. "By embarrassed silence and inaction we have allowed venereal disease to reach epidemic proportions in our state."[19] She proposed a bill that would exempt "venereal disease instruction" from the parental consent requirement. Around the same time, state senator Albert Rodda introduced a complementary bill that "would allow teachers to introduce sex education materials not previously inspected by parents without jeopardy to teachers' credentials."[20]

But anti–sex ed activists quickly grabbed onto the issue. Republican Assembly Education Committee member Robert Burke argued that education about STIs would expose "clean wholesome kids" to a sordid subject, and a group called Concerned Parents of Contra Costa and Marin charged that it would "give the sex educators the tool they need to get around the regulations."[21]

But the Assembly Education Committee was not convinced by the antis' pleas.[22] In May 1971, they overwhelmingly approved Fong's bill 50 to 8. The bill also had support from many government and community groups, including, the *Los Angeles Times* reported, Governor Reagan's Task Force on Venereal Disease, the state board of education, the California Medical Association, the California Federation of Women's Clubs, the Association of California School Districts, the California School Nurses Organization, and the California Teachers Association.[23] In September, it passed in the senate, 21 to 10.[24] Despite this, Governor Reagan vetoed the bill in October 1971, arguing that it would "remove from the parents their right to consent to their children's participation in venereal disease instructions."[25]

Assemblywoman Fong initially attempted to override Reagan's veto but was not successful. Then, she changed her tactics, working *with* Reagan on a new version of the bill, which she resubmitted in February 1972. It was similar to her original bill, but now with the stipulation that parental approval was required for a student to take a sex ed class (an "opt-in" clause). This watered-down, Reagan-endorsed bill was still not immune to Republican criticism. In March 1972, Republican assemblyman John L. E. Collier accused the bill of "using VD as a veil to come in the back door on sex education."[26]

Nonetheless, the bill—which was not as strong as Fong's original one, and which did not actually mandate VD education—passed the legislature and was signed into law in August 1972.[27] A few months later, in December, California took another important step for rational sex ed when the state board of education officially rescinded its ban on "SIECUS materials" in public schools.[28]

TAKING SEX ED TO COURT

The strategy of banning sex ed via legislation had proven ineffective, at least in California. And so, anti–sex ed activists pivoted. In 1969, Gordon Drake had published another book about the evils of sex ed, *SIECUS: Corruptor of Youth*. In it, he presented to parents a new tactic: a constitutional argument against sex ed. "The legal framework," he wrote, "is provided through the Tenth Amendment of the Constitution of the United States which provides that 'the powers not delegated to the United States by the Constitution nor prohibited by it to the states, are reserved to the states respectively, or to the people.'"[29] He urged individual parents to claim for themselves the right to control their children's education—and to back their claim with legal action.

Parents answered the call. In February 1970, the *Daily News* reported that the board of education in Norwalk, Connecticut, was having difficulty hiring a high school sex ed teacher, in part because "a group calling itself concerned parents has opposed the course and has threatened to file a lawsuit against any teacher who teaches it."[30] In the same month, Paul Clemmer, the leader of an anti–sex ed group called TASTE (Topekans Against Sex Training Education) in Topeka, Kansas, sued the city, charging that the school system's human growth and development course was unconstitutional under the Fourteenth, Ninth, and Tenth Amendments. Referring to the Fourteenth Amendment, which reads that the state won't "deprive any person of life, liberty, or property without due process of law," Clemmer argued that the course violated "the personal liberty of a parent to determine the subjects taught his children, and the influences to which they will be exposed." Referring to the Ninth Amendment, which reads, "The enumeration, in the Constitution, of certain rights, shall not be construed to deny or disparage others retained by the people," Clemmer argued that "the People, acting through the Legislature, have not empowered defendant to carry on such a program." As to the Tenth Amendment, which reads, "Any powers not given to the federal government are reserved for the states or the people," Clemmer argued that "authority to conduct the program has not been given the defendant by constitutional or legislative provision, and therefore authority to instruct children in sex education is reserved to the people."[31]

However, the state district court judge disagreed with Clemmer on all counts, arguing that the school *was* "authorized by Constitutional and statutory authority to conduct programs of education in promotion of the public health, welfare and morals," that the sex ed program in question was a "reasonable exercise" of this authority, and that it did not "unreasonably restrict the liberty of the plaintiff." It was an open-and-shut case in favor of sex ed.[32] Planned Parenthood lawyer and SIECUS board member Harriet F. Pilpel commented approvingly on the decision, saying, "The court has paved the way for a recognition" that children have "the *right* to be educated about sex, a central phenomenon of their personal lives."[33]

Meanwhile, in Howell, Michigan, in 1970, a group called Parents Concerned About Curriculum attempted to abolish their school district's optional sex ed course by bringing a lawsuit against the district—complete with a sheriff's deputy delivering subpoenas to board members during a board of education meeting.[34] Led by a Mr. and Mrs. Hobolth, the group's argument hinged on the First Amendment—claiming that "sex education is not legal or valid because it does not foster religion or morality, yet deals with a subject closely associated with matters of religion or morality."[35] Then there was the fact, the suit went on to claim, that the course's materials were "designed to question parental authority by encouraging analysis, appraisal and criticism of parental authority."[36] Circuit judge Paul Mahinske found the program constitutional, but ordered one change to the enrollment procedure. Mahinske recommended that the district switch from an "opt-out" arrangement to an "opt-in."

Unwilling to give up, the Hobolths hired attorney William Ball, who was counsel for a group called the Defenders of Essential Rights, Inc. (DOER).[37] DOER's president, Ruth E. Gotberg, described the group as "a national interfaith organization which supports cases involving parental rights."[38] Gotberg and DOER implored their members to donate funds for Hobolth and his case, noting that "little people like Mr. and Mrs. Hobolth who have been game enough to stand up all alone to challenge a monstrosity like the Michigan sex education program are left to fight and suffer all alone. . . . We can't let that happen any longer."[39]

With Ball on their side, the Hobolths' argument became more pointed. Ball claimed that the sex ed class went so far as to establish its own religion—a clear violation of the First Amendment—by espousing, teaching, and promoting "Secular Humanist practices, values, and concepts."[40]

Secular humanism broadly refers to a nonreligious worldview that centers human reason and rejects religious positionality when it comes to morality and decision-making. Humanism has a long history in the United States. The American Humanist Association was formed in 1941 and was, as the group explains, meant to "recognize the nontheist and secular nature of humanism, organize its advocates, and align the organization for the mutual education of both its religious and nonreligious members."[41] By the early 1970s, as James E. Wood wrote in an editorial for the *Journal of Church and State*, among the religious right secular humanism had become "a code word for explaining all the evils in American society, largely replacing 'communism,' as used in the fifties and sixties as the greatest threat facing America and its democratic institutions."[42] By the time Michigan's court of appeals was ready to hear Ball's argument, the American Humanist Association had published its *Humanist Manifesto II*, which, among other things, called for "universal education" and the "right to birth control, abortion, and divorce," proclaiming that "varieties of sexual exploration should not in themselves be considered 'evil.'"

As Ball explained in his brief of October 1973, "the Plaintiff and associated parents . . . stress their recognition of the right of all religious groups—including Secular Humanists—to express their religious views and to live according to them. But such groups may not utilize public funds and public institutions in their efforts to impose those views upon others," and further, that "the Michigan sex education and family program is an expression of Secular Humanist ideology."[43]

Michigan's court of appeals did not agree, and in April 1974 the court upheld Judge Mahinske's ruling, finding sex education classes constitutional.[44] Mr. Hobolth, ever persistent, then asked Michigan's supreme court to hear the case.[45] That court declined, and so affirmed the validity of the sex education classes.[46]

In November, Hobolth penned a letter to the editor of the Livingston County *Daily Press and Argus*.[47] "The courts," the letter read, "have finally said in effect that God's word can be perverted in practically any way a local school may wish."[48] He wrote of the "Biblical requirement of resisting the evil" of the program and thanked his supporters. As Hobolth saw it, Michigan was now a staunchly pro–sex ed state. But at the same time his protracted legal battle over sex ed in Michigan was coming to an end, another was gearing up.

BIRTH CONTROL EDUCATION IN MICHIGAN AND BEYOND

Michigan's regulations pertaining to physical education and "sex hygiene" had been on the books since 1949. The law read that it was "the duty of boards of education in all school districts of having more than 3,000 [students] to engage competent instructors of physical education and provide the necessary place and equipment for instruction and training in health and physical education."[49] It went on to specify that "any program of instruction in sex hygiene be supervised by a registered physician, a registered nurse, or a person holding a teacher's certificate," and also that "any child upon the written request of a parent or guardian, shall be excused from attending classes in which the subject of sex hygiene is under discussion."[50] However, it also clarified that it was not "the intention or purpose of this act to give the right of instruction in birth control, and it is hereby expressly prohibited to any person to offer or give any instruction in said subject of birth control or offer any advice or information with respect to said subject."[51]

When this legislation had passed, ASHA had lauded it as "an outstandingly important piece of legislation, and a milestone on the road to better social hygiene education."[52] By the 1970s, however, the law did not come across as a safeguarding of social hygiene education, but as a ban on birth control education. Between the practical problems it created—like not being able to answer student questions—and the deep relevance of birth control information in a world that was still concerned with "teenage illegitimacy," this ban was significant.

Michigan was not alone in banning birth control education. In 1971, four states dictated that "the medical aspects of birth control were not permitted in the public schools," an article from the *Journal of School Health* reported. In nine states, "discussion of specific methods and technique of birth control was not permitted." And in one state, "the discussion of population problems was not permitted in the public schools."[53]

At the same time, some experts were coming to believe that birth control should be taught in schools—even though most sex ed classes still by and large prioritized a message of abstinence. H. S. Hoyman, the head of the Department of Health and Safety Education at the University of Illinois, suggested a model in which "we should teach *about* contraception in our high schools within a social, moral, legal, and ethical context. . . . This means that the topic of contraception should be handled in a way that does not place the high schools and society in the position of giving tacit approval, or an open invitation, for high school boys and girls to engage in premarital sexual intercourse."[54]

In great part, the need for including birth control information was due to the fact that birth control was nearly impossible to ignore, even for teenagers.

The Pill was more popular than ever in America—even though it was not necessarily easy for young people to access, as the law did not guarantee minors the right to contraception.[55] Indeed, it had only been in the last several years that a series of Supreme Court cases had taken down the "little Comstock" laws that had categorically banned contraception in some states. In 1965, the Supreme Court had heard *Griswold v. Connecticut*. At the time, Connecticut had a law, dating back to 1879, that made it illegal to use anything for "the purpose of preventing conception," or aiding anyone in doing so.[56] And so, in order to challenge the law, the executive director of the Planned Parenthood League of Connecticut, Estelle Griswold, opened a birth control clinic in New Haven. She and a gynecologist who was volunteering at the clinic, Dr. Lee Buxton, were arrested, tried, and found guilty of breaking the law.[57] They appealed the decision until it reached the Supreme Court.[58]

The Supreme Court's decision held that banning birth control was, indeed, unconstitutional—but only for married couples.[59] The court agreed 7 to 2 that within marriage, there was a right to privacy guaranteed by the First, Third, Fourth, and Ninth Amendments, and Connecticut's law restricting a married couple's ability to gain information about, or access to, contraception violated that right.[60]

In 1972, *Eisenstadt v. Baird* expanded birth control access to single people as well.[61] *Eisenstadt v. Baird* was tried initially in Massachusetts, where at the time it was illegal to give contraception to unmarried people.[62] William Baird, the clinical director of a birth control manufacturer called EMKO, had been instrumental in a number of cases that had tested the legality of restricting contraception access.[63] In order to test the Massachusetts law, Baird gave a lecture to Boston University students in 1967, during which he distributed a sample of contraceptive foam.[64] He was arrested, and the case was eventually tried by the Supreme Court in 1972.

The court found 6 to 1 that Massachusetts's law was unconstitutional—not, as in *Griswold*, on the grounds of privacy, but rather under the Fourteenth Amendment's Equal Protection Clause; there was no "rational basis," the justices found, to differentiate between single and married people when it came to the question of access to contraception.[65] This ruling opened access to birth control more than ever, even as it did not open access to minors. Yet, teenagers were likely to be aware of the Pill's existence and to expect to be able to ask a sex educator about it. As a result, laws like Michigan's made it difficult for teachers to do their jobs.

In March 1974, just a month before Michigan's supreme court would decline to hear Mr. Hobolth's appeal, two men—a teacher and a physician—made the first attempt to challenge the state's ban on birth control education.[66] They were Alexander Mercer, the head of the science department at Redford High School in Detroit, and Dr. Richard Goldfine, a resident in obstetrics-gynecology.

Together, they filed a lawsuit alleging, according to Louis Heldeman of the *Detroit Free Press*, that "the prohibitions violate constitutional free speech rights of students and teachers . . . as well as keep them from vital knowledge for their well-being."[67] They enumerated the practical difficulty that had resulted from this ban. Mercer, as head of the science department, explained that he had to "screen textbooks and curriculum materials to make sure they don't contain birth control information and limit his effectiveness with students by refusing to answer their questions about reproduction, population control and related issues."[68] Meanwhile,

Goldfine had "stopped accepting speaking appearances in public school classes because it is impossible to talk about his specialty of population growth and control without discussing the means of control."[69]

The assistant state attorney general asked that the lawsuit be dismissed on the grounds that the ban did not have a direct effect on the plaintiffs, and further that the two men were "attempting to usurp parental rights. They want to compel students as a captive audience to endure their lecture on birth control and sex education."[70] In July, a panel of judges assigned to the case granted the assistant attorney general's request, dismissing the suit "on the ground that the plaintiffs had failed to show any specific instances where a teacher had suffered 'any threats or reprisals . . . for conduct or speech in connection with family planning courses.'"[71] One of the judges, federal circuit judge Albert J. Engel, wrote in an opinion: "This is a classic example of a cause in search of a controversy."[72]

Dr. Goldfine acknowledged his disappointment, noting that the ruling "leaves the people of Michigan with a law that will continue to prevent students and young people from obtaining information they need." Then he predicted: "We will probably continue to see an increase in teenage illegitimacy that we have seen constantly in the last few years."

In Michigan, neither the Hobolths, who believed that the state was too permissive with sex ed, nor Mercer and Goldfine, who believed the state was too strict, had received the outcomes they had sought by taking the issue to trial. In January 1975, Dr. John Porter, Michigan's superintendent of public instruction, wrote that he hoped any change in sex ed policy would come from the legislature rather than from litigation.[73]

It appeared that he might get the legislative solution he wanted when, in March 1975, Republican state senator Gilbert Bursley of Ann Arbor explained that he felt it was "ridiculous" that teachers had to "refuse to answer a student question on 'what is the pill.'"[74] He introduced a bill that would lift the ban on teaching birth control information. A similar bill had been introduced the year prior, but it died in the House Education Committee after what the Ironwood *Daily Globe* called "emotional controversy."[75]

Bursley's bill proposed two measures: it would first remove the state's ban on discussing birth control in public schools, and it would also, the *Hillsdale Daily News* explained, "require the state board of education to establish guidelines on birth control, sex hygiene and venereal disease in the classroom."[76] In July 1975, the Senate Education Committee approved the bill.[77]

Opposition came out in force when the bill was debated in the full senate later that month. Groups like MOTOREDE had largely died out by the 1970s. But they had been supplanted in name, if not in spirit, by groups like HOW, short for Happiness of Womanhood, Inc.—a pointed jab at the feminist organization NOW, the National Organization for Women. NOW had been founded in 1966 and became especially active around the Equal Rights Amendment (ERA), which would have amended the Constitution to guarantee equality to all Americans, regardless of gender. The ERA had been passed by Congress in 1972, but it still needed ratification from thirty-eight state legislatures in order to become a constitutional amendment. And the political right mobilized effectively to prevent these ratifications. These efforts were led in large part by anti-feminist activist Phyllis Schlafly, a former JBS member who had made a name for herself in 1964 by publishing a book called *A Choice Not an Echo*, an endorsement of Barry Goldwater. In 1972 she founded a conservative political group called the Eagle Forum. In the same year, she published a widely circulated essay that condemned "women's lib" as "anti-family, anti-children, and pro-abortion. It is a series of sharp-tongued, high-pitched whining complaints by unmarried women."[78] In her world view, sex ed landed squarely on the side of liberals and feminists, and so should be demonized. In this framework, the issues of abortion, sex ed, feminism, and the ERA were impossible to separate from one another—a phenomenon seen clearly in Michigan as debate raged on over teaching birth control in schools.

As Geraldine Strozier of the *Detroit Free Press* reported, "Each side claims the other is being manipulated by sinister forces. NOW people claim HOW is just a front for the John Birch Society, and HOW claims NOW is being manipulated by fascist and communist elements. . . . Both groups compared the other side's tactics with Hitler's."[79] Strozier went on to elucidate the issue: "In talking about the birth control issue, women from HOW and NOW easily slip into arguing about abortion or the ERA, as if the issues were one and the same."[80]

In July, the Michigan senate voted on the bill. It failed, with 23 senators against it and 13 in favor.[81] But Bursley, its sponsor, was not content to let that be the end of it, and he exercised his right to motion for another vote while the senate was still in session.[82] He also introduced an amendment that would put more control over the content of a course in the hands of local school districts and local health departments rather than in the state board of education and Department of Public Health.[83] The senate postponed the vote until October, which gave more time for the arguments to spiral.[84]

As the October vote approached, Bursley was busy tacking on conciliatory amendments everywhere he could. One required parent review boards to assess proposed materials and modes of instruction.[85] Another, offered by Democratic senator Dale Kildee, made sex ed classes opt-in rather than opt-out. Ultimately, though, the bill was defeated in the senate, 22 to 12.[86] "Members of [HOW] who have been campaigning against the bill," Paul Varian reported in the *Petoskey News-Review*, "let out a cheer from the galleries when the final vote was announced."[87]

Three months later, however, interest in the topic of sex ed was renewed when some counties in Michigan began to show higher rates of STIs among teenagers.[88] In addition to its law against teaching about birth control, Michigan also had laws that required, as Millicent Lane in the *Lansing State Journal* explained, "public schools to provide information about dangerous communicable diseases."[89] Gonorrhea and syphilis fell into that category, but educators in Michigan were reluctant to address STIs following the defeat of Bursley's bill, much like the educators in California who had been unsure what they could and could not teach after regulations were tightened there.[90]

There was such confusion around the legality of discussing anything having to do with sex that the state education director, Dr. John Porter, and the state public health director, Dr. Maurice Reizen, cowrote a letter that was sent to all public school superintendents and principals in the state.[91] They clarified that the defeat of Bursley's bill did "not nullify or change" existing laws about teaching about infectious diseases, and that there was "an urgent need for young people to continue receiving factual information on venereal disease."[92] It was clear that regardless of these attempts to separate "venereal disease education" from the larger topic of sex ed—as people like Maurice Bigelow had urged—the average administrator or educator was not interested in walking that line.

A year after Porter and Reizen's letter, in April 1977, state representative Barbara-Rose Collins, a Democrat from Detroit, introduced yet another bill that would lift the ban on birth control instruction.[93] All the same dramas played out, with the same allegiances, battles, protests, debates, and concessions. But this time, the house approved the bill. As Donald Woutat, an Associated Press writer, explained, this gave "local school districts the option of offering voluntary instruction in family planning, human sexuality, reproductive health and venereal disease."[94] In October, the bill also passed in the Senate Education Committee.[95] On November 3, it passed in the full senate.[96] On the last day of November, it was signed into law, lifting the decades-old ban on birth control instruction in Michigan public schools.[97]

Michigan's law against birth control instruction had functioned, in many ways, as a ban on sex ed, or at the very least as a ban on the modern sex ed of the 1970s. With it struck down, Louisiana stood alone as the state with the most restrictive sex ed law.

ALPHONSE JACKSON FIGHTS FOR SEX ED IN LOUISIANA

Louisiana had placed its ban on sex ed in 1969, ostensibly so that a committee could gather more information on it. The committee had originally planned to report back to the legislature in 1970. In 1970, the committee announced it needed more time to come to a conclusion and recommended that the ban stay in place until it could complete its study.[98] Louisiana's legislature approved this recommendation in June 1970.[99] But by 1974, there was no sign of the committee or its report, and the ban on sex ed remained firmly in place.

That May, state representative Alphonse Jackson, a Democrat from Shreveport, introduced a bill that would repeal the ban and allow local school boards to make their own decisions about sex ed.[100] Jackson explained the necessity of sex ed, citing "a very high increase in terms of social disease," and also noted that "it just doesn't make sense in 1974 for us not to educate people relative to what is a natural biological function." The *Shreveport Times* reported that Jackson's bill had support from many reputable organizations, including "the State AFL-CIO, the Louisiana School Boards Association, the New Orleans Area Health Council, the League of Women Voters, the Caddo Parish School System, the Louisiana Education Association, the Louisiana Teachers Association and various psychologists and physicians."[101]

Representative Jackson had been elected two years prior, the first Black legislator elected from Caddo Parish since Reconstruction.[102] He had been a teacher and then an administrator in Louisiana, and he had worked as principal of a largely white school during desegregation. His commitment to desegregating schools, and education more broadly, had led him to rise to prominence among Louisiana's professional educational groups.[103] Jackson was thinking deeply about the needs of Louisiana's schools at the time—and in addition to his bill to repeal the ban on sex ed, he also introduced a resolution that would direct the state's Department of Education to survey the "available instructional materials for sex education programs."[104]

But at the state legislature hearings in June, it was clear that many of the old protestations of the late 1960s had not lost their power. The House Education Committee chair called sex ed "teaching raw sex," while Senator Jesse Knowles called it "the greatest plan I've ever seen to destroy a republic."[105] Opposition came in from Louisiana communities as well. As the hearings were going on, the Catahoula Parish School Board took it upon itself to go "on record opposing sex education in public schools."[106] Jackson's bill did not make it out of committee, but he was successful on one measure: a resolution that would direct "the state Department of Education to study sex education instructional materials," as John Hill of the *Shreveport Times* explained.[107]

The task force, which included, Hill reported, "parents, school board members, teachers, sociologists, doctors and legislators," ultimately "recommended that the ban be lifted."[108] Their reasoning, following six months of study, was that "the home and the church, the two institutions which traditionally have been responsible" for teaching sex ed, had failed to do so. In addition, the report explained, the onset of the state ban on sex ed seemed to be related to increases in STIs. In 1970, there had been 8,373 reported cases of gonorrhea in Louisiana. In 1974, there were 22,826 cases.

With the task force findings now in hand, in May 1975 Representative Jackson reintroduced his bill.[109] But the antis remained firmly anti, and their arguments became more sophisticated. According to the *Shreveport Times*, conservative legislators argued "that there is nothing in the present law which prohibits the teaching of a sex education course as described by the task force." All the pertinent information could be taught in the hygiene section of a biology course, they said.[110]

Such slippery arguments were possible because Louisiana had not legally defined what sex ed was. Jackson now attempted to pin down a definition from the attorney general, especially as it related to the 1970 moratorium. The moratorium, as the *Shreveport Times* explained, still allowed schools "to teach science, biology, hygiene, physical education and about venereal diseases."[111] Did that also mean, lawmakers queried, that the moratorium included "a prohibition against a course by the name of family planning, family health . . . specifically relating to the human reproductive cycle?" On that note, was the moratorium still even legally valid? It was only supposed to be in effect "until the final report and recommendation" of the committee formed in 1969, which had disbanded before ever filing a final report.[112] The attorney general's office responded that the moratorium *was* still valid, and that it would prohibit any course under any name that primarily dealt "with the human reproductive system as it pertains specifically to the act of sexual intercourse."[113]

With that point clarified, Jackson could now address arguments that educators in Louisiana could teach what they needed to without teaching "sex ed" per se. Like Assemblywoman Fong in California, Jackson argued that Louisiana teachers were often afraid to discuss sex at all for fear of the heavy punishment associated with it—"a suspension of 15 to 60 days . . . and withholding of state funds from the guilty school systems."

A hearing for the bill was held in May 1975. It was six hours long and garnered a group of "housewives" protesting against it. The housewives wore buttons that, according to Guy Coates of the *Town Talk*, read "Stop Sex Education," and they carried signs blaring "Clean Up Our X-Rated Schools": the 1960s was not so far in the past.[114]

Before the vote, Jackson made an impassioned appeal for the bill. "Bodies are being destroyed," he said, "and futures shattered because we're not willing to provide what the [Louisiana] Constitution mandates the public education system to provide: 'learning environments and experiences, at all stages of human development, that are humane, just and designed to promote excellence in order that every individual may be afforded an equal opportunity to develop his full potential.'"

The bill was once again defeated. "I'll try again next year," Jackson said.[115] And he did, this time with a version of the bill that allowed for sex ed only with written permission from parents.[116] Asked if he thought his chances were better that year, Jackson responded: "No, it's about same. But I'm going to continue to try."[117] He was right about his chances. His measure was voted down in committee in July 1976.[118] "I'm going to keep offering this legislation," he said. "I know that we ought to offer it."

So he introduced the bill again in 1977. That year, one witness testified that "the chapter on human sexual reproduction" had been ripped out of the life science book used by seventh graders "on orders of her West Carroll Parish school board," the *Town Talk* reported, because most Louisiana educators believed there was a total ban on teaching anything to do with sex.[119] The bill failed again—this time in the House Education Committee. The *Town Talk* noted that the committee vote was "divided along racial lines"—the three supporters of the bill, including Jackson himself, were Black.[120]

"I'll see y'all back next year," he remarked.[121]

And he did, in 1978. And his bill failed, again. But then, an ally emerged to help Jackson: Senator Nat Kiefer of New Orleans, as the *Shreveport Journal* reported, "simply took the text of Jackson's bill and introduced it" in the Senate Education Committee. There, it was approved, even by people who had previously disagreed with it. Senator Don Williamson of Caddo Parish had voted against sex ed in 1969, but now cited "'the high number of pregnancies existing among high school girls in Caddo Parish'" for his change of heart—and vote.[122] "My friends," Williamson said later that June, "the church has not taken care of it. The home hasn't taken care of it. It's an idea whose time has come."[123]

The bill passed in the senate 28 to 8 later in the month, its one concession being an amendment that would require any sex ed course to be separated by gender.[124] When the bill moved to the house, its opponents became more outspoken, bolstered by members of the Christian Defense League, a white supremacist group, who said the measure would "increase promiscuity."[125] And, then, the bill was yet again killed—though this time the cause of death differed from that of prior years, with the House Education Committee voting to defer action.[126] Jackson called the move "a dirty way" to end the skirmish because, as the *Shreveport Journal* explained, "once a bill is deferred in committee, it cannot be heard on the floor unless the full House votes to order the panel to report the bill. The action is used rarely because most legislators prefer to respect the sanctity of the committee system."[127]

Jackson wasn't the only one outraged this time. Now he had Senator Kiefer on his team, who announced his plan to "find me an education House bill on final passage and amend it over here and put it right back on them."[128] By this time, public opinion seemed to favor sex ed more than ever, even if stalwart conservative lawmakers didn't. Three Louisiana newspapers—the *Shreveport Journal*, *Shreveport Times*, and *Town Talk*—published editorials or opinion pieces voicing their support for the bill and bemoaning the state of sex education, and teen pregnancy, in the state.[129]

That being said, some of Jackson's allies in the legislature reported receiving hate mail. One was sent a letter that charged him with being "a Jewish, Zionist, Communist pig who is trying to undermine America"— all simply because he supported sex ed. Senator Kiefer also reported that he had been accused of being a communist for his support of sex ed.[130]

But Kiefer was successful in finding a house bill that he could amend with the sex ed measure, forcing it up for debate in July 1978.[131] He also found a coauthor for the amendment, Senator Edgar "Sonny" Mouton of Lafayette.[132] The *Shreveport Times* reported that Governor Edwin Edwards had already announced his intention to sign the bill into law if it passed.[133] It was piled high with safeguards: it called for classes to be separated by gender and for curricula to be approved by local school boards, committees, and the state board of elementary and secondary education.[134]

The bill died in the house. However, many house members, according to the *Shreveport Journal*, voted it down not because they disagreed with it but because of the convoluted tactics that had been used to get it there.[135] And, so, Jackson, Kiefer, and Mouton went back to the drawing board, with plans to introduce a *new* bill. Senator Mouton said, "We're going to give them a clean bill . . . We're not going to find anything else to hide behind."[136]

The new bill, this time penned by the long-suffering Jackson, was padded with even more safeguards, including provisions for it to be "fully explained to parents that sex education will be taught in a family life course," and a stipulation that "no instructor may quiz a student about the personal sex habits of the student's family."[137] But this bill, too, was unsuccessful. The *Town Talk* reported that the house voted to table it "just hours before the annual session came to an end."[138] However, the proponents of sex ed remained undaunted, per usual.

"It's that time of year again," John Hill wrote in the *Shreveport Journal* the next year, in April 1979. "The birds and bees are busy and the Louisiana legislature is engaged in its annual rite of spring consideration of a sex education bill."[139] It was a surprise to no one that Representative Jackson returned with his bill. This time, he had the explicit support of Governor Edwards, who now not only promised to sign the bill but actively urged its passage to help those "hundreds and thousands of Louisiana citizens who have no idea what causes pregnancy."[140]

Several members of the House Education Committee introduced their own sex ed bill around the same time. Authored by Representatives Lanny Johnson and B. F. O'Neal, this bill did not provide for sex ed classes per se, but allowed sex ed content to be taught as part of other classes.[141] The *Shreveport Journal's* opinion page pointed out that Johnson and O'Neal's bill "would do little more than maintain the status quo," preserving "Louisiana's dubious distinction of being the only state without public-school sex education per se."[142] And, so, it was perhaps unsurprising that their bill was the one to pass in the House Education Committee, while Representative Jackson's bill was killed.[143]

Also unsurprisingly, sex ed's opponents came out in full force even for this extremely weak bill. "The unyielding opponents of sex education," the *Shreveport Times* reported, "are planning mass rallies at the Capitol."[144] On April 30, 1979, dozens of people rallied at the state capitol,[145] singing "God Bless America" and carrying a portable electric sign that flashed "Vote No on Sex Education," reported Ronni Patriquin of the *Shreveport Journal*.[146] Another sign read, "Who's going to teach our kids sex ed? Homos, lesbians, rapists?"[147]

Ten days later, another anti–sex ed protest was held at the capitol, this time attended by what United Press International referred to as "busloads of fundamental Baptists."[148] Reverend Bill Burrows of the Merrywood Baptist Church outside of Shreveport was one of the speakers, exhorting: "Are you going to allow bald-headed, pot-bellied, cocktail-sipping buzzards to sit around a round table and tell you your kids are going to learn about sin. . . . What we need is some old-fashion, window-rattling, hell fire and damnation, brimstone fundamentalist preachers to tell these low-life politicians that God's way is the right way."[149]

This diatribe garnered considerable criticism, and calls ensued for Burrows to issue a public apology. Burrows instead doubled down, noting that "the state has no right to step in and take the place of the parent. The children are still God's gift to parents, not the state."[150]

Debate on this bill got underway, but the negotiations took a discouragingly familiar turn. Floor amendments severely weakened the bill, rendering it virtually useless: one amendment reinstated the penalties against teachers, while another prohibited the use of the term *sex education*. Alphonse Jackson called the amendments "a mockery," and said that "the bill as amended would be a cruel, cruel hoax to play on the parents and children of this state."[151] In the end, this version of the bill was voted down—this time because proponents of sex ed, "disgusted with amendments," also voted against the measure.[152]

But that was not the end of the sex ed fight that legislative session— Senators Kiefer and Mouton still had their bill. After a flurry of amendments that weakened its original proposal, the bill eventually passed in both Louisiana's house and senate. It did *not* lift the ban on separate sex ed classes, but instead took a different approach. Although it required that sex ed content must be taught in existing courses like biology or physical education, it also clearly delineated key topics that could be discussed, including, as the *Town Talk* reported, "factual biological or pathological information that is related to the human reproduction system and may include the study of venereal disease, pregnancy, childbirth, puberty, menstruation and menopause."[153] No school was beholden to teach these things, however, with local school boards having control over whether or not they wanted to include such content. Amendments stipulated that such instruction must happen "in the context of existing health, biology, physical education and home economics courses," and only for seventh grade and up. In July 1979, the governor signed off on the bill. After a decade of outright prohibition, sex ed was now legal in Louisiana—though it could be taught only in existing courses, and only for grades seven through twelve.[154] It did not technically repeal the 1969 moratorium, but it effectively allowed sex ed to be taught in Louisiana, the last state to hold onto harsh restrictions from the 1960s.

And, so, as the 1980s approached, it seemed clear that anti–sex ed activists were not going to find success blocking sex ed through either legislative measures or court cases.

CHAPTER 13

A DECADE OF FEDERAL ACTION

While sex ed battles were fought and won in Michigan and Louisiana throughout the 1970s, teenagers continued to have sex and continued to get pregnant. Newspapers across the country took notice and ran multipart series on teen pregnancy statistics and programs in their communities. Each article highlighted the wide-eyed innocence of the girls before they became pregnant. In April 1970, the *Daily News-Post* quoted the father of a pregnant teen as saying, "Last year my daughter wanted a giraffe. This year she wants a baby."[1]

"Mostly they are poor," a *Miami Herald* reporter remarked, in 1970, about young pregnant women in Florida at Dade's Maternity and Infant Care Project. "Mostly they are black," the article went on. "The problem goes largely unrecorded among middle and upper-class whites. They can afford the luxury of careful abortion or quiet delivery."[2] In 1972, a *Los Angeles Times* article opened: "The girl—barely 16, unmarried, pregnant and on record that she would keep her baby—sat in her high school English class, licking a lollipop."[3]

ROE V. WADE

The next year, in 1973, the United States Supreme Court decided the case of *Roe v. Wade*. "Jane Roe," a pseudonym for a woman named Norma McCorvey, had become pregnant in 1969. In her home state of Texas, abortion was illegal except when it was necessary to save the life of the mother. At the same time, a pair of lawyers—Sarah Weddington and Linda Coffee—were seeking a plaintiff through whom to bring litigation around legalizing abortion. McCorvey seemed to be an ideal candidate, and she agreed to be their client.

Weddington and Coffee argued that Texas's abortion ban was unconstitutional. Texas's law was similar to those of the majority of states at the time.[4] Ten states had slightly less restrictive laws, allowing for abortion in the case of "substantial risk that continuance of the pregnancy would gravely impair the physical or mental health of the mother or that the child would be born with grave physical or mental defect."[5] A few states permitted abortion in cases where the pregnancy was the result of a rape. Only four states—Alaska, Hawaii, New York, and Washington—had no laws restricting abortion before the fetus was viable.[6] This meant that a person in need of abortion was often compelled to travel to a state with less restrictive laws—if they could afford it.

Initially, *Roe v. Wade* was reviewed by a judicial panel. The panel sided with Roe, finding Texas's law unconstitutional. This finding was appealed to the Supreme Court, which in January 1973 ruled also in favor of Roe, providing a constitutional right to some abortions, citing the Due Process Clause of the Fourteenth Amendment, which provides a right to privacy. This meant that, going forward, any state law that restricted abortion would be subject to strict scrutiny in terms of constitutional review.

The court's ruling also stated, however, that the right to an abortion was not absolute. It instituted—and essentially invented—the concept of trimesters. As per the ruling, no law could be made limiting abortion in the first trimester; a state could place some regulations on abortion in the second trimester, so long as those regulations were tied to health; and a state could ban abortion in the third trimester, unless the abortion was medically necessary for the pregnant person.[7]

It was a landmark ruling. Individuals were no longer at the whim of geography when it came to whether or not they could access abortion care.[8] And it was a ruling that had the potential to lower rates of teen pregnancy, at least in theory.

TITLE X

But, by 1976, despite *Roe v. Wade* and increased access to birth control, experts were calling teen pregnancy an epidemic. "One out of 10 women aged 15–19 gets pregnant each year—one-quarter of those who are sexually active," Joy Dryfoos and Frederick Jaffe wrote in *Family Planning Perspectives*, a journal put out by the Guttmacher Institute, a research and policy organization founded in 1968, originally part of Planned Parenthood. "In addition," the article explained, "about 30,000 youngsters under age 15 become pregnant annually. The epidemic of adolescent pregnancy and childbearing poses one of the most difficult challenges remaining to a society which has otherwise brought fertility under a high degree of control."[9]

The looming question, posed by journalists as well as researchers, was *why* the number of adolescent pregnancies had grown so high. After all, the past decade had seen so many advances in the development of contraception, in legal access to that contraception, and, crucially, in funding for family planning. The 1970 Family Planning Services and Population Research Act—also known as Title X—had allocated federal funding for family planning services for low-income families, as well as for population research.[10] This act created the Office of Population Affairs,[11] which issued grants to and worked with organizations that helped with family planning programs—like health departments, Planned Parenthood affiliates, hospitals, free clinics, and community groups.[12] The act specified that none of this federal funding could be used for abortion, but it did fund a wide range of other reproductive care, including contraceptive counseling, other birth control options, and referrals to other health services.[13]

Once this federal funding was made available, the number of women who received services from organized family-planning programs jumped dramatically: from 863,000 in 1968 to 2.6 million in 1972. These programs overwhelmingly served younger women in their twenties and women living in poverty, and they provided care for adolescents as well.[14] Title X also made possible a number of significant studies and books on teen pregnancy in the early 1970s. Johns Hopkins University's study on adolescent sexuality, contraception, and pregnancy and Robert Sorensen's book *Adolescent Sexuality in Contemporary America* were two important achievements in this category. Both pointed to similar conclusions: young people were having sex, and they tended not to use contraception.

A 1973 study of five hundred thirteen- to seventeen-year-old "unwed, never-pregnant" girls found that those who sought contraception had already been sexually active: "Most of them had been having intercourse for more than a year; few were using any contraceptives, and fewer still were using one of the most effective methods."[15] A study from 1975 came to a similar conclusion.[16]

How could these trends be explained? Didn't young people want to avoid pregnancy? Researchers identified a number of reasons, among the most significant being ignorance, lack of access to contraception, stigma, and dislike of contraception. Those last two reasons—stigma around contraception and dislike of contraception—were not particularly high on the list of responses, but they did offer an important view of young people's thoughts about sex. In a 1975 study, one-quarter of adolescent respondents reported that they didn't use contraception "because it interfered with the pleasure, spontaneity or convenience of sex."[17]

The question of access was more important, especially to the researchers—many of them worked at clinics that helped young people access family planning resources. Young people were reporting that they didn't know where to obtain contraceptives, that they thought contraception was too expensive, or that they didn't know that contraception was actually available to them.[18] In part, this may have been due to the fact that, through the 1960s, various state laws still banned advertisements and sales of contraception through the relics of the Comstock Law. Other state laws restricted minors from accessing contraception and contraceptive information.[19] Condoms were not allowed to be advertised on national television as dictated by a 1950 policy enacted by the National Association of Broadcasters, which would not be overturned until 1979.[20]

But a 1976 study suggested there may have been a more important barrier to access: the healthcare system itself. The study cited as examples the Pill and the intrauterine device (IUD)—a small object inserted into the uterus and which has existed in some form or another since the early 1900s but by 1970 had developed into the copper or hormonal T-shaped device similar to today's—finding that both "presently require medical supervision, and their distribution is controlled by physicians and health institutions." As such, the researchers concluded, "The health system serves as gatekeeper for the most effective existing methods."[21]

But the most commonly reported reason for not using contraception was ignorance or misinformation. A 1975 report revealed that most of the young women in its study were having what was then becoming called "unprotected" sex simply because they did not think they could become pregnant.[22]

Federal funding through Title X attempted to quell the tide of teen pregnancy, and state actions repealing the bans on sex ed were positive indications that the issue was being taken seriously. But, of course, opposition mounted too—in a new form.

Throughout the 1970s, the overall political climate of the country was shifting. Lines previously drawn were hardening and deepening. By 1980, the relatively niche groups that had formed in reaction to second-wave feminism—such as JBS and HOW—had morphed into full-blown political movements. "Religious Right Becomes Potent Political Force," read the headline for the KNT News Service in May 1980. In the article, author Patrick Riordan chronicled the myriad ways that religion and politics were coalescing to extreme productive ends nationwide.[23]

A NEW NATIONAL FORCE

In Maryland, Riordan reported, a group called the Christian Coalition for Legislative Action was attempting to unseat a current senator because he was "too liberal on abortion and wrong on taxation of private schools." In the lead-up to the presidential election in November, a political action committee (PAC) called the Christian Moral Government Fund had pledged to "raise $1 million to help elect Ronald Reagan president and defeat up to 50 'immoral' members of Congress."[24] These groups, Riordan argued, were part of a "new and potent political force . . . the Religious Right . . . a network dedicated to the vision of making American politics more 'Christian' and 'moral.'" Other groups could also be said to be part of this network, like Phyllis Schlafly's Eagle Forum and the Moral Majority.

The Moral Majority, a political organization headquartered in Lynchburg, Virginia, had been formed in 1979 by Jerry Falwell, a Baptist minister and televangelist, along with conservative activist Paul Weyrich. The group was dedicated to bringing conservative Christian values to American law through political action and lobbying. Falwell's biggest asset as the head of the Moral Majority, as author Daniel K. Williams argues in his 2010 book *God's Own Party*, was that he "gave the Christian Right a national voice that it would not otherwise have had. . . . By the end of the summer of 1980, Republican Party leaders were treating him like an influential lobbyist and the leader of an important swing constituency."[25]

The timing of this new political force, and Riordan's article, was not coincidental: the 1980 presidential election loomed. Conservative evangelicals who made up this coalition knew that they had real power—in numbers, in money, and in connections—to make a difference in this election. As Williams put it in *God's Own Party*, while there hadn't been the same interest or action prior to the 1980 election, now "the leaders of the newly emerging Christian Right were determined to transform their movement into an influential voting bloc within the GOP."[26]

Ronald Reagan, a divorcé who had been an actor in liberal Hollywood and infrequently attended church, would not have been the religious right's first pick for an ideal candidate. As governor of California, he had made "therapeutic abortion" legal. Later, he spoke out against an anti–gay rights measure. But he had some things going for him, as evangelicals saw it. He supported prayer in public schools. He hated communism. He described a "born again" religious experience. [27]

And the religious right was nothing if not shrewd; Reagan was simply the best candidate they had to support. The election that year would be the Republican nominee up against incumbent Democrat Jimmy Carter, who had lost the affection of many Christians, and Southern evangelicals in particular—in great part because of his strong dedication to the separation of church and state.[28]

Reagan knew that support from the religious right could be extremely powerful, so he began courting their vote ahead of the election, even bringing on members of the movement as campaign advisors. Beverly LaHaye, wife of evangelical minister Tim LaHaye, was hired on the campaign as a "family policy" adviser.[29] And family policy was certainly high on the list of the things that the religious right cared about as the 1980s dawned. The new decade was seeing a rise in divorce rates, a burgeoning acceptance of homosexuality, and more women working outside the home—all apparent affronts to the "traditional family."

The Associated Press reported that the religious right (speaking specifically of the Moral Majority, although the same could probably be said for the movement as a whole) was also against "the Equal Rights Amendment, abortion, gay rights, sex education, the Department of Education, [and] national health insurance."[30] And in September 1980, two months ahead of the presidential general election, the Associated Press reported that the Moral Majority was "declaring war against America's liberal politicians and marching ambitiously from the pews to the election booths." Ahead of the election, another group that was part of the religious right, the Religious Roundtable, created report cards for legislators, scoring them on their voting history and encouraging voters to cast their ballots only for the most conservative lawmakers.[31]

CAPTURING ELECTIONS

In September 1980, the Christian right claimed an early victory when Jeremiah Denton, a conservative Vietnam War veteran with no political experience, won the Republican primary for the senate in Alabama against an eight-term Republican incumbent.[32] His "only one real source of support," Brian Kates of the *Daily News* reported, had been the "Christian New Right."[33] "The entire Republican Party establishment," noted Moral Majority leader Paul Weyrich, had actually supported Denton's incumbent opponent. But with the Moral Majority and other evangelical groups' help, he had won the primary—and later that fall, he clinched the senate bid. It was a prelude to bigger wins ahead.

In November, Reagan won the presidency. The Harris Survey, a popular poll, found that "conservatives—particularly the white moral majority" had lent him "massive support," giving "him a more than 12 percentage point overall lead, before the votes of the rest of the electorate were counted."[34] With Reagan voted in, and the religious right to thank—a fact they would not forget—his administration could now begin work, including on sex ed.

The 1970s had primarily been a decade of individual states sorting out their laws around sex ed, although the specter of teen pregnancy had also haunted legislators at the national level, leading to increased federal funding for sex ed programs. The Department of Health, Education, and Welfare (HEW) had helped fund programs in schools that were meant to prevent unplanned pregnancy.[35] President Carter's HEW secretary, Joseph Califano, said in June 1977 that the administration had a duty to "move more vigorously in the area of sex education," specifically because the president had made it clear that he opposed federal funding for abortion. As such, Califano explained, he believed he had "an obligation to provide a whole host of alternatives to abortion."[36] The next year, in 1978, the federal Office of Adolescent Pregnancy Programs (OAPP) was created in response to the high rates of unplanned teen pregnancy in the nation.[37] Carter's 1979 fiscal budget had earmarked $2 million for sex ed—not a huge amount, compared to the $142 million total appropriated for teen pregnancy prevention, but something.[38]

Reagan's secretary of Health and Human Services, Richard Schweiker, had different ideas about how the federal government should handle sex ed. In 1981 Schweiker explained that he did "not believe . . . the federal government should be in the sex education business." Schweiker oversaw two other Reagan appointees who would be assumed to share this opinion: Surgeon General C. Everett Koop and Marjorie Mecklenburg, head of the OAPP. Both were also outspoken anti-abortion activists. Koop had been a member of two anti-abortion organizations, the National Right to Life Committee and Americans United for Life, and had also narrated the controversial anti-abortion film *Whatever Happened to the Human Race?* Mecklenburg was the cofounder of an anti-abortion group called American Citizens Concerned for Life.[39]

In April 1981, journalist Nicholas von Hoffman wrote that "the Reaganauts are going back past conservative to have a try at staging a sexual counterrevolution. Abortion is to be banned, contraception discouraged, if not prohibited, and, furthermore, sex education is to be chased out of school."[40] Von Hoffman called it the "New Chastity." And indeed, there was a real sense of newfound intensity and vitriol around anything to do with sex: where sex ed had once been considered a means of preventing abortions, it was now being decried alongside them.

NEW BATTLES IN NEW JERSEY AND THE RISE OF "ABSTINENCE ONLY"

In February 1980, New Jersey's board of education announced their plan to mandate "family life courses" for all its public schools, grades K to 12.[41] This was to replace a policy that dated back to 1967, which had encouraged sex ed courses but had not required them. The *Daily Register*, out of Red Bank, explained that this new policy "would, in effect, remove from the jurisdiction of municipal or regional school boards the question of whether to provide 'Family life' courses, which include sex education."[42] The state board, made up of individuals appointed by the governor, had the power to mandate that each school district offer the course. And as the state board president, P. Paul Ricci, put it, the districts had had "13 years in which to act voluntarily. . . . Now it's time for the state to act."[43]

Around the same time, the *Paterson News* reported that Governor Brendan T. Byrne had "signed legislation that would permit parents to have their children excused from sex education, if they so desire."[44] But this safeguard—not to mention the fact that the state board of education's plan allowed for parents to dismiss children from the courses if they conflicted with the family's religious beliefs—was not enough to stem the tide of outrage toward the state board of education's action.[45]

First, opponents attempted to stop the state board from going forward with their mandate at all. In April 1980, Mark Magyar of Red Bank's *Daily Register* reported that "the state Board of Education sat stonily through eight hours of predominantly anti–sex education testimony."[46] The opponents' arguments could have been from any of the previous three decades, if not earlier. They took offense to the fact that the classes, in their words, functioned "outside a Judeo-Christian moral context," and that they would condone "premarital sex, abortion, birth control, homosexuality, incest, masturbation, and necrophilia." Others invoked SIECUS as the problem, accusing the group of plotting to promote "the religion of secular humanism, an aggressive atheism that shuns God, religion and patriotism." "Most of the almost 90 speakers," Mary Ellen Schoonmaker for the Hackensack *Record* reported, "were fundamentalist Christians."[47]

But the state board nonetheless announced their mandate in April 1980, joining Kentucky and Maryland as the only states that required sex ed to be taught in all grades of public schools. New Jersey's new mandate called for implementation of the courses by 1983, giving local school districts time to find a suitable curriculum and teachers.[48] Throughout the spring and summer of 1980, however, opponents chipped away at the mandate until it looked more like a suggestion. By August, the "mandate" dictated that sex ed no longer had to be offered in all grades, some topics had been eliminated from the curriculum entirely, parents would receive an outline for the year before the classes began, and provisions were made for "doctors, clergy and community representatives" to help design the curriculum.[49]

But opponents were still not content. By November, a coalition had formed between four conservative New Jersey groups: the Coalition of Concerned Parents, United Taxpayers Association of New Jersey, Monmouth County Right to Life, and New Jersey Moral Majority.[50] The Reverend Harry Vickery, chairman of the New Jersey Moral Majority, claimed that government-mandated sex ed was "an indoctrination of a religion of secular humanism."[51]

In truth, New Jersey's proposed sex ed was much more socially conservative than Vickery made it out to be. By April 1981, a year after the original mandate had been announced, the courses had been weakened even more in response to pushback from opponents. Now the state education commissioner was saying that the sex ed courses were meant to, among other things, "reinforce the traditional family unit."[52] By that time, too, the state board of education had changed its messaging: the education commissioner, Edward Burke, was advising school districts that they would have local control over what subjects they taught, and that the state guidelines were merely suggestions.[53]

Despite the loosening of the guidelines and the conventional monogamy espoused in the proposed courses, opponents remained unmoved. In May 1981, Phyllis Schlafly announced she was coming to New Jersey to speak on "Forced Sex Education."[54] She arrived in Morristown in June to great applause—and also to some protests. About twenty people from the New Jersey Chapter of the National Coalition to Stop the Moral Majority picketed outside the venue. They held signs bearing slogans like "The 'Moral Majority' is Neither" and "Who's Teaching Her Sons Family Life?"[55]

Schlafly was undeterred. Once inside the venue, she confidently and incorrectly informed the four hundred people assembled that "forced sex ed" leads to "a tremendous increase in pregnancy, V.D. and promiscuity." She recited the litany of anti–sex ed talking points and even revived some decades-old classics, including that sex ed "shreds away a girl's natural modesty, which is her defense against promiscuity."[56]

Schlafly portrayed sex ed classes as "'how-to' courses where the main purpose is to have sex without having a baby and without having guilt." They never taught, she charged, that "something is wrong, that it is immoral—that it is a sin." The fact that nearly all sex ed classes did teach within a moral framework was immaterial to Schlafly, because she was only interested in morals that were expressed in religious terms. She further claimed, "The purpose of these courses is not to give the facts but to change the attitudes of the students."[57]

For Schlafly, this was an indictment of sex ed. But was it true? Did sex ed classes change the attitudes of young people? The efficacy of sex ed was still an open question, but studies on the subject were becoming more and more pointed. Some dealt specifically with this question of attitude changes. Two well-regarded studies of the mid-1970s did determine that sex ed could affect changes in attitude—provided that was one of the goals of the course. A teacher who aimed to cultivate a more "liberal or permissive" mindset on topics like masturbation and homosexuality, for instance, was often successful in changing students' attitudes.[58]

For some, this was a positive outcome. Of course, Schlafly would find such a thing a travesty. Even more terrifying to Schlafly and her ilk was another common tenet of sex ed, which held that, in order to discourage teen pregnancy, instructors should encourage young people to feel *less guilt* about having sex. As one study explained, "Sexual guilt discourages the recognition of one's sexual activity and thereby hinders the use of effective contraception. Thus, when guilt is reduced, contraception is more likely to be used and pregnancy is less likely to occur."[59]

For those who wanted to reduce the rates of teen pregnancy, this was a good thing. But it was becoming clearer that Schlafly and her allies were not interested in preventing teen pregnancy—they were interested in preventing teens from having sex altogether. And so, even though established sex ed courses already centered the monogamous married model of love and sex *and* appeared to encourage contraceptive use, Schlafly and company began to demand courses that discussed nothing other than abstinence: no STI information, no birth control instruction. Abstinence only. And based on their political machinations in New Jersey and beyond, they were clearly committed to pushing this model.

WHOSE SEX ED?

All this debate was pointing to a much larger question: Who was properly "in charge" of sex education? Was it SIECUS and Planned Parenthood, which believed in providing young people with any facts they wanted, or was it the Moral Majority and the Eagle Forum, which believed that instruction began and ended with abstinence?

The answer seemed to be whoever controlled the money. Planned Parenthood had been federally subsidized through Title X for years.[60] There had been some protests over this fact, as Planned Parenthood provided some abortion services in some locations, but overall it had not been incredibly controversial. By the 1980s, however, Planned Parenthood began to unseat SIECUS as the ultimate evil in the eyes of the religious right. That Planned Parenthood offered contraception, abortion counseling, and services to teens without parental approval (unless mandated by state or local law) was perceived by many on the Right as an invasion of parental rights.[61] And when Planned Parenthood developed a secondary school sex ed curriculum and began presenting it in public schools, the Right saw that as a threat too.

In December 1980, a group called Parents Who Care convened a meeting in Santa Cruz, California, to purge the perceived dangers of Planned Parenthood from their schools.[62] Although parents were able to withdraw their students from the classes that Planned Parenthood had developed, were advised of the classes in advance, and were kept apprised of all course materials, Parents Who Care were still outraged. Some of their criticisms seemed manufactured or relied on misleading arguments. The leaders of the meeting, for instance, criticized the materials that Planned Parenthood had recommended for teachers to read, implying that they were also meant to be read by students.[63] One of the books that Planned Parenthood suggested that teachers read for background information, for instance, was *Our Bodies, Ourselves*, originally published in 1970.[64] The book encouraged women to take control of their sexuality, and included information on abortion, birth control, and lesbian sexuality. It was meant for adults. But this clarification was not impactful—the accusation itself was enough to spark controversy.

Such attacks on Planned Parenthood unfolded nationwide. In April 1981, Karen DeMasters reported in the *Asbury Park Press* that the County Board of Freeholders in Monmouth, New Jersey, had voted to "cut off a $28,000 grant to Planned Parenthood, Inc."[65] The local Planned Parenthood office sponsored an abortion clinic and had taught free sex ed programs in area high schools, hospitals, and nonprofits. When the grant was revoked, the office's executive director explained that, going forward, they would now need to charge fees for their educational services.[66]

THE CHASTITY BILL

There were larger schemes coming. In 1981, Senator Denton of Alabama—who had been elected thanks in great part to the Moral Majority—introduced legislation that would reallocate $30 million in federal money away from programs that provided adolescents with birth control—including Planned Parenthood—and into programs that had a "pro-family" emphasis and which specifically advocated for teens to use "self-discipline" and "chastity."[67] In particular, the Associated Press reported, the bill would prevent centers that received federal funds from "referring pregnant teen-agers to abortion clinics."[68] The bill—officially called the Adolescent Family Life Act (AFLA) and nicknamed the "chastity bill"—was initially proposed as an amendment to the Public Service Act of 1970. It also forbade "federally funded development of new contraceptives" and only allowed "federally funded abortion research . . . if it is directed 'to the negative consequences of abortion.'"[69] Denton referred to this as a *reversal* of "government influence": In his mind, the money that had been allocated to clinics like Planned Parenthood gave the message that the American government believed that "sex was OK." He knew his bill would be controversial. "You can say," he exhorted in May 1981, "that we are going back to 1450. There is going to be a great pillorying about this."

He was correct. An editorial in the *Los Angeles Times* noted that the bill was "yet another case of attempting to impose, through legislation, one group's moral standards on every group."[70] And, as the *Boca Raton News* pointed out, defunding clinics as the bill proposed had real practical consequences—rendering them "virtually worthless."[71] Even conservative columnist James J. Kilpatrick took issue, writing, "If the two senators' chastity bill is a conservative bill, the principles of conservatism have been turned upside down."[72] Kilpatrick explained that "one of the principal doctrines of American conservatism today" was that "the government . . . should leave the citizens alone to lead their lives as they see fit; further, that public institutions should not intrude upon private morals."[73] Denton's bill was a textbook example of such an intrusion, Kilpatrick noted, calling it a "melancholy example of federal paternalism."[74]

But on the side of the pro-chastity camp was the simplistic but undeniable fact that abstinence was, of course, effective in preventing pregnancy and STIs. This became the intellectual underpinning of the bill, the realities of teenage sexual life be damned. The bill became popular enough that it gained support from across the aisle. Democratic senator Edward M. Kennedy became interested in the bill and softened its language. He struck the phrases "promiscuity means having sexual intercourse out of wedlock" and "the purpose of the bill is 'to promote self-discipline and chastity.'"[75] With his changes, the legislation was given a newly defined purpose: "to find effective means, within the context of family, of reaching adolescents before they become sexually active in order to maximize the guidance and support available to adolescents from parents and other family members and to promote self-discipline and other prudent approaches to the problems of adolescent premarital sexual relations, including adolescent pregnancy."

The bill passed in the Senate Labor and Human Resources Committee on June 24, 1981.[76] At the end of July, senators negotiated the health package that Denton's proposal was considered under. In the end, the bill went forward with Denton's proposed $30 million, becoming Title XX of the Public Health Service Act, and "providing $10 million for research on teen-age chastity and up to $6.75 million of counseling on the prevention of promiscuity."[77] As Rebekah Saul explained in an essay for the *Guttmacher Report on Public Policy*, Title XX kept true to its original promise of "virtually prohibiting funding for family planning services or the provision of any abortion-related information to AFLA program participants."[78]

By 1984, Denton's legislation had given funding to fifty-nine so-called "demonstration" projects, "including 16 prevention projects, 30 care projects and 14 projects that offer a combination of care and prevention services." Grantees included "county health departments, Catholic charitable organizations, universities, local YWCAs, hospitals, rural health services, and multi service agencies."

CHAPTER 14

CURRICULA WARS

THE FIRST AFLA PROJECTS

In 1982, Adolescent Family Life Act (AFLA) funding became available for the first time. One of the recipients was Teen-Aid, Inc., an abstinence-only education group based in Washington State and led by LeAnna Benn.[1,2] Teen-Aid's goal, as stated in its charter, was to "reduce the many adverse consequences of premarital sexual activity among teens by encouraging abstinence as a premarital lifestyle." Benn explained, "We want to help marriage be the most beautiful thing possible."[3] Teen-Aid was actively opposed to what it called "contraceptive education"—that is, classroom sex ed that included information about contraceptives.[4] Teen-Aid argued that typical sex ed, or "contraceptive education," was a "band-aid approach," as opposed to the "long-term solution" that the abstinence-before-marriage lessons offered.[5] As such, Teen-Aid "did not advise teens regarding contraceptives or abortion." It even rejected the label of "sex education," the Associated Press reported, favoring language like "programs that encourage abstinence."[6]

By 1983, with help from a $140,000 grant from AFLA, Teen-Aid produced a high school curriculum called Sexuality, Commitment and Family. The *Tri-City Herald* out of Pasco, Washington, explained that this curriculum's emphasis was not "on the consequences of teen-age sexual activity but rather on the advantages of abstinence."[7] By May 1983, Teen-Aid reported that its curriculum had been sold to three hundred private and public high schools. By 1986, Teen-Aid had produced a film meant to pitch its approach to administrators at prospective client schools. Benn, who appeared in the film, revealed much about the curriculum's underlying sexism when she explained its value. She explained that "young men respond best to the Teen-Aid course, because they are more likely to have set goals for themselves and look toward their own future." Benn also stated that sixteen-year-old males tended to be most receptive to the curriculum's message, because "they want the girls they are going to marry to remain virgins."[8]

Another key AFLA-funded project from this time period was Coleen Kelly Mast's curriculum Sex Respect: The Option of True Sexual Freedom. Mast worked as an education consultant for the Catholic diocese in Joliet, Illinois. Until the mid-1980s, her work in sex ed had been geared primarily toward Catholic schools. But in 1986, with help from an AFLA grant, she published a curriculum intended for public school audiences.[9] Though Sex Respect was marketed to public schools and therefore ostensibly free of overt religious messaging, it was arguably free of any practical messages at all. It contained no anatomical information and certainly no information about birth control. The slim "textbook" simply bombarded the reader with catchphrases and slogans that urged them to wait until marriage to have sex. Among them were "Sex is like driving—you need a license to do Both," "Don't be a Louse; Wait for your Spouse," and "Pet your dog, not your Date!"[10]

Mast and Benn, along with other abstinence-forward proponents gaining in popularity through the 1980s, argued that their positive emphasis on abstinence was a welcome change from the assumption that all young people would have sex, which they claimed was the foundation of "traditional" sex ed programs.

Not everyone bought their arguments. The *Shreveport Journal* reported that when the sex ed subcommittee in Caddo County, Louisiana, examined Sex Respect in July 1986, some members "said the program underestimated the sophistication of teens and took a negative approach." A Louisiana State University Medical Center doctor on the committee was quoted as saying that it "promotes guilt, fear and self-hatred" and "doesn't invite you to have self-respect and learn to make decisions."[11]

But for many conservatives, programs like Teen-Aid and Sex Respect offered attractive alternatives to what they had long decried as amoral, or immoral, sex ed curricula. So now, when school boards were faced with decisions about sex ed—whether to implement it at all, what textbook to use, and so on—they could choose between "abstinence only" or traditional sex ed. And thanks to AFLA funding, abstinence-only programs now had the endorsement of the American government and the appearance of legitimacy.

CURRICULA WARS IN SOUTH CAROLINA

The decision of what curriculum to use was before a health and sex education committee in Beaufort County, South Carolina, in June 1986. The committee—like the ones that SIECUS had advocated for twenty years prior—had been put into place to review curricula and make recommendations to the county school board and had been at work since October. Aileen Mulhern of the *Beaufort Gazette* reported that the committee was composed of "teachers, parents, and health professionals."[12] Originally, the committee had recommended using a curriculum called Health Skills for Life, but it was rejected by the school board, in part because of rumors that the program was linked to Planned Parenthood.[13]

Now, the district had gone back to the drawing board. It looked seriously at three curricula: Sex Respect, Teen-Aid, and the 3R Project: Reproductive Risk Reduction, a state-funded project that had existed since 1979.[14] The 3R Project urged teens to delay sexual activity but, in contrast to Sex Respect and Teen-Aid, also provided information about the ways to "reduce the risk" of sex "and protect oneself and others from damaging relationships." The curriculum covered reproduction, puberty, anatomy, fetal development, "birth control responsibilities," and STIs, among other things.

It was this curriculum that the superintendent of Beaufort County schools, Robert G. Salisbury, recommended in June 1986.[15] The next step was to go to the school board for approval. However, the vice chairman of the board objected: "It appears to me that the administration did not review the sex education curriculum with objectivity, without giving fair review to the other curriculums available."[16] He recommended that Sex Respect and Teen-Aid be given more review.

In the months that followed, local right-wing opponents took the 3R Project's materials out of context and rallied against it. In the summer of 1986, a pamphlet called *An Evaluation of the 3R Project*, produced by "Concerned Parents," circulated widely in Beaufort County.[17] The *Beaufort Gazette* noted that the pamphlet contained no actual "evaluation" of 3R, but instead "was composed of excerpts from reference material suggested for teachers," including "discussion on masturbation, homosexuality and virginity."[18]

A hearing on the county's proposed adoption of the 3R Project was held in August 1986. It lasted two hours and drew 160 people.[19] The Concerned Parents group trotted out what had become a "21-point list of objections." A spokesperson for the Raymond G. Bennett Council of the Knights of Columbus, a Catholic organization that espouses conservative social values, claimed that "The 'Three R' project appears to be an attempt in pragmatic hedonism." A local Catholic priest, Father Philip Hamilton, promised that if Beaufort County chose the program, he would challenge it in court.[20]

Among school board members, it was a deadlock. One school board member suggested teaching all three curricula—the 3R Project, Sex Respect, and Teen-Aid—and allowing parents to choose one for their child. This generous and ambitious option was dismissed, but the committee did agree to look into both AFLA-funded curricula more closely.[21] One committee member was quickly skeptical of them, noting that "some medical facts . . . don't seem to be absolutely correct." Of Sex Respect in particular, they remarked that the curriculum "beats them over their heads and tells them not to do it. It's not going to help them when Mother Nature takes over in the back seat of a car."[22]

In late August, the Beaufort School Board voted not to use Teen-Aid or the 3R Project.[23] They were unable to reach agreement about anything else and, as Mulhern in the *Beaufort Gazette* put it, "threw the issue back to parents."[24] They announced they would poll parents in the district, and then delegate the creation of a curriculum to a task force specifically created for the purpose.[25] But then, a month later, one of the board members, Carol Arberg, announced she had changed her mind and favored Teen-Aid after all. "I think it's better," she said, "to establish a moderate program [than] no program." Her change of mind was enough to give Teen-Aid a majority of supporters on the board: on October 1, the board voted in favor of the abstinence program, five to four.[26] Board chair Paul

Siegmund summarized his displeasure: "Teen-Aid, educationally," he said, "is the equivalent of teaching that the earth is flat."[27]

THE SCHOOL-BASED CLINIC MODEL

While young people in Beaufort were receiving government-funded platitudes about abstinence, other American students were getting government-funded sex ed and comprehensive care through school-based clinics. Although this model didn't gain national momentum until the 1980s, one of the earliest school-based clinics had opened in 1973, in a junior-senior high school in Saint Paul, Minnesota. The city had been home to the Saint Paul Maternal and Infant Care (MIC) Project since 1968.[28] An article in *Family Planning Perspectives* described the MIC Project as offering "comprehensive, multidisciplinary health care to adolescents."[29] By 1980, the MIC Project had established clinics in two "inner city" senior high schools. Each clinic was staffed with a family planning nurse practitioner, a clinic attendant, and a social worker, among others.[30] There were on-site day-care programs affiliated with the clinics, meant to "give the adolescent parents an opportunity to complete high school, and at the same time learn good parenting skills." Funding for the project came from a number of sources, including Title V Maternal and Child Health (MCH) block grants, Title XIX funds, and Title XX funds for the day-care facility. State funding came from the Minnesota Community Health Services Act.[31]

The MIC Project set out to "address the total health care needs of adolescents" and also "developed a comprehensive medical and educational program." The results seemed promising. After two years, Laura Edwards, the director of the MIC Project, reported that "the clinic was being used by about two-thirds of 12th grade students and by more than nine in 10 pregnant students," and "fertility rates among female students fell by 56 percent between 1973 and 1976—from 79 to 35 births per 1000."[32] Subsequent research found that the dropout rate for student parents fell "from 45 percent in 1973 to 10 percent in 1976," and further, that "no repeat pregnancies occurred among those students who delivered with the project and returned to school."[33]

The MIC Project served as a model for other clinic projects nationwide. By 1985, Joy Dryfoos in the journal *Family Planning Perspectives* noted that "in at least 14 American cities . . . comprehensive health services—including family planning services—are being offered in clinics located in or near public high schools and junior high schools."[34] These clinics, Dryfoos noted, served patients who tended to be "from low-income families, a reflection of the neighborhoods in which programs are located."[35] Dryfoos also reported that, in a study of nine school-based clinics, all surveyed provided not only general medical care, like treatment of "minor acute illnesses" and physical exams for sports and employment, but also "individual counseling about sexuality [and] gynecological examinations. . . . They either offer contraceptive prescriptions in the clinic or refer students to off-site birth control clinics. . . . They perform laboratory tests, screen for [STIs], provide nutrition education and refer students . . . to social service agencies."[36]

Other clinics varied school to school. Some served as classrooms for sex ed. Most provided pregnancy tests, and many provided prenatal care. Many offered referrals to abortions, although lack of public funding for abortions made it hard for low-income students to actually receive them. And clinics that received funding through AFLA were, of course, prohibited from providing abortion counseling. One researcher noted that while such clinics would refer pregnant students to information about adoption, "teenagers appear to have little interest."[37] Although there was no long-term data on the clinics, as they were still so new, Dryfoos noted that the "school-based programs [had] been credited with improving students' health, lowering their birthrates, raising their levels of contraceptive use and improving their school attendance."[38]

At last, here in the school-based clinic was an evidence-based, research-backed solution to reducing adolescent pregnancies—the avowed goal of so many programs, organizations, municipal officials, federal policymakers, public healthcare workers, medical professionals, educators, and parents. The clinics were meeting young people where they were, providing them with the active care they needed to address their specific situations. As such, it was only a matter of time before the religious right began to decry them.

ATTACKS ON THE CLINIC MODEL

"In Room 165 at DuSable High School, teen-agers can receive not only general medical care but also birth control pills and condoms," read an article in the Sunday *New York Times* on September 22, 1985, entitled "Sex and School Clinic: A City at Odds," by E. R. Shipp.[39] Three months earlier, DuSable High School, a majority-Black school located on Chicago's South Side, had opened a clinic in conjunction with Provident Medical Center.[40] It was funded by the Illinois Department of Public Aid and, the Associated Press reported, "a coalition of private foundations." The year prior, the same article reported, "about 300 DuSable girls—one-third of the female students—gave birth."[41] In the clinic's first two months, Shipp reported it "saw 476 students, and dispensed contraceptives, mainly condoms, to 169 of them."[42] The manager of the clinic, a nurse practitioner, explained that receiving contraceptives required parental consent. "We don't just pass out birth control pills and condoms. . . . Family planning is just one of 10 health functions we perform," she said in an interview.[43]

Local protest against the clinic occurred in the months after it opened. The Associated Press reported that anti-abortion groups and others opposed to "family planning" asked that the clinic be shut down.[44] But the school board, after a multi-hour debate in September 1985, remained strong on the side of the clinic. The board did concede that there could be stronger guidelines around parental consent, which it planned to implement.[45]

The clinic at DuSable remained a topic of controversy as the year went on. The AP's reporting on the clinic found its way into local newspapers, and "letters to the editor" pages were filled with the same old arguments against sex ed. In January 1986, the Black economist and commentator Walter E. Williams—who often espoused libertarian and unorthodox views—cited DuSable's clinic as an example of the way that he believed that Black Americans were being used as political pawns. Williams charged that putting the clinic in a majority-Black school was no accident. "People wishing to lace public schools with sex clinics," he wrote, "have discovered a new use for Blacks."[46]

In April, the Scripps Howard News Service, a wire service that supplied content to papers across the country, published two head-to-head op-eds on the controversy, both penned by stalwarts of the sex ed world: Phyllis Schlafly against school clinics and the president of Planned Parenthood; Faye Wattleton, for them.[47] "These sex clinics in public schools,"

Schlafly wrote, "promote the promiscuity of minors by giving them devices to assist in engaging in illicit acts with 'sex partners.' . . . They are saying 'Step right up, little girl, and get your contraceptives here; have fun with your sex partner; the only thing that's wrong is having a baby.'" Schlafly cited Sex Respect as a good alternative to these houses of promiscuity, lauding the curriculum for its "creative lessons, cartoons and jargon that appeal to teen-agers."

Wattleton, on the pro side, pointed to data showing that communities with school-based clinics tended to have declining pregnancy and childbirth rates among teenagers. She added that parents in those communities typically supported the clinics. Further, the clinics not only proved that family planning worked; they were also providing other healthcare services—like physicals, nutritional counseling, and treatment of minor injuries—that students may not be able to get any other way.[48] Wattleton's and Schlafly's views mapped neatly onto Democratic and Republican policies, respectively. In February 1986, the House Select Committee on Children, Youth, and Families released a study on teenage pregnancy that recommended, among such other measures as sex ed and contraception, "comprehensive health care through school-based clinics."[49] The Democrats on the committee said, "We know contraception works. We know sex education can make a real contribution. We know comprehensive care is essential."

The Republican minority report on the same study came to different conclusions altogether—ones that favored what one journalist called "a family-oriented approach that encourages children to refrain from sexual activity."[50] It argued that teaching young people to embrace abstinence was hard, while teaching them about contraception was easy. Therefore, they concluded, the Democrats had merely taken the easy way out. "We have, as a nation," the minority report read, "decided that it is easier to give children pills than to teach them respect of sex and marriage." The report falsely attributed the nation's rising rates of teen pregnancy, "drug abuse, venereal disease, suicide and other forms of self-destructive behavior" to the liberal practice of "[giving] children pills."[51]

It was easy to tick off these sobering statistics, but it was simply not accurate to attribute them to birth-control access or to birth control itself. The research of the 1980s had shown that if the goal was to lower teen pregnancy rates, the solution was to give young people clinics through which they could access birth control or, at the very least, information about birth control. However, if the goal was to prevent young people from having sex—which seemed to be what the Right wanted, whether they would say it or not—that was an entirely different story.

CHAPTER 15

AIDS

A FRIGHTENING NEW EPIDEMIC

In 1981, the year AFLA was signed into law, five young men in Los Angeles—all previously healthy, and all gay—died following a "rare lung infection" coupled with what appeared to be a weakened immune system. More such cases began to appear—mostly in gay men, mostly in big cities like New York and San Francisco. They presented with an aggressive cancer, Kaposi's sarcoma, as well as the lung infection *Pneumocystis carinii* pneumonia. In June of that year, the CDC began following this strange and tragic phenomenon. In July, the *Bay Area Reporter*, a weekly gay paper out of San Francisco, mentioned "Gay Men's Pneumonia." By the end of the year—just six months later—337 cases had been reported. One hundred thirty men had died.

By May 1982, the mysterious illness had the name GRID: gay-related immune deficiency, so called because it seemed to affect only gay men. By September, it had a new name, and one that would stick: AIDS—acquired immune deficiency syndrome. As researchers would come to find out, AIDS is caused by the human immunodeficiency virus (HIV), a sexually transmitted infection that can be contracted by anyone—not just gay men. HIV can also be spread through contact with blood, like when using shared needles, and it can be transmitted from parent to baby during pregnancy or childbirth.

The virus spread quickly and viciously. The CDC would eventually report that "the estimated number of infections increased from 20,000 in 1981 to 130,400 in 1984 and 1985."[1] A report from 1986 showed that AIDS patients usually died roughly fifteen months after diagnosis.[2] It was a brutal and stunning epidemic, one that the American government ignored, stigmatized, and failed to fund research for. Like the syphilis outbreaks at the turn of the twentieth century, when an infection was often viewed as the price one paid for the sin of extramarital sex, some now felt that AIDS was a punishment for the sin of being gay. Perhaps no group claimed this more explicitly than American Evangelists. Jerry Falwell would express this belief most succinctly in 1987: "AIDS is a lethal judgment of God on the sin of homosexuality."[3]

THE SURGEON GENERAL CALLS FOR SEX ED

Reagan's surgeon general, C. Everett Koop—who had a penchant for wearing a full general's uniform while in office—once called the gay rights movement "anti-family," was a born-again Christian, and was staunchly anti-abortion. One might have assumed he would agree with Falwell. But his report on AIDS, released in October 1986, showed a different side of the nation's doctor.

Koop wrote that "the threat of AIDS should be sufficient to permit a sex education curriculum," and should start at the "lowest grade possible." He mentioned third grade as a good starting point. "The need is critical," Koop explained, "and the price of neglect is high. The lives of our young people depend on our fulfilling our responsibility."[4] In addition to his call for sex ed in public schools, he also urged compassion. Recognizing a prevailing attitude that "people from certain groups 'deserved' their illness," he stated in no uncertain terms: "Let us put those feelings behind us. We are fighting a disease, not people. Those who are already afflicted are sick people and need our care, as do all sick patients."[5] In addition to sex ed, Koop also urged widespread condom use and testing, and—with echoes of Dr. Morrow—explained that "we can no longer afford to side-step frank, open discussion about sexual practices."

Koop's report was shocking, given his political and religious affiliations. As an editorial in the *Washington Post* put it: "It isn't often that Planned Parenthood and the Reagan administration see eye to eye, but a national crisis has brought them together."[6] Some believed that Koop's call might be just the thing to at last usher in a new era of sex ed in the United States. Just days after Koop's report was released, journalist Ellen Goodman wrote that "AIDS, of all things, may be the tragic impetus to bring frank and explicit talk about human sexuality to the young."[7]

But angry responses came from those on the right who had regarded Koop as an ally. Phyllis Schlafly remarked, derisively, that the report sounded "as though it was written by the National Gay Task Force."[8] In February 1987, Koop reported that he had received a "tremendous amount of hate mail," from conservative Christians who, like Schlafly, felt he had betrayed them.[9]

Even some educators condemned his call for sex ed—though with less passion than Schlafly and her ilk. R. Camille Dorman, assistant superintendent of Palm Beach County, Florida, took issue with Koop's recommendation that the instruction begin as early as third grade. "I think it would be very, very difficult to break down the material so the young children could understand it in a way that it doesn't scare the daylights out of them," she said.[10] Others worried more about the fact that AIDS education would apparently necessitate acknowledging the existence of homosexual sex. Howard Carroll of the NEA said, "To explain to children of that age what homosexuality is, this is what raises the red flag."[11]

There were logistical concerns as well. In some states, existing laws made it difficult to implement Koop's suggestions. As the *Salt Lake Tribune* pointed out, per Utah's state board of education, public schools could not teach about the "'intricacies of intercourse,' 'the acceptance of homosexuality' and 'how to do it approaches to contraceptive techniques.'... Utahns," the article concluded, "obviously cannot teach their children how to avoid AIDS infections—and death—if they refuse to discuss its causes."[12]

But despite the mixed reactions, the federal government was willing to put its money where Koop's mouth was. In November 1986 the Reagan administration announced that $10 million in federal funding would be allocated to "state education agencies to help them design and introduce comprehensive AIDS sex and drug education programs into the classroom."[13] The initiative was sponsored by the CDC. "A year from now," Dennis Tolsma of the CDC said, "you'll see things being taught in schools that aren't being taught now."

TEEN PREGNANCY IN THE 1980S

One epidemic did not cancel out another, and though AIDS was taking center stage nationally, teen pregnancy continued to be a pressing concern for those who were paying attention. In 1985, the Guttmacher Institute reported on a study that compared "adolescent pregnancy and childbearing in developed countries . . . to gain some insight into the determinants of teenage reproductive behavior, especially factors that might be subject to policy changes."[14]

The study compared the United States with five other countries: England and Wales (categorized as one country), France, Canada, Sweden, and the Netherlands. Those countries were chosen because each had "considerably lower" rates of teen pregnancy than the US but similar rates of sexual activity among young people. Compared to them, the United States had an "exceptional position," the researchers explained. "American birthrates, abortion rates, and pregnancy rates were much higher than those of all the other countries."[15]

As to *why* this was the case, an array of societal factors emerged, but probably the most remarkable was these other countries' "tolerance of teenage sexual activity." These nations had approached teen-pregnancy prevention with the very methods that America had doggedly rejected for decades.[16] In the other nations, the study reported, "public attention was generally not directly focused on the morality of early sexual activity but, rather, was directed at a search for solutions to prevent increased teenage pregnancy and childbearing." In the United States, meanwhile, "sex tends to be treated as a special topic, and here is much ambivalence: sex is romantic but also sinful and dirty, it is flaunted but also something to be hidden."[17]

Crucially, not one of these other countries had what the United States had fought so hard for: "official programs designed to discourage teenagers from having sexual relations." The governmental obsession with abstinence was a purely American phenomenon. "The other countries," the report noted, "tended to leave such matters to parents and churches or to teenagers' informed judgments."[18]

In December 1986, the National Research Council—an arm of the National Academy of Sciences—recommended that pregnancy prevention be given "highest priority" among schools and governments, and specifically called for "more extensive sex education and the dispensing of 'contraceptive service' by schools and community clinics"—not the kind of programming that was funded by AFLA.[19] Unsurprisingly, the president of Planned Parenthood supported the council's recommendations. Reagan's education secretary, William Bennett, did not, instead calling school-based clinics "dumb" and predicting that they would "damage our schools and children."[20]

REAGAN BELATEDLY CALLS FOR SEX ED

Stepping in at last, in March 1987, after "nearly seven years of silence," as Julie Johnson of the *Baltimore Sun* put it, Reagan himself finally spoke out on AIDS. He called it "Public Health Enemy No. 1" and spoke in favor of sex ed in schools, so long as it was "taught in connection with values." He noted that he [didn't] "quarrel" with Koop's public-health philosophy on sex ed, though he also opined: "When it comes to preventing AIDS, don't medicine and morality teach the same lessons?"[21]

This was the same conclusion that Dr. Morrow had reached eighty years prior. And it was certainly still true that abstinence from all sexual activity did necessarily preclude someone from becoming pregnant, and it also considerably reduced the risk of contracting an STI. But now medicine offered options that hadn't been available at the turn of the century. The modern condom in particular had emerged as an almost miraculous little device: cheap, relatively simple to use, easy enough to manufacture, and highly effective at preventing both pregnancy *and* STIs, including AIDS.

But for people who saw abstinence as *the point*, educating students on condoms was identical to promoting sex. No argument, however reasonable and fact based, could sway Schlafly and her vanguard of this notion—and now they had curricula like Sex Respect and Teen-Aid, which theoretically provided sex ed while excluding all information about contraception. With this deceitful framework now in place, states could comply with Reagan and Koop's call for sex ed in schools without having to teach young people a single thing about how to actually prevent pregnancy or avoid STIs.

By December 1987, seventeen states and Washington, DC, had newly mandated AIDS education in their public schools—twelve more states compared to the five that had done so just seven months earlier.[22] However, these programs differed wildly in content, showing again just how much terms like *sex education* could be used and abused. Language was finessed in other ways, too. For instance, California passed a bill that declared abstinence *"the* primary" rather than *"a* primary" way of preventing AIDS.[23] The bill's language also claimed that other methods, like condoms, *"may* reduce the risk of spreading the disease."

When it came to sex ed, the late 1980s were a time of immense debate in school districts nationwide. Yet for all the drawn-out meetings and heated deliberation, the end results were often nothing more than a vague guideline that sex ed needed to "stress abstinence," which really meant a program that differed very little from any standard sex ed class of previous decades.

NEW BATTLES IN SOUTH CAROLINA

In January 1988, the South Carolina legislature considered a bill that required comprehensive health education in schools, including sex ed. The bill specified that "abstinence and the risk associated with sexual activity outside of marriage must be strongly emphasized" and that "abortion must not be included as a method of contraception." It also banned contraception distribution and abortion counseling within schools.[24] At the time, according to Democratic state senator Nell Smith, South Carolina had an "incidence of teen-age pregnancy" that was "90 percent higher than the national rate." The bill was endorsed by the state board of education, the South Carolina Medical Association, and the Baptist Education and Missionary Convention, among others.[25]

The most controversial part of the bill included an option for local school districts to include "pregnancy prevention education" in their curricula. But the bill also included plenty of parental-rights safeguards around that portion of the class. For a student to attend a class that addressed pregnancy prevention, a school district would have to notify parents and allow them to opt out their children. And parents were assured that any discussion of pregnancy prevention would "stress the importance of abstinence before marriage." Senator Smith accused critics of the bill, especially conservative religious groups, of creating a "well-organized misinformation campaign" around the proposed health-education measure. She also cited Bob Jones University—a conservative evangel-ical Christian school located in Greenville, South Carolina—as one of the bill's staunchest opponents.[26]

During a senate debate, *The State* newspaper reported, a small group of Republican senators "began a detailed, almost line-by-line review of the bill." Their comments revolved around their concern that the bill's language did not reflect "traditional, family values."[27] As an editorial from the Rock Hill *Herald* marveled in January 1988, "to hear some of these folks tell it, almost *any* learning about sex . . . is dangerous to your young people."[28]

In the end, the bill passed the senate with only a few additional con-cessions: classes would be postponed until the 1989–90 school year, and discussion of contraceptives was banned until the sixth grade. The bill's tone remained unrelentingly conservative, insisting that teachers couldn't "discuss abortion except to explain its complications." "Alternate lifestyles" (presumably meaning same-sex relationships) were not to be "discussed except in the context of sexually transmitted disease." Teachers, the bill read, "must preach abstinence."[29]

In March, a legislative panel began work on reconciling the house and senate versions of the bill.[30] One conservative on the panel was con-cerned that the language wasn't strong enough to make it crystal clear to students that "homosexual behavior is illegal and immoral."[31] (South Carolina's Code of Laws, under the category "Offenses Against Morality and Decency," included "buggery"—another word for sodomy.[32] This type of law, which was relatively common in the United States, was usually only enforced to harm LGBTQ+ people, and in some very limited ways functioned as a "ban" on homosexuality.) But the bill passed in April, and then South Carolina's schools got to the work of deciding how to meet its new requirements. What followed was a waterfall of problems, as schools were forced to reckon with individual, local, and now state dictates about sex ed.[33]

In May, school board members in Rock Hill, South Carolina, were presented with a petition. Organized by "Concerned Citizens," the pe-tition bore the signatures of 536 residents who had some specific sug-gestions for the now-mandatory sex ed program. They wanted sex ed to be opt-in, not opt-out; they wanted no discussion of contraception until twelfth grade; and they wanted "neither homosexuality nor abortion" to be "presented as acceptable." They also wanted the course material to "promote moral values and the benefits of postponing sexual activity until marriage," and to "uphold the traditional institution of the family and encourage parental involvement."[34]

As the school board contended with the Concerned Citizens, students themselves entered the debate. One high school senior argued that "contraceptive awareness should be taught in late elementary schools." Another student said that sex ed shouldn't "beat around the bushes, because you're going to find out from kids and stuff. It's better if someone just comes and tell you about it." And more than one of them pointed out that they had classmates who were already pregnant.[35] To address the situation—and prolong it—the school board appointed a committee that would, as Lisa Buie in the Rock Hill *Herald* explained, "oversee a state-mandated comprehensive health education program."[36]

And then it was all too familiar. Tedious sessions taken up with minutiae. Old grievances aired anew. Awkward compromises and concessions. Next came harangues about a state-approved textbook called *Human Sexuality*, which was decried for being "too explicit" based on a "description of sexual intercourse."[37] Parents wanted something with more of an abstinence focus. Both Teen-Aid and Sex Respect were suggested.[38] In December, a compromise was struck. Students would be taught about "both abstinence and contraceptives." *Human Sexuality* would be the textbook, while Teen-Aid would be used as a teacher resource.[39]

Abstinence education was clearly finding its way into public school curricula nationwide, often at the behest of lawmakers at every level. But the American public was showing strong support for sex ed that covered more than "just say no." By mid-1988, one study found, the US "generally supported sex education and instruction" about "AIDS, other STDs, abstinence and the prevention of pregnancy."[40] Clearly, the matter of sex ed remained complicated, controversial, and cloudy—with no one-size-fits-all solution in sight.

CHAPTER 16

THE RISE OF COMPREHENSIVE SEX ED

SEX ED, STATE BY STATE

By the late 1980s, sex ed in the United States had truly morphed into its own particular quagmire, complicated by varying state laws, competing agendas, and disparate funding streams. What one student was taught in rural Mississippi could be different from what another student was taught in New York City. This was not unlike educational trends across other subjects.

In 1981, Reagan's education secretary had appointed a National Commission on Excellence in Education. In 1983, the commission released its report, *A Nation at Risk: The Imperative for Educational Reform.*[1] As the title suggests, the commission's findings were bleak. The report cited declines in SAT scores, increases in the need for remedial courses in college, high rates of illiteracy among adults and teenagers, and America's overall poor academic standing in comparison to other countries.[2] The report was a call for action, and it suggested innovation and reform in "content, expectations, time, and teaching."[3]

Following the commission's report, education policy analyst Diane Ravitch recalled in 1990, "in a shift of major proportions, the locus of educational policymaking moved from the federal government and local governments to the states."[4] As Ravitch explained, "American education is highly decentralized," and so "state legislatures pursued reform in different ways."[5] But for subjects other than sex ed, reports and guidelines were released, replete with best practices and up-to-date thought. States and schools began to implement assessments to measure their students' progress in learning—the phenomenon known as "standards-based education."[6] Although there was some hope of implementing national standards for each discipline, in practice each state tended to develop its own standards.[7]

Sex ed, however, existed in the pressure cooker of politics, taboos, state-mandated AIDS education, and the ongoing battle over whether to teach abstinence only. This meant that there were, as SIECUS's director of program services Diane De Mauro commented in 1990, "great inconsistencies in program objectives, provisions for teacher training, program design, and course implementation and evaluation." In great part, that was because each community's program was shaped by its political and cultural context, and "the mandates and recommendations often have caveats and restrictions that seriously call into question the usefulness of the program."[8]

And those restrictions and caveats could be considerable. In 1989, *Family Planning Perspectives* reported that "sex education teachers often do not have a free hand in determining what topics to cover." Some schools provided specific curricula, others had "formal restraints" on topics, and still others had what were called "informal restraints."[9]

Another 1989 study showed great variance in instruction about condoms. In Michigan, the study reported, students were taught where to purchase condoms, while in New Jersey, there was an activity showing how to use them. In Alabama, North Carolina, Ohio, and Oklahoma, however, "condoms are treated relatively negatively," and in New York and Alabama, the curriculum emphasized only "the failure rate of condoms." In other states, condoms were mentioned, but the curriculum provided "no specifics on how they are to be discussed."[10]

Moreover, teachers simply didn't always know how to teach the material in the curriculum. A 1989 survey reported that 80 percent of teachers needed "assistance with factual information, teaching materials or teaching strategies."[11]

SIECUS WEIGHS IN

To address these myriad problems, SIECUS was ready to step in. Since the right-wing attacks on the organization in the 1960s, SIECUS had been relatively quiet, though diligently working. They continued fighting for sex ed, publishing their journal and articulating open-minded positions on sexuality. Now, in the late 1980s, they positioned themselves as the perfect group to provide tools with which to evaluate sex ed programs—just the kind of thing that was needed in the era of standards-based education reform. In 1988, the group undertook a "Curricula Review Project." Diane de Mauro explained that the group evaluated programs based on how comprehensive they were. For a curriculum to meet SIECUS's standards, the content needed to be "thorough, up-to-date, and accurate," and its view of sexuality had to be "accepting and natural" rather than "prohibitive and judgmental."[12] A curriculum also must have "a discussion of changing family structures," "a presentation of new reproductive technologies," "an affirmation of sexuality as a natural part of human life," "a presentation of the variety and range of human sexual behaviors," and "the inclusion of comprehensive family planning information."[13]

SIECUS also evaluated AIDS curricula, which were distinct from sex ed curricula in many states. Here, SIECUS looked for programs that aimed for "the elimination of misinformation about HIV/AIDS; the postponement of premature sexual involvement; the reduction of experimentation with drugs; the encouragement of increased condom use; and the encouragement of compassion for people with HIV/AIDS through effective education methodologies."

In their project, SIECUS reviewed state sex ed guidelines or curricula from twenty-three states, as well as AIDS education programs from thirty-four states. They found that "overall . . . most of the sexuality education curricula did not focus specifically on human sexuality as an area of study and exploration and a large percentage of the guidelines were out-of-date, particularly those on AIDS education." This was especially troubling given how fast conditions changed during an epidemic. "Almost one-third of the states," SIECUS stated, "are using curricula published prior to 1984," thereby rendering it unacceptable by their standards.

De Mauro reported that while AIDS education was presented with significantly more "urgency and alarm" than general sex ed, actual facts about AIDS and its transmission were frequently lacking. But most of the curricula, de Mauro said, "gloss over the sexual transmission of HIV and focus on the development of 'just say no' skills, with an emphasis on abstinence." These curricula shortchanged students, she argued, because they did not focus on functional information about how to protect themselves from infection.

The SIECUS report also criticized programs that provided little information on how to actually use contraception—mainly condoms, but also dental dams and the spermicide nonoxynol-9. A useful, comprehensive program had to cover it all: buying, using, and disposing of prophylactics. SIECUS took issue with faulty information and half-truths about condoms that were flourishing during this time, like one New York program that claimed, incorrectly, that "the use of condoms" was "extremely high-risk behavior." De Mauro concluded that "much work lies ahead before students will have access to comprehensive programs that will adequately prepare them for healthy, sexual adult lives, and that will help them to adequately protect themselves."

SIECUS, of course, had long held doubts about the efficacy of abstinence programming. In their early days, however, there hadn't been much data available to back up those suspicions. But by the late 1980s, researchers had found that while students who took an abstinence course "became significantly more supportive of abstinence and significantly less likely to intend to engage in sexual intercourse," in at least one case, "the effects quickly diminished with time, and by 3 to 4 months after the course, were no longer statistically significant."[14]

STUDIES FAIL TO SUPPORT ABSTINENCE EDUCATION

New data also contradicted a favorite myth of abstinence proponents: that more comprehensive sex ed classes promoted sexual activity. In fact, the results were rather surprising: they suggested that sex ed appeared to have *no* real effects on sexual behavior. One study, authored by Douglas Kirby, looked at fourteen programs from eight organizations and found that none of them had a measurable effect on "the frequency of sexual intercourse without any method of birth control . . . the frequency of intercourse with relatively ineffective methods of birth control . . . or the frequency of intercourse with relatively effective methods of birth control."[15] But Kirby noted that while this may have been surprising at first glance, "additional knowledge, in general, does not have much impact on behavior." He explained—as others had before him—that "many important factors other than knowledge undoubtedly affect teenager sexual and contraceptive behavior," including "parents' values, peer pressure . . . media messages, the availability of sexual partners and birth control, sexual desires," and others. In that light, he explained, "one would not expect a small amount of additional information about sexuality to have much impact upon behavior." There were things that a good program could do to attempt to encourage behavior changes, specifically attempting to "help adolescents personalize . . . information, improve their decision-making and communication skills, increase their motivation either to avoid sex or use birth control, [and] change their perception of peer group norms regarding having sex and using condoms."[16] Role-playing activities, he suggested, seemed like a particularly promising way to do that. He was also clear that this kind of program deserved to have information about birth control in it, even though current data did not suggest that much behavioral change would occur regardless.

There was less research on the abstinence programs that AFLA had funneled so much money into. As an attempt to rectify that, the Office of Adolescent Pregnancy Prevention, which administered AFLA grants, contributed to the funding of an evaluation of some of those projects. It concluded that there was "little support for abstinence-only approaches to the prevention of adolescent sexual behavior."[17] The researchers also pointed out that the result "provide[d] strong arguments for questioning the basic premise that pregnancy prevention programs should be limited to abstinence-only approaches." This was a major strike against AFLA, and it was not the only one.

KENDRICK V. SULLIVAN

There had been major concerns about AFLA's legality since it was signed into law in 1981. In 1983, the ACLU brought a legal case against the program, arguing that it violated the First Amendment. They were joined by "a diverse group including federal taxpayers, clergy, and the American Jewish Congress," according to the federal court's decision.[18] In the case that became known as *Kendrick v. Sullivan*, ACLU's lawyer, Janet Benshoof, argued that AFLA had censored information about abortion, acted as an indoctrinator by subsidizing a government program aimed at inculcating teenagers with an anti-abortion message, and violated the free speech of teachers because they were "prohibited from providing full information." In short, Benshoof argued, "Inculcation, not education, is the goal of the Act."[19] Benshoof argued that AFLA was unconstitutional both "on its face and as applied."[20] A law that is unconstitutional "facially" is *always* unconstitutional; but a law that is unconstitutional as applied might be unconstitutional only in specific situations or when applied to specific people or groups. In 1987, a district judge ruled that AFLA did indeed violate the Establishment Clause of the First Amendment, which reads, "Congress shall make no law respecting an establishment of religion." The decision was appealed straight to the Supreme Court in 1988, where a 5 to 4 majority reversed one part of the lower court's ruling. Where the district court had found that AFLA was unconstitutional both "on its face" and "as applied," the Supreme Court held that the law was facially constitutional. "AFLA," the decision read, "has a valid secular purpose."[21] However, in order to determine if it was unconstitutional as applied, the Supreme Court remanded the case for more information. The court directed the inquiry to determine whether aid from AFLA was "flowing to grantees that can be considered 'pervasively sectarian' religious institutions," and if there were times that "AFLA aid has been used to fund 'specifically religious activit[ies] in an otherwise substantially secular setting.'"[22]

As with almost all the fights over sex ed, from local school boards to First Amendment cases, there was an element of intensity to this fight that was somewhat surprising. In the district court's decision, they noted, "The ferocity and magnitude of the battle over the critical facts distinguishes this action from other Establishment Clause cases."[23] It was such a battle that they were not able to find summary judgments in either party's favor, and in 1991, they decided they would have to go to trial.

Two years later, in 1993, the parties reached a settlement. The agreement, which was for a five-year term, created stricter guidelines for AFLA grants. As an ACLU publication explained, these guidelines stipulated that "AFLA-funded sexuality education may not include religious reference, may not be offered in a site used for religious worship service, or offered in sites with religious iconography." It also required that programs be "medically accurate."[24] About a decade after the rise of abstinence education, here at last was some widespread skepticism about its intentions. The

Sex Respect and Teen-Aid curricula in particular were being subjected to scrutiny as well: researchers noted that "both focused on developing personal skills, especially concerning abstinence, but failed to address sexual behaviors. Students may be taught to 'say no,' but they are not taught exactly to what they are saying no. Further, "both assume all students are heterosexual."[25]

A BATTLE IN DUVAL COUNTY TO TOPPLE TEEN-AID

As the flaws of abstinence-only sex ed continued to mount, the alternative—sex ed that *did* address sexual behaviors and, crucially, that provided information and instruction about birth control—began to gain political support. In April 1992, Planned Parenthood of Northeast Florida, along with six local families, filed a lawsuit to stop the Duval County School Board from using Teen-Aid. Planned Parenthood called the program "incomplete, inaccurate, biased, sectarian."[26] Florida had a law that specified that public schools had to teach health education, including sex ed, but it let districts choose their curricula.

The Associated Press reported that the Florida Department of Education's Center for Prevention and Student Assistance and the Department of Health and Rehabilitative Services had conducted, unrelatedly, "at the request of an unidentified school district," a study of Teen-Aid and had conceded that the program was certainly not without its faults. The deputy secretary for health said that "the overall tone of the curricula is one of sensationalism, which appears to be an attempt to produce fear rather than to provide information." The curriculum falsely claimed that "the only way to avoid pregnancy is to abstain from genital contact," and that "correct usage of condoms does not prevent HIV infection, but only delays it."[27] The Florida Medical Association, the *Shreveport Times* reported, had also "weighed in" and found that "Teen-Aid falls short of state sex education requirements."[28]

Teen-Aid also held that "the majority of teens are not sexually active," a claim that the Florida Department of Education dispelled. The curriculum also made troubling and incorrect statements about abortion, like, "After one has aborted a child, an individual loses instinctual control over rage." The text displayed biases about racial and sexual diversity as well, with one reviewer noting that it "does not represent the cultural diversity and differing family structures present in the student population throughout the United States."

As the lawsuit proceeded, the Christian Coalition—a group led by conservative Christian broadcaster Pat Robertson—footed the legal bills for the Duval County School Board. Robertson's American Center for Law and Justice hired attorney Jay Sekulow (who, nearly thirty years later, would go on to be lead counsel for President Donald Trump in his first impeachment trial).[29]

The case brought much attention to Teen-Aid. LeAnna Benn protested that the dispute, because of "bad publicity," was costing her organization "thousands of dollars a month in sales."[30] For this reason, Teen-Aid itself got involved in the Duval County issue and moved to dismiss the case. By October 1992, the nation was watching, with many seeing it as a test case for abstinence-based sex ed. Circuit Judge Bernard Nachman disagreed. "Protracted litigation," he wrote, "would not serve the public interest." He wanted the parties to mediate out of court.[31] The Duval County School Board, however, voted 4 to 3 against mediation, forcing the trial to go forward. The board predicted: "Planned Parenthood is going to get waxed. It's fun to be right."[32]

Then, in October 1993, the Duval board introduced a competing lawsuit against Florida's state board of education, claiming that it had "forced schools to teach sex education but never set up rules for the schools to follow. . . . Without set rules for the state, the county should be able to adopt any program it sees fit, thereby making the suit by Planned Parenthood of Northeast Florida subject to dismissal."[33] Planned Parenthood attorney Betsy White called it a "stall tactic."

It wasn't until April 1996 that Planned Parenthood and the local families announced their plans to dismiss their 1992 lawsuit. Their decision came after the school board approved a new sex ed plan that the *Miami Herald* reported "met approval of both Planned Parenthood and the Christian Coalition."[34]

The new sex ed program included lessons on birth control but also held that abstinence was the "expected" standard. The chairman of the Christian Coalition of Florida noted that "although many in the Christian conservative community would prefer not have sex ed taught at all . . . this is the best we can hope to achieve."[35]

SEX RESPECT IN LOUISIANA

Around the same time, a similar lawsuit was filed in Louisiana, this time targeting Sex Respect rather than Teen-Aid. Updated from its original 1986 version, the Sex Respect curriculum now addressed the AIDS crisis—sort of. A 1991 *Shreveport Times* article described Sex Respect's message succinctly: there was no such thing as safe sex. The curriculum's fear mongering was intense. When a student in a Sex Respect film inquires about the consequences of having sex before marriage, the teacher says: "I guess you're just going to have to be prepared to die."[36]

The curriculum now also included a chastity pledge, a new phenomenon that had originated in conservative evangelical Christian churches but was spilling into abstinence-only classes in public schools. The Sex Respect curriculum directed students to lace their fingers together and say "I choose chastity. I will do the right thing and wait for the rings."

The seeds of the Louisiana lawsuit began in November 1991, when the Caddo Parish School Board abided by a parent review committee's recommendation and voted to use the Sex Respect curriculum. Their decision went against the recommendation of the school administration, which had not yet been able to review the curriculum. Several administrators had expressed concerns "as to whether such a curriculum [would] really address Caddo Parish's staggering teen pregnancy rate."[37] At the time, Shreveport, the largest city in Caddo Parish, claimed the distinction of having the fourth-highest teen birth rate in the nation.[38] Of the school board decision, LSU Medical Center's chief of obstetrics and gynecology predicted: "We're on the road to . . . disaster. . . . A lot of lives are going to be ruined and a lot of money wasted, and that's pretty horrendous."[39] A two-hour board meeting ensued, during which Sex Respect was thoroughly discredited. A petition opposing the curriculum, signed by 1,100 students and teachers, was also presented.[40] But rather than come to any decision, the board opted to delay the proceedings and reorganize the parent review committee. Finally, in August 1992, the committee announced it was now considering five curricula, including Sex Respect and Teen-Aid.[41]

In September, the committee announced that it was again endorsing their original choice, Sex Respect. They had not yet decided on "program supplements," however. As Diana Murphy of the *Shreveport Times* reported, school board guidelines required that "any sex education program approved [must] include material on sexually transmitted diseases—including HIV-AIDS—and the effectiveness of contraceptives in reducing the risk of disease and pregnancy."[42] Because Sex Respect did not include such material, they needed to choose supplementary resources that did.

The *Shreveport Times* condemned the curriculum decision in an op-ed by the editorial board: "Why would the Caddo Parish School Board willingly vote to deceive the children of the parish by adopting . . . 'Sex Respect'?"[43] The editorial noted that the program was "racially, gender and religious biased. Their medical inaccuracies gird a fundamentalist agenda to remove comprehensive sex education from public schools."

At the end of September, the Caddo Parish School Board officially voted to implement Sex Respect, along with those supplemental materials that would make the course compliant with school board guidelines.[44] But now the board was met not only with criticism but also with legal action. Diana Murphy of the *Shreveport Times* reported that a group of about ten "parents, teachers, and citizens" pledged to fight the decision in court, arguing that Sex Respect was "sexually and racially biased and contained religious and moral overtones."[45] The suit went to trial, and in March 1993, district judge Frank Thaxton barred the use of Sex Respect in local schools, ruling that it presented "inaccurate medical information, subjective religious beliefs and improper counseling on abortion."[46]

The director of Project Respect, the group that made Sex Respect, commented: "With all the garbage being brought up in school, it's incredible that anyone would spend time and money to bring charges against a health message of abstinence." The attorney who had represented the Shreveport parents responded that "abstinence absolutely should be taught, it's just that it should be taught in a manner that presents accurate information, not just scare tactics and inaccurate information which confuses children."[47]

STOP PLANNED PARENTHOOD, INC.

By the early 1990s, it was becoming clear that abstinence-only curricula were falling short educationally, medically, and legally. Nonetheless, some school districts continued to teach them. This was in part because the Right was producing what appeared to be unbiased evidence in their favor.

In 1990, Dr. Dinah Richard published a report called *Has Sex Education Failed Our Teenagers?* Though the report had some extratextual trappings of legitimacy—it was formatted in an official-seeming pamphlet, and it billed itself as a "research report"—Richard's piece had not actually been published by a peer-reviewed journal but by Focus on the Family, a fundamentalist parachurch organization. Moreover, Richard's doctorate was not in any health- or science-related subject but in speech communications. She did, however, have experience as a "volunteer director of a pro-life speaker's bureau."[48]

Richard's report was essentially the 1990s version of the anti–sex ed pamphlets of the late 1960s. She took grains of truth and spun them into conclusions that didn't match the data. Richard began by citing the legitimate research from Douglas Kirby that had shown sex ed to have a minimal effect on behavior. But then she claimed that the "old" style of sex ed (i.e., curricula that included information about contraception) was therefore categorically ineffective, and promised that the "new" abstinence-only approach would make up for all of comprehensive sex ed's shortcomings. She wrote that "while the results" of abstinence-only education evaluation "have not yet appeared in major journals, early reports are promising."[49] She handpicked studies with small sample sizes that showed those promising statistics.

Kirby, however, had actually included both comprehensive and abstinence-only programs in his research and had found abstinence-only to be just as ineffective at changing behavior, if not more. Nonetheless, many in the media received Richard's work as unbiased reporting. "There is conclusive evidence," Mike McManus wrote in 1991, in the *Indiana Gazette*, "that 'contraception education' is a failed strategy, while abstinence education has proved effective, according to Dr. Dinah Richard."[50] The media's credulousness might have come in part because Richard presented a reductive narrative of data that was, in reality, very hard to parse. The efficacy of sex ed had always been difficult to measure. It was much simpler to say that sex ed didn't work than to analyze the intricacies of the different curricula, competing goals, and other factors that contributed to sexual-health outcomes and activities.

Others on the right parroted Richard, bringing with them additional "evidence" ripped straight from 1968. In April 1994, Jim Sedlak, national director of Stop Planned Parenthood, Inc., wrote an op-ed published in the *News and Record* out of Greensboro, North Carolina, in which he claimed that sex ed was "harmful to our children, dangerous for society and fails to reduce teen sexual activity or teen pregnancies. It is a failed social engineering program that must be halted everywhere."[51] Sedlak cited Melvin Anchell, the anti–sex ed activist and psychoanalyst who had risen to prominence in the late 1960s promulgating Freud's theory of a latency period.

In May 1994, economics professor and pro-life activist Jacqueline Kasun wrote an essay for the conservative journal *Policy Review*, founded by the Heritage Foundation, in which she fell back on the old argument that sex ed classes promoted promiscuity. She cited the debunked myth that that "in California . . . children model genital organs in clay."[52] A month later, she took the "con" side in another set of pro-and-con essays on sex ed prepared by the Scripps Howard News Service. Kasun argued that "the only conclusion to be drawn is that belief in sex-ed programs has attained the status of dogma among its adherents, and is impervious to the facts."[53]

The "pro" essay was written by Planned Parenthood's director of education, Trish Moylan Torruella. She focused on the efficacy and popular support of what she called "real sex education," which was also increasingly referred to as "comprehensive sex education." She cited a 1994 study that found that "about 85 percent of American adults support sexuality education in public schools, while 73 percent support making information and contraceptives available through health centers in schools."[54]

Torruella also pointed out the biggest flaw in the conservative argument against sex ed. "Comprehensive, realistic, sexuality education that provides accurate, balanced and straightforward information," she wrote, "hasn't even been put to the test in America." There had simply never been large-scale implementation of comprehensive sex ed—in part because of the whims of history; in part because of aggressive opposition. She concluded with a sober warning: "There was never a time when censorship and distortion of truth would be accepted as responsible education. In the age of AIDS, it's a deadly form of child abuse."[55]

Pro-abstinence supporters ignored such well-reasoned opinions, instead relying on two complementary claims: that their approach to sex ed was new and that it was taught in only a minority of classrooms nationwide. Therefore, they asserted, abstinence-only represented an alternative to the "failed" status quo. But a 1993 SIECUS report had found that among "state sexuality education curricula and guidelines . . . fewer than one-third of state guides include any sexual behavior topic other than abstinence."[56] Clearly, the abstinence approach was by far the more popular—in execution if not in theory.

Unfortunately, this fact was lost on cultural commentators. In October 1994, the *Atlantic* published a cover story called "The Failure of Sex Education" by Barbara Dafoe Whitehead. Whitehead was vice president of the Institute for American Values, a think tank that promoted the traditional nuclear family. She wrote, inaccurately, that "At the moment, the favored approach is called comprehensive sex education,"[57] basing her claim on the fact that comprehensive programs had been endorsed by the AMA and the surgeon general. Her article ignored the decades of research that had found that abstinence-only programs were not particularly effective, as well as the reality that abstinence-based programs had in fact been implemented widely in American schools. Instead, it outlined the "failure" of comprehensive sex ed. She claimed, among other things, that if such "easy sex talk" was really "a key determinant of sexual behavior . . . it would be our tongue-tied grandparents who had high rates of illegitimacy and STDs, not today's franker and looser-lipped teenagers." But this claim was ahistorical—the reality was that teenagers in the 1930s *had* had high rates of illegitimacy and STIs. Whitehead concluded that "what sex educators are offering now is training in sexual survival. Once the kids have been equipped with refusal skills, a bottle of body oil, and some condoms, 'reality-based' advocates send them into the world to fend for themselves. It's not realism. It is retreat."[58]

Whitehead's cover story was reprinted in newspapers nationwide. Syndicated *Los Angeles Times* columnist Cal Thomas commented positively on her piece, concluding: "What makes us think that children, who are forbidden to drive cars in most states until they are 16, can handle sex at even earlier ages? The state ill serves the public by attempting to put children in the sexual driver's seat before they are ready—and with incorrect sign posts that have led them astray."[59]

Thomas's enthusiasm assumed that Whitehead's research was accurate. There was one seemingly eternal problem with sex ed, though, and that was that it was hard to draw any one conclusion about its efficacy when it came to changing behaviors. Then there was the fact that different groups had beliefs about what behaviors needed to be changed. For the abstinence-only crowd, the standard that mattered the most was if sex ed led to delaying sexual activity, ideally until marriage. On that the data was unclear, with different studies coming to different conclusions. A 1995 article in *Family Relations* highlighted this challenge. In "the relation between education and initiating coital activity," F. Scott Christopher admitted, "findings on the issue have been mixed." One study found "no association between sex education and initiating sexual intercourse for teens 17 to 18"; but for young teens, ages 15 to 16, sex ed seemed to lead to "initiation to coitus." Another found that teens of the same age were "less likely to have engaged in sexual intercourse than those who had not participated."[60]

The study in *Family Relations* did find that there was one behavior that tended to change when students were given comprehensive sex ed, although writers like Whitehead and Richard were unlikely to give it much ink. Several studies had found a "positive relationship" between sex ed and contraception use—it seemed that young people who learned about contraception were likely to use it. Christopher also raised a familiar complication for sex education researchers in the United States. He warned that because there was such "little consistency in what constitutes 'sex education' across different communities . . . it may be unclear what is actually measured" when asking youths if they have taken sex ed.

In the mid-'90s, the disparities among sex ed curricula continued to grow, as did the support for both abstinence-only and comprehensive approaches—even as the data continued to conclude that abstinence-only programs were ineffective.

CHAPTER 17

THE A-H DEFINITION

CLINTON, WELFARE REFORM, AND SEX ED

Despite the growing body of evidence against abstinence-only sex ed, and despite a Democratic president, Bill Clinton, seated in the White House, the government continued to fund programs based on this discredited approach. In 1996, President Clinton signed the Personal Responsibility and Work Opportunity Reconciliation Act, known also as the "welfare reform" bill. It had been drafted in the Republican-controlled Congress that had resulted from the 1994 midterm elections.[1] Clinton had vetoed two welfare-reform bills that had emerged from that body, but after negotiations with House Speaker Newt Gingrich, he signed into law the third bill that was produced. Even that was more conservative than he would have liked, but, as *Politico* reported, "with his reelection campaign in high gear it was too politically risky for him to veto yet another welfare reform bill."[2]

Republicans had written into the bill provisions meant to reduce rates of illegitimate pregnancy. Under that umbrella was an allocation of $50 million per year for abstinence-only education, paid through maternal and child health (MCH) block grants. To be eligible for the funds, programs had to abide by strict criteria to qualify as "abstinence education." The federal government defined an abstinence education program as one that

A) has as its exclusive purposes, teaching the social, psychological, and health gains to be realized by abstaining from sexual activity

B) teaches that abstinence from sexual activity outside marriage is the expected standard for all school age children

190

C) teaches that abstinence . . . is the only certain way to avoid out-of-wedlock pregnancy, sexually transmitted diseases, and other associated health problems

D) teaches that a mutually faithful monogamous relationship in the context of marriage is the expected standard of human sexual activity

E) teaches that sexual activity outside of the context of marriage is likely to have harmful psychological and physical effects

F) teaches that bearing children out-of-wedlock is likely to have harmful consequences for the child, the child's parents, and society

G) teaches young people how to reject sexual advances and how alcohol and drug use increase vulnerability to sexual advances; and,

H) teaches the importance of attaining self-sufficiency before engaging in sexual activity[3]

This list came to be known as the "A-H definition" of abstinence (in reference to its eight points, lettered A through H). It was extremely detailed and extremely biased toward conservative Christian norms. It also had not gone through a proper vetting process. As SIECUS's director of public policy, Daniel Daley, later pointed out, the list had been added without debate "in the final version of the legislation usually reserved for correction and technical revisions." By the time anyone was paying attention, it was too late. "The welfare reform legislation," Daley wrote in the spring of 1997, "represents . . . the broadest attack on the provision of comprehensive sexuality education to young people in the United States."[4]

Under this legislation, a program would be ineligible for funding if it taught abstinence but included even a sentence about contraception. As such, states whose sex ed curricula contained any kind of contraceptive information were now forced to choose between accepting money from the government or keeping their programs comprehensive and forfeiting the funds. Some states outright refused the funding. The director of Maine's health department protested that "the limits on what you can say are so restrictive [that] youths might raise issues you couldn't address under the law."[5]

STATE WORKAROUNDS AND UNINTENDED CONSEQUENCES

Other states created workarounds. In July 1997, New Jersey applied for $4 million from the program, with its own stipulation that it would be used only by "private, non-profit groups . . . outside of school hours."[6] New Jersey governor Christine Todd Whitman believed that this would allow the state to receive the federal funds while also continuing to teach comprehensive sex ed in public schools. New Jersey officials also announced their plan to focus on only three of the eight points of the definition, which was explicitly what the definition's authors had tried to avoid.[7] (New Jersey did get the funding in 1998, but because state curriculum standards required education on contraception, it was not used for public schools).[8]

Conservative members of Congress weren't pleased to hear about workarounds like Whitman's. In early 1998, Republican representative Thomas J. Bliley Jr. wrote to the Health and Human Services secretary that it was "imperative that . . . the Department . . . approve applications [that] are consistent with the letter and spirit of the legislation."[9] To ensure that states were acting in accordance with the law, Bliley called for extensive "documentation of state plans and the criteria HHS used to evaluate them."

Despite Bliley's best efforts, however, much of the funding that made its way to states was not used in exact accordance with the A-H definition. As Joan Lowry reported for the Scripps Howard News Service in 1998, some of the money was in fact being used to "fund afterschool activities that have little to do with abstinence like golf lessons and hockey teams, or underwrite broadly disseminated media campaigns that are unlikely to have a significant impact on behavior." Lowry pointed to an Atlanta Catholic school that had received $35,000, which it used to "pay for afterschool abstinence classes combined with golf and African dance lessons."[10] As such, the program drew criticism from both sides. Liberals charged that it placed too much emphasis on abstinence, which had no data to support its efficacy; conservatives were angered that funds were being used for things other than abstinence curricula.

Nonetheless, by 1999, it was clear that abstinence was going to remain a staple of sex ed courses nationwide. *Family Planning Perspectives* reported that "among the 69% of public school districts that have a district-wide policy to teach sexuality education, 14% have a comprehensive policy that treats abstinence as one option for adolescents in a broader sexuality education program"; 51 percent had what was called an "abstinence-plus" policy, meaning that while abstinence was emphasized, contraceptive information was included; and 35 percent of school districts with sex ed programs ("or 23 percent of all U.S. school districts") taught abstinence "as the only option outside of marriage, with discussion of contraception either prohibited entirely or permitted only to emphasize its shortcomings (an abstinence-only policy)."[11]

During the late 1990s and early 2000s, an unintended consequence of the abstinence-only approach revealed itself. Researchers found that, for all the talk of abstaining from sex, students did not understand precisely what activities they were supposed to be abstaining from. As journalists Yomi Wronge and Lisa Fernandez reported for the Knight Ridder media company in January 2001, "A growing number of adolescents believe that when it comes to abstinence, everything but intercourse is acceptable."[12] Abstinence-only programs typically focused primarily on teen pregnancy prevention. This meant that they failed to address the risks of activities like oral and anal sex, which could—and in many cases did—lead to STIs.

THE GEORGE W. BUSH YEARS

As the 2000 presidential election approached, the stakes for sex ed seemed higher than ever, especially as it appeared that federal funding was the key to determining its nature. Ahead of the election, the two major presidential candidates, Republican George W. Bush and Democrat Al Gore, were asked about their views on federal funding for the subject. Gore explained that he supported a "comprehensive strategy to prevent teen pregnancy and the transmission of sexually transmitted diseases" that included "abstinence education and other measures." Bush, meanwhile, responded that he strongly supported abstinence programs . . . and favored "spending at least as much on teen abstinence programs as on teen contraception programs."[13]

And indeed, when Bush became president, he and his cabinet continued to fund abstinence-only programs. Under Bush, the AFLA program was better funded than during the Clinton years.[14] This was despite the fact that, in keeping with what had become something of a tradition in its own right, the surgeon general, David Satcher, had himself criticized the abstinence approach. Satcher was a holdover from the Clinton administration—his term had not yet expired when Bush took office. Reporting in 2001 on a study that Clinton had commissioned, Satcher said of abstinence programming: "There was insufficient research to back claims that courses teaching abstinence until marriage have any success in delaying sexual activity among unmarried teenagers."[15] The White House distanced itself from the report, and conservative operatives quickly denounced it.[16]

Peter Brandt of Focus on the Family called Satcher's report "ideology disguised as science" and charged that it called into "question the surgeon general's ability to remain the chief medical officer of the United States."[17] But Satcher stood by his report. "I think it will stand the test of time," Satcher said in August 2001, "and I don't think any surgeon general will come behind and look at the public health science and reach a different conclusion."[18]

But many conservatives continued to insist that abstinence-only education had merit. This was largely for religious reasons: abstinence before marriage had long been baked into Christian doctrine. However, political figures could not explicitly allude to religious values when defending this type of education. Instead, they continued to perpetuate the myth that the programs had simply not existed long enough to be properly evaluated. Kevin Keane of the US Department of Health and Human Services claimed in August 2001 that while a lot of critics were saying that abstinence-only education hadn't been proven to work, "it hasn't been proven not to work either."[19] The reality was that researchers like Douglas Kirby had been studying the efficacy of abstinence programs for decades, but the talking point remained a useful rhetorical strategy.

By fall 2001, however, chinks were starting to form in the conservatives' defenses. In September, the National Institute of Child Health and Human Development reaffirmed what an earlier Kirby study had found: that abstinence programs tended to have only short-term effects and that student commitments to abstinence quickly wore off. And if teens who had received abstinence-only education did have sex, reports found, "they are more likely to become pregnant than teens who have received comprehensive sex education."[20] This particular finding was especially damning, as it proved that abstinence-only was actually *counterproductive* when it came to reducing rates of teen pregnancy.[21]

Nor was it always medically accurate. A report by Democratic representative Henry Waxman from California found that "two-thirds of the abstinence-only education curricula studied contained incorrect scientific information regarding condom failure, sexually transmitted diseases, the health consequences of abortions, and mental health. Much of this information directly contradicted the scientific findings of government agencies such as the Centers for Disease Control and Prevention."[22]

Remarkably, this consensus was forming even with abstinence-only proponents allegedly putting their thumbs on the scale. Dr. John Santelli, chair of the Columbia University Mailman School of Public Health and senior fellow at the Guttmacher Institute, relayed in 2006 that there may have been governmental interference in data collection about the lack of efficacy of abstinence programs. Santelli explained that the CDC's Division of Adolescent and School Health (CDC-DASH), which was overseen by the Department of Health and Human Services, had devised a system called Programs That Work that used a "rigorous peer reviewed process to identify programs that were effective in changing adolescent sexual risk behaviors." But then, one day in 2002, Programs That Work simply disappeared. Santelli and his colleagues believed he knew why. The audit of programs, Santelli wrote, resulted in a "failure to identify any abstinence-only programs as effective."[23] Rather than report this massive failure, the institution silently made the whole thing vanish.

However, by the mid-2000s, it became clear that no amount of data would sway abstinence-only adherents from their cause; federal funding for abstinence programs actually grew. One report found that, between 2001 and 2005, funding for abstinence-only sex ed increased from $73 million to $158 million.

Santelli argued that funding such ineffective and misleading educational programs in fact constituted a human rights violation. As L. P. Freedman had articulated in 1995, "Access to complete and accurate HIV/AIDS and sexual health information has been recognized as a basic human right, as complete and accurate health information is essential to realizing the highest attainable standard of health." It was not a bridge too far to assert that the US government was violating the rights of its students by enabling abstinence-only curricula and promoting it over programs that provided information about HIV/AIDS. Yet those programs continued apace, frequently with codicils about morals and chastity tacked on for good measure.

The year 2006 saw the then-highest amount of federal funding for abstinence programs—a total of $176 million. Some of the states were defending abstinence education as well. In May 2006, Wisconsin's Democratic governor signed a bill requiring that "sex education teachers must present abstinence as the preferred behavior for unmarried people."[24] And in November 2007, picketers protested outside a school board member's home in Saint Lucie County, Florida, because she had approved a comprehensive sex education program called Get Real About AIDS.[25]

But there were, of course, countermovements as well. By 2007, nearly half of the states, along with Washington, DC, chose not to apply for Title V funds—the mechanism through which A-H abstinence funding was provided. This was due to the restrictions around the programs, according to reports by the National Coalition Against Censorship, but also because the grants required matching funds from the state.[26] In April 2007, following a rally, abstinence-only sex education was *banned* in Washington State public schools.[27] Actions like these fueled the flames of the sex ed debate, which became even more heated in the run-up to the historic 2008 presidential election.

OBAMA AND TEEN PREGNANCY PREVENTION

"The latest hot quote from U.S. Sen. Barack Obama leads me to wonder exactly what values and morals he's instilling in his daughters and what values and morals he will advocate if he becomes the next president," wrote conservative columnist Fran Eaton in April 2008 in the *Southtown Star*, located in a suburb of Chicago.[28]

As the presumptive Democratic presidential candidate and the first Black American to rise to that position, Obama had already been derided by the right for a host of perceived offenses, including his pro-choice stance on abortion. As for the "hot quote" Eaton had referenced, he had merely stated that he was going to teach his daughters "first about values and morals, but if they make a mistake, I don't want them punished with a baby. I don't want them punished with an [STI] at age 16, so it doesn't make sense to not give them information."[29]

Eaton interpreted Obama's response as an endorsement of comprehensive sex education. She then trotted out a series of unsubstantiated reports on the supposedly scandalous state of sex ed in Illinois: "Kids [are] sent to the grocery stores for grape jelly to use as sex play lubricant," she said. "The kids are encouraged to take showers together." Like Phoebe Courtney and Gordon Drake fifty years earlier, Eaton was circulating unverified anecdotes with a single purpose in mind: to terrify the public.[30]

It wasn't just a lone local journalist weaponizing Obama's views on sex ed. The Republican presidential candidate, John McCain, aired a thirty-second campaign ad in which a narrator ominously claimed that "Obama's one accomplishment" in education has been "legislation to teach 'comprehensive sex education' to kindergarteners. . . . " Then John McCain's voice boomed in: "Barack Obama. Wrong on education. Wrong for your family."[31]

The ad was full of inaccuracies. First, the legislation McCain referred to had never actually become law—and Obama had not sponsored it.[32] He had, however, voted for a bill, in committee, that would have modified Illinois's sex education law to require curricula to be "age and developmentally appropriate" and also enable parents to opt out their children, according to the *New York Times*.[33]

It was true, however, that Obama did support comprehensive sex ed, and when he took office in January 2009, his budget reflected that. It eliminated most of the funding for abstinence programming. Instead, Obama's first fiscal year saw funding for "teenage pregnancy prevention programs" (TPP). A congressional report on reducing teen pregnancy explained that, under TPP, grants could be awarded to public and private entities to fund 'medically accurate and age appropriate' programs."[34] TPP, in contrast to abstinence-only, was committed to comprehensive methods and evidence-based practices. Melody Barnes of the White House domestic policy team also made clear that Obama was "open to innovation [which] could include abstinence-only if there is indication it would work."[35]

Abstinence-only advocates were—unsurprisingly—displeased. *USA Today* reported that Valerie Huber of the National Abstinence Education Association believed that her "organization must work harder to persuade Congress to continue funding abstinence education."[36]

In response to Obama's initiatives, some states created their own strong comprehensive sex ed programs. Wisconsin passed the Healthy Youth Act in February 2010, which required "public schools to teach contraception."[37] A year later, an Illinois bill called for the end of abstinence-only sex education, though it didn't pass in the senate.[38] Other states crafted guidelines around sex ed for the first time—an important step forward.

But having guidelines in place did not mean that states were following them. In South Carolina, for instance, a comprehensive sex ed law had been on the books since 1988. Yet a 2013 study from a South Carolina sex ed advocacy group found that three out of four of the state's school districts were not in compliance.[39] There were procedural violations, like not having an advisory board or filling out a survey, but also, as another report noted, the study found that 75 percent of schools [were] not in compliance with at least one of the six measurable requirements of the reproductive health education components" of the law.[40] Some states had no guidelines at all.

Meanwhile, the need for effective teen pregnancy prevention remained high. In 2009, a study showed that the US had seen "39 births per 1,000 girls ages 15 through 19."[41] Though it was the lowest rate on record, it was still high when compared to those of other countries. In the Netherlands, the rate of teen pregnancy was 4 for every 1,000 girls. In Japan, it was 5; Sweden, 8; Canada, 13. The study, like so many before it, confirmed that young people in countries with lower teen birth rates had easier access to contraception, and that "teachers, parents and physicians tend to be more accepting of teenager sexuality and more likely to encourage use of contraception."

Indeed, it was not just the educational system that neglected the sexual health of adolescents. A study from early 2014 found that in only 65 percent of checkups did doctors "talk to the teenage patients about sex"; and when those conversations did happen, they lasted "for only 36 seconds, on average."[42] In 2015, Professor Ann Ramsdell at the University of South Carolina School of Medicine wrote an opinion piece for the Columbia *State* in which she decried the lack of sex ed among undergraduates taking classes in women's health. "I often find myself," Ramsdell wrote, "teaching basic sex education because of all the misinformation my students had before they reached my classroom. . . . It is concerning that so many of them are beginning college without being able to name parts of their own bodies or how they function."[43]

Ramsdell voiced her support for South Carolina's House Bill 3447, which required "students to receive age-appropriate, medically accurate information about pregnancy prevention and sexually transmitted disease protection." The state's established sex ed guidelines dated back to 1988 and required "stressing abstinence."[44] House Bill 3447 died in the House Public Works Committee.[45]

South Carolina was not the only state to see sex ed reform proposed and killed in the mid-2010s. It was an era in which polarized debates on the subject raged. The sides lined up as usual: Team Comprehensive Sex Ed protesting that existing guidelines were too restrictive, and Team Abstinence condemning new guidelines as utterly outré. In 2015, legislators in Texas—which had abstinence-only education and the "fourth highest teen pregnancy rate in the nation"—introduced a bill that would still require that sex ed classes stress abstinence but also be "age-appropriate, medically accurate . . . evidenced based . . . and should provide information and methods to prevent pregnancy and disease including HIV."[46] The bill died in the Public Education Committee the next month.[47]

BATTLES IN OMAHA

And while all this was happening—or, more accurately, not happening—some school board meetings were proceeding like reruns from the late 1960s. In the spring of 2015, Omaha Public Schools (OPS) in Nebraska planned to overhaul the sex ed curriculum for the first time since the 1980s.[48] OPS already taught comprehensive sex ed. But now, as part of their curriculum overhaul, the district surveyed residents about the current topics covered in OPS sex ed and potential topics that could be added. In April, the district held a public meeting on the subject that drew about 150 people. Some parents brought up the idea of adding abortion and sexual orientation to the curriculum, while others wanted more emphasis on abstinence.[49] Throughout the spring and summer OPS worked toward the overhaul, and another meeting was held in October. By then, the tenor had changed. Erin Duffy of the World-Herald News Service reported that "various groups" had spread their belief that if OPS updated the curriculum to include gender identity, sexual orientation, and abortion, it "would encourage, even promote, teen sex." Before the meeting, picketers gathered on the sidewalk to hand out pamphlets condemning comprehensive sex ed.

Officials, Duffy explained, had expected about four hundred people, but more than a thousand showed up: "The crowd quickly overflowed the school board room where the meeting was originally supposed to take place and soon packed [a] large auditorium."[50] Officials cut short the "chaotic public forum," where people "cheered, jeered, and demanded answers." One parent described a rumor he had heard that "the new curriculum would teach student different sex positions and how to masturbate." Others leveled charges that some of the attendees "weren't necessarily district parents."[51] The drama continued. In November, Erin Duffy reported that "roughly 300" people showed up for a school board meeting—at which sex ed was *not* on the agenda. This did not stop people from speaking on the subject during the public comment portion of the meeting, however.[52]

In early January 2016, sex ed *was* an agenda item, and it drew a crowd of 350 people. The public comment portion of the night lasted three hours. The same old charges were voiced: Duffy reported that opponents of sex ed were concerned that the curricula "would strip children of their innocence." Some urged the schools to "focus on the essentials" rather than on sex ed. And these opponents expressed their grievances beyond the hearing room. At the meeting there was "a truck parked outside . . . flashing graphics with messages . . . opposing the sex education overhaul. One featured a condom and the question: 'Is this appropriate for 8th graders? OPS says yes.'"[53]

Though the supporters of sex ed didn't resort to flashing lights, they were just as adamant about their own argument. Duffy reported that these supporters noted, in general, that "students deserve an up-to-date curriculum that teaches consent and healthy relationship, respect for students regardless of sexual orientation or gender identity, and ways to protect against STDs and pregnancy." At long last, schools were beginning to recognize that not every student was cisgender and heterosexual.[54]

All of this debate was happening even though there was a clear consensus among local parents in favor of sex ed. The board was set to vote on the curriculum on January 20. Several weeks before the vote, a newspaper advertisement paid for by the Women's Fund of Omaha explained that "93% of Omaha Public School Parents Support Comprehensive Sex Education."[55] But the anti–sex ed contingency, like their counterpart in the 1960s, ignored the data and unearthed experts of their own. An anti–sex ed group called Nebraskans for Founders' Values hosted a free public event at Omaha's Liberty Christian Center featuring psychologist Miriam Grossman. Grossman had written a book called *You're Teaching My Child What? A Physician Exposes the Lies of Sex Education and How They Harm Your Child*, and she was now bringing her message to Omaha just before the scheduled vote.[56]

On January 20, the board voted overwhelmingly in favor of broadening the topics covered in the curriculum. It would now include "abortion, sexual orientation and gender identity." It was an important victory for modern sex ed, one that acknowledged LGBTQ+ students, gender identity, and abortion. Next up was the challenge of actually selecting a curriculum that would align with the new standards.[57]

The district reviewed twenty-five programs. Some they discounted quickly; any related to Planned Parenthood were "automatically discounted," Erin Duffy reported, as a concession to the "frequent concern of those opposed to the sex education update" (the concern, presumably, being that Planned Parenthood was too extreme to be used in public schools). The district narrowed the pool down to fifteen. In February 2016, OPS outlined the curriculum review process to the public: families and teachers would all be involved, and all were invited to "leaf through and grade health and sex education textbooks and handouts at curriculum night."[58]

The school board set up four curriculum nights. Given the recent community fervor around sex ed, they planned for 300 attendees. But "only about 30 people," the *Omaha World-Herald* reported, "turned out." Performing outrage at school board meetings was one thing, but when it came to the actual work of hammering out the details of a sex ed program, not many were interested.[59]

In the end, Omaha Public Schools staff were the ones to make recommendations to the school board about what materials to use. In May, they were ready with their picks.[60] Now the school board would vote from among those options. Opponents of the broader standards, in classic delay-tactic style, urged that the board take additional time to "review curriculum options." But the board did not capitulate, and they proceeded to cast their votes. The materials they approved for the district included HealthSmart, an evidence- and skills-based program from ETR Associates; Human Sexuality from Pearson Education; and Teen Health from McGraw-Hill Education.[61] These materials, Duffy reported, "got the highest ratings from teachers and school nurses who piloted different options."[62] Among the "supplemental resources" the board approved was the Rights, Respect, Responsibility (3R—distinct from, and not to be confused with, the "3R Project," discussed in chapter 14) curriculum from a notable nonprofit group called Advocates for Youth. AFY had been formed in the 1980s with the goal of promoting "effective adolescent reproductive and sexual health programs and policies in the United States and the global south." They described their 3R curriculum as "LGBTQ inclusive and covers all 16 topics recommended by the [CDC] as essential components of sexual health education."[63] AFY, like many sex ed programs, used role-playing as a teaching strategy. Omaha Public Schools planned to use AFY's 3Rs to teach about some of the new topics, specifically gender identity and sexual orientation.[64]

Joe Dejka reported in the *Omaha World-Herald* that AFY's curriculum "was one of the few options available" that covered these topics, and that "OPS officials . . . always knew they'd have to revise portions of the curriculum to fit the Omaha community."[65] But before the "Omaha version" of the 3R material was made public, opponents of the expanded sex ed program circulated "a version they found online." This version was then shared by the conservative group Nebraskans for Founders' Values, and then on the website of the Archdiocese of Omaha. Even after the school board explained that they had made many modifications to the 3R program for Omaha schools, including omitting the role-playing portion, the vitriol remained.

It was clear that the old narratives around sex ed activism were not going to die, even in the Obama era. And, then, in November 2016, Donald J. Trump was elected president of the United States.

CHAPTER 18

TRUMP, BIDEN, AND TODAY

W hen Donald Trump—the failed businessman posturing as successful mogul, completely lacking political experience, and with a bevy of financial and sexual scandals under his belt—was elected president in 2016, many liberals and progressives predicted the worst for people of color, reproductive rights, immigrants, and all marginalized individuals and causes. His supporters, meanwhile, applauded what they perceived as a return to bygone halcyon days. His lip service to "family values," his vow to "make America great again," and his (relatively recent) pro-life stance spoke to a certain sector of Americans, many of whom had bought into the myth of the inherent value of an abstinence-only approach.

TPP IS DEFUNDED
Six months into his term, Trump appointed Valerie Huber as chief of staff to the assistant secretary of Health and Human Services.[1] Ten years earlier, Huber had established the National Abstinence Education Association, which had been recently rebranded as Ascend.[2] Huber also had the distinction of having served as the "abstinence education coordinator" for the state of Ohio.

Democracy Forward reported that before she was officially appointed, Huber had reportedly met with Trump appointees to discuss her desire to "immediately halt" the Obama-era comprehensive Teen Pregnancy Prevention Program (TPP) in favor of an abstinence-only approach.

Huber, however, avoided using the word *abstinence* when describing her approach, rebranding it as *sexual risk avoidance* (SRA or SRAE for *sexual risk avoidance education*). This phrase was meant to show that her approach would enable youth to avoid risks entirely as opposed to merely reducing them, as comprehensive sex ed (or CSE, as it was becoming known) was purported to do.

Jennifer Haberkorn in *Politico* reported that advocates of CSE feared that Huber would "funnel money away from groups that provide contraception and toward crisis pregnancy centers . . . or groups that promote abstinence-only education."[3] And indeed, two months after she was appointed, Democracy Forward reported that Huber's office had "cut 81 Teen Pregnancy Prevention Program grants to evidence-based sex education programs, despite the success of the program and bipartisan support from Congress." Obama's last round of TPP funding was not due to run out until 2020, but Huber had taken it upon herself to end the funding early and without notice.

Schools and curriculum directors were blindsided. Taylor Goldenstein reported for the *Austin American-Statesman* in July 2017 that a TPP grantee called EngenderHealth, which worked with charter schools in Travis County, Texas, had received a letter from the government "quietly, without warning," informing the program that "$4.6 million in funding over the next four years . . . was being eliminated."[4] In Rochester, New York, $2 million in TPP funding was slashed from a CSE health education program called THRIVE. In the state of Arizona, the cuts amounted to $2.8 million, which would have funded sex ed for students who received no such classes in their public schools.[5] In total, the Trump administration cut more than $213 million from teen pregnancy prevention programs nationwide, well in advance of their planned expiration dates. The editorial board of the *New York Times* wrote in August 2017 that the cuts were "an assault on efforts to prevent teenage pregnancy."[6]

By March 2018, Huber had been given even more power over sex ed funding. Haberkorn reported for *Politico* that Huber had been made the "final arbiter of which groups receive federal family planning funds," which was a "change from prior years, when a group of officials made the decision."[7] And, in 2018, Trump's budget reflected increased funding for abstinence education.[8]

RESTRICTED ACCESS TO TITLE X FUNDS

Trump didn't just cut TPP and increase funding for SRAE; he also put new strictures on other federal family planning funds and regulations. Whereas under President Obama, Title X—the federal funding stream for family planning and related services—had been made available for grantees that offered all types of contraception, the Trump administration's application for the funds stressed "natural family planning methods and eliminat[ed] the [prior] focus on all types of contraception," according to *Politico*. In particular, the application seemed designed to make it hard for Planned Parenthood to qualify for federal funds. The executive vice president of Planned Parenthood called the restrictive application "a clear attempt to roll back access to the type of birth control that most women want to use."

The president of the American College of Obstetricians and Gynecologists charged the administration with "turning back the clock on women's health." In May, the Associated Press wrote that "step by methodical step, the Trump administration is remaking government policy on reproductive health—moving to limit access to birth control and abortion and bolstering abstinence-only sex education."[9]

CONSENT EDUCATION

But the need for real, comprehensive sex education was more important than ever. And it wasn't just because CSE provided essential information about the risks of pregnancy and STIs. Advocates were realizing that CSE could help address related problems that were finally coming to light on a national level—such as sexual assault. The #MeToo movement, originally founded by activist Tarana Burke, took off in full force in 2017 as an effort to bring awareness to the shocking prevalence of sexual assault. Sexual assault survivors used the phrase "me too," stylized as the hashtag #MeToo for sites like Twitter, to share their experiences and show the magnitude of the problem. When film producer Harvey Weinstein was accused of sexual assault under the #MeToo banner, the issue became the focus of a full national conversation—at last.

Consent, if not named as such, had been an important aspect of liberal sex ed since the 1960s. A foundational concept of "respect" had been embedded in the sex ed of that era as theorized by people like Lester

Kirkendall. Now, with the momentum of #MeToo behind it, consent was emerging as a topic all its own within sex ed. Progressive curricula like AFY's had included the concept in their work throughout the 2000s, and now it was becoming more and more common. The *Seattle Times* argued in an editorial in early 2018 that "schools can combat cultural influence that contribute to sexual assaults . . . by emphasizing that students should ask for and receive a 'yes' before proceeding with sex, rather than stopping only if their partner says 'no.'"[10] By May 2019, the Associated Press reported that nine states—California, Connecticut, Maryland, New Jersey, Oregon, Rhode Island, South Carolina, Vermont, and Virginia—along with Washington, DC, "require that consent be part of the sex ed curriculum."[11]

LGBTQ+ VISIBILITY IN SEX ED

There was also, at long last, real action toward repealing the anti-LGBTQ+ sentiment—and outright discrimination—that had been built into traditional sex ed curricula. In early 2019, the *Arizona Daily Star* reported that the state's new superintendent of public instruction, Kathy Hoffman, was calling "on lawmakers to repeal a law that prohibits any courses on AIDS and HIV from portraying homosexuality 'as a positive alternative lifestyle.'"[12] The law in question, which dated back to 1991, also forbade "teachers from suggesting 'that some methods of sex are safe methods of homosexual sex.'"

Democratic state senator Martin Quezada had for the last four years proposed repealing the law, but without success.[13] But thanks to Hoffman's encouragement—and, probably, a lawsuit filed by a group called Equality Arizona—Republican state representative T. J. Shope introduced a floor amendment that would repeal what was colloquially known as the "no promo homo" law. In April 2019, the amendment passed in the Arizona house, 55 to 5. After it passed the senate as well, Lily Altavena, reporting in the *Arizona Republic*, wrote that "in an usually fast move, Gov. Doug Ducey . . . signed the bill into law" that very month.[14] This, of course, did not mean that sex ed in Arizona now adequately met the needs of queer students—only that it could not overtly discriminate against them.

Washington state also saw real progress on LGBTQ+ equality when Laurie Dils, who oversaw sexual health education within the Washington state superintendent's office, introduced one of the most ambitious sex ed plans of the modern era. She wanted the legislature to pass a measure requiring CSE for all public school students, K–12, by the 2022–2023 academic year.[15] Prior to this, Washington had an HIV/AIDS education requirement. On March 10, 2020, after hours of debate and reconciliation, the bill requiring CSE in Washington made it all the way to Governor Jay Inslee.[16] A large group of anti–sex ed protesters—a hundred or more, the *Spokesman-Review* reported, with signs decrying "government overreach, infringement of parents' rights and the loss of children's innocence"— gathered to attempt to convince Inslee to reject the bill.[17] But at the end of March, even as COVID-19 began to make its way throughout the country, Inslee signed the bill into law.[18]

The many Washington parents opposed to the law did not give up, even as schools in the state—and across the nation—closed down due to the pandemic. They announced their plans to collect enough signatures (129,811, to be precise) to force a referendum, which would put the question of CSE on the ballot for voters to decide on directly. One of the opposed parents, Julia Ditto, was also a columnist for the *Spokesman-Review*, and she wrote in May 2020 that she found it "very telling that, even amid a pandemic, groups across Washington who oppose [the bill] have still managed to—from a safe, social-distance, mind you—collect more than 88,000 signatures."[19]

Enough signatures were gathered, and the question went to the 2020 ballot.[20] It became a hot-button issue. Republican state senate hopeful Dave Lucas boasted in a text ad that he was the "only state Senate candidate standing in opposition to . . . mandatory graphic sex education.'"[21]

This was the first time in American history—somehow, after decades of debates, bills, pickets, anger, and passion—that sex ed had ever appeared on a state ballot. And comprehensive sex ed won. Fifty-eight percent of voters voted in favor of the courses. Washington became, the *Tri-City Herald* reported, "among only 17 states . . . that require content be medically accurate, among 26 plus D.C. that require it be age-appropriate, and among nine that require instruction be appropriate for a student's cultural background and not biased against race, sex, or ethnicity."[22] (Schools were still required to notify families of the course, and parents could opt-out their children.)

BIDEN TAKES OFFICE

Democrat Joe Biden was elected president in the fall of 2020, and when he released his budget in May 2021, SIECUS—which now goes by the name SIECUS: Sex Ed for Social Change—issued a statement saying they were "grateful to the Biden administration for proposing a budget to Congress that addresses an evidence-based, holistic approach to family planning and reproductive health."[23]

Biden's budget increased Title X Family Planning funding by 18.7 percent and included a request for $101 million for the Teen Pregnancy Prevention Program that had been so thoroughly gutted by the Trump administration. But Biden also continued allocating funds for SRAE.

Biden's budget was clearly, then, a mixed bag. But it was, admittedly, a swing toward evidence-based practices. And, by 2021, the evidence in favor of CSE couldn't get much clearer. In January, the *Journal of Adolescent Health* published a paper called "Three Decades of Research: The Case for Comprehensive Sex Education," which found "strong support for comprehensive sex education across a range of topics and grade levels." There was evidence, the paper continued, for "the effectiveness of approaches that address a broad definition of sexual health and take positive, affirming, inclusive approaches to human sexuality."[24]

COVID, CRT, AND BOOK BANS

But schools across the nation did not immediately implement new sex ed curricula in 2021—not only because of longstanding political affiliation and funding, but also because COVID-19 had made Americans reexamine their beliefs about what the government, and the public school, could or could not ask them to do. Face-mask mandates, which were an evidence-based way to reduce the spread of COVID-19, had become demonized by the right as a symbol of state overreach. At the same time, critical race theory (CRT), which views race as a social construct embedded deeply in social and legal structures, was cast in the spotlight after the highly publicized murder of unarmed Black man George Floyd by a white police officer. Conservatives greatly misconstrued, or perhaps deliberately misrepresented, the theory, labeling it as dangerous and imposing outright bans on teaching about race and racism. Book bans flourished in conservative areas, often targeting books with content around sexuality and race. And so, in the spring and summer of 2021, as the United States tired of COVID-19 restrictions, schools announced they were opening back up. They quickly became a battleground for these culture wars. Sex ed couldn't avoid the fray.

In June 2021, the Pinellas County, Florida, school board held a public meeting to consider expanding the COVID mask mandate. Parents opposed to the mandate commented for two hours. "Several wove other themes into their remarks about the masks," Marlene Sokol wrote for the *Tampa Bay Times*, "how they were against the teaching of critical race theory and sex education, for example."[25] In Illinois, a parent who opposed mask mandates in Wesclin Community Unit School District #3, Jeremy Rakers, said that masks were the "tip of the iceberg," and commented forebodingly: "If you haven't seen what Illinois is trying to throw down our throats with CRT and sex education."[26]

In New Jersey, meanwhile, the state board of education had in 2020 approved standards for sex ed that ensured, according to the executive director of Answer, the Rutgers education center, that "children in grades K–12 will continue to learn information that is age appropriate, medically accurate, and shown by research to help keep them safe."[27] Like the guidelines of many states, New Jersey's also included an opt-out measure. But just as the standards were poised for implementation in 2022, the all-too-predictable outcry went up. Many conservative parents, invoking "parental freedoms," a popular term of the early 2020s, decried the standards as another example of governmental overreach and "woke" education. After what one journalist called "severe backlash in conservative ranks," the state capitulated and announced it would review the standards. But New Jersey governor Phil Murphy stood by the original standards, claiming they had been "intentionally misrepresented."

Likewise, the head of the state department of education found nothing wrong with the standards and went forward with them, reminding parents that they could opt their children out of any lessons that went against their moral or religious views.[28] Despite parental protests, New Jersey remains something of a leader in sex ed nationwide.

THE FALL OF *ROE* AND THE RISE OF "DON'T SAY GAY"

In June 2022, the stakes for sex ed got higher when the US Supreme Court reversed *Roe v. Wade*, dismantling Americans' constitutional right to some abortions. By restricting abortion access, the need for accurate information about sex and contraception became even more crucial.

Attacks on sexual freedom unfolded at the state level as well. In August 2022, Republican Florida governor Ron DeSantis signed into law a provision that would come to be known as Don't Say Gay. The law, citing parental rights, stated that "classroom instruction by school personnel or third parties on sexual orientation or gender identity may not occur in kindergarten through grade 3 or in a manner that is not age appropriate or developmentally appropriate for students."[29]

Much like the restrictive anti–sex ed laws that had been passed in the late 1960s in states like California and Louisiana, this law led to confusion and fear in application. Jo Yurcaba for NBC News reported in 2022 that the Florida law "doesn't give examples of what is age or developmentally appropriate, and it doesn't outline what breaking the law would look like. As a result, school districts' interpretations of how to best implement the law vary widely."[30] But most implementations of the law looked pretty draconian. "Duval County public schools," Yurcaba reported, "removed a 12-minute anti-bullying video that taught middle and high school students how to support LGBTQ peers." In Miami-Dade County, school administrators announced plans to "remove chapters that cover gender identity and sexuality" from textbooks that had been purchased less than a year earlier, the Associated Press reported.[31]

In 2023, Florida legislation expanded the Don't Say Gay provisions— prohibiting, Yurcaba reported, "sexual orientation or gender identity instruction in prekindergarten through eighth grade," and restricting "reproductive health education in sixth through 12th grade."[32] As of September 2024—as this book was in its final edits—Florida sex ed has become even more restrictive. Florida does not require sex ed—but, as

SIECUS reports, its laws specify that if sex ed is taught, it has to "include the benefits of abstinence as the expected social standard." If HIV/AIDS information is taught, it has to "emphasize the benefits of heterosexual marriage."[33] Now, as the Associated Press reports, thanks to a provision that requires the Florida Department of Education to approve materials on "reproductive health and disease information . . . about a dozen districts across Florida have been told by state officials to restrict their sex ed instruction plans."[34] In Broward County, officials advised that "pictures of reproductive anatomy and demonstrations on how to use contraceptives" were not appropriate and should not be used in any grade.

Christopher Pepper, a health educator whose work is funded by the CDC-DASH notes that "the obstacles folks in Florida face have just grown higher and higher with each year; to the point where they started to cry during our meetings."[35] Meanwhile, he writes, "states on the West Coast have all passed strong laws mandating comprehensive sex ed and are moving in the opposite direction . . . and the places that got the CDC funding and haven't faced roadblocks have developed really innovative, high quality curriculum that is largely available to the world for free."

THE FUTURE OF SEX ED

And so, this is where we find ourselves. Decades of irrefutable evidence have shown that comprehensive sex ed reduces rates of teen pregnancy and STIs, and that abstinence-only sex ed does not. Yet our country has so politicized the subject that it is hard to see it clearly. Sometimes sex ed is reduced to a punch line or an awkward memory, a shared trauma from one's preteen or teen years. It is very rarely considered for what it is: a class intended to teach young people about their bodies and about the risks of sex.

And because of this, it is the young people who are harmed. The content of sex ed in public schools and other government-funded venues is often changed by the political party in control. When Republicans are in power, funding is made most available for abstinence programming. When Democrats are in control, most funding goes to comprehensive sex ed (CSE). This is most visibly true of decisions made in the White House, but it is also true of decisions made by state and even local legislatures and school boards. This inimical flip-flopping has wreaked an appalling disparity in the quality of sex ed for our young people. Must schools be prepared to revise their textbooks with each election cycle? One might be tempted to say this is an untenable situation. Yet, it has endured for decades with no end in sight.

Part of the reason that this situation has remained as stuck as it is, is because of the appearance of open questions. If we believed what anti-sex-ed proponents had to say, we would all think that there was no settled conclusion about sex ed. But there are good and solid conclusions about good and solid sex ed. The American Academy of Pediatrics (AAP) explains clearly and succinctly that comprehensive sex ed gives young people the information they need to "develop a safe and positive view of sexuality, build healthy relationships" and "make informed, safe, positive choices about their sexuality and sexual health."[1] The evidence is in, the conclusions have been drawn. The AAP continues, explaining that CSE has shown "demonstrated success in reducing rates of sexual activity, sexual risk behaviors, STIs, and adolescent pregnancy and delaying sexual activity." And in addition to those specific health and sex-related outcomes, CSE has also "been shown to support social-emotional learning, positive communication skills, and development of healthy relationships." CSE is also associated with other beneficial outcomes like reduced rates of homophobia, an increased recognition of gender equality, decreased rates of domestic and intimate partner violence, prevention of childhood sexual abuse, and media literacy.

Meanwhile, opponents still have us debating the foundational questions, as if it is 1906 and we are at Dr. Morrow's first meeting of the American Society of Sanitary and Moral Prophylaxis. Will teaching about sex open some horrible, depraved pit of sin in our children? How young is too young? Who will do the teaching? Won't teaching young people about prophylaxis encourage them to have sex?

It's a maddening situation—one where experts are forced to relitigate foundational ideas over and over again in bad faith debates. It's almost enough to make one want to give up entirely, which, I suspect, is part of the opposition's playbook. It is a strategy that they have applied not only to sex ed but to abortion, gun control, and climate change. There are very real questions and concerns about sex ed, none of which should be discounted. But the space for real conversation has been so diminished by the manufactured arguments of Republicans that we hardly have space to breathe.

And on that note, the abstinence-only framework is not only useless but intellectually dishonest. It is a travesty—and a tragedy. A national shame. And yet so many Americans fight against its alternative, portraying CSE as pornographic and damaging to young people. On its website, the World Health Organization defines CSE as a sex ed program that is accurate, age appropriate, and comprehensive, "meaning they cover a range of topics on sexuality and sexual and reproductive health, throughout childhood and adolescence." This is not a radical agenda. In fact, it feels very much like the bare minimum of what should be required. It is an approach that we should use and indeed improve on so that it adequately addresses the needs of LGBTQ+ students, especially trans students.

In 1906, a single group, the American Society for Sanitary and Moral Prophylaxis, believed that the STI epidemic of its day could be solved by two complementary projects: sanitation, or medicine; and morals, or religion. More than one hundred years later, the nation has had countless groups devoted to sex ed, each falling into one of two camps: those who claim the best way to reduce the rates of STIs (and pregnancy) is through evidence-based approaches and access to medicine, and those who claim the best way to minimize these risks is by merely telling young people to abstain from having sex until they marry.

In the early years of the ASSMP, members imagined a future when the problems of STIs could be solved by "sanitation," alone. In a world where a drug or other medicine could cure all syphilis and gonorrhea, where unintended pregnancies were not a concern, where would a group like their own focus their efforts? They believed they would still have an important job: the need to train young people in the healthiest ways to have sex relations of all types. They believed that abstinence was the only standard worth living up to, and the one that would still need to be emphasized.

Now, we live in a world where a huge number of STIs and unwanted pregnancies could be cured, treated, or handled. But what the ASSMP did not anticipate, perhaps, was that the pursuit of the "moral" and the emphasis on abstinence have left many ignorant of medical means.

The American obsession with abstinence borders on the absurd. There is still impressive buy-in to the popular idea that all people should first date, then marry, and only then have sex—even though this is simply not a factual description of the sex lives of many Americans. And, at the same time, it also remains a bedrock tenet of American marketing and media that the whole point of life is to have sex, married or not.

That young people sometimes have sex (and that those young people might not be straight!) is particularly difficult to fit into many peoples' conceptions of reality. But the sooner we can accept that adolescents can and do have sex, the sooner real movement toward equitable education can happen. Sex ed is about our fundamental rights and deeply interwoven with issues of reproductive justice, healthcare, self-esteem, the nature of education, public schools, and social equity.

In the process of writing this book, I have found that one of the things I have to do frequently is contextualize sex ed as an important part of reproductive justice. It is lower stakes than some other direct services, like abortion and birth control. But it is foundational, the first and sometimes only information young people get about sex and reproduction. And because it takes place in schools, where most children and adolescents spend their time and most adults do not, I believe that leads to an overall feeling that sex ed is unimportant or unserious.

But it is really for those two reasons that it is most important to me.

It is the foundation of reproductive health and thus of reproductive justice, and it is found in a public institution that serves most American youth.

That institution—the public school—is of particular interest to me because it is such a fertile site for activism and action, even if we don't think of it as one. So many landmark Supreme Court cases revolve around public schools—*Brown v. Board of Education* on segregation; *Tinker v. Des Moines* on free speech; *Wisconsin v. Yoder* on the First Amendment; *Engel v. Vitale* on school prayer—in part because we have never quite decided the purpose of American public schools. It is paid for by taxpayers and populated by minors. It is decentralized, perpetually underfunded, and its culture and curricula vary based on location and donations. We haven't decided if it's supposed to train students for jobs, or college, or both, or neither. It is still a grand experiment, as is America.

Another question that often comes up—to me but also throughout the history of sex ed—is whether sex ed "belongs" in schools. I have kept myself out of this book for many reasons, but here, finally, in these last pages, I can tell you what I really think (on that question and on others!).

Does sex ed "belong in schools"? Who knows. We—humans—invented schools. Nothing inherently belongs in them. We also invented sex ed. And marriage. And the concept of abstinence. The data firmly points to the fact that comprehensive sex ed is an effective tool for reducing STIs and rates of teen pregnancy, and for this reason alone, I posit that yes, it does belong in schools. The other reason that sex ed belongs in schools is that I do not believe that parents are a child's best sexuality educators. Parents do tend to be their children's de facto primary sex educators, but this does not mean they are best suited for the task. In fact, I think this notion that parents are their children's best sex educator has mostly been used to appease conservatives opposed to sex ed in schools. What's more, talking about sex *at all* is hard for many people, and with your parent and/or child it becomes doubly or triply so. Finally, parents do not inherently possess information that equips them to teach about sex, though they certainly may have moral beliefs about sex that they want their child to hold, which is completely appropriate.

Of course it's fine to teach your child, in your home, that abstinence before marriage is what you expect of them. Abstinence prevents pregnancy and STIs. And what you tell your kid is, frankly, none of my business. (But if you ask, I will tell you that the statistics are not on your side, and you should tell your teenager what a condom is, even if you don't think, for whatever reason, they are going to use them.)

However, when it comes to lessons of puberty, contraception, STIs, self-esteem, gender identity, sexual orientation, and the other elements of a strong comprehensive sex ed curriculum, a parent is just not automatically an expert—in the same way that they are not automatically their child's best math teacher or English teacher.

I also think that abstinence-only sex ed has no place in public schools. It is a waste of taxpayer money, and it is unethical. More often than not it is a clear violation of the separation of church and state. "Abstinence-plus" is a concession to Republicans and seeks to portray comprehensive sex ed as radical when really it is just basic instruction.

And while abstinence truly is effective at reducing rates of STIs and pregnancy, it is effective in the same way that avoiding water is the best way not to drown. It's technically true, but if you're at the beach and all your friends are swimming or have life jackets, I think you'll probably want swimming lessons.

I have also come to believe that the "lessons" of abstinence are far more intrusive to students than comprehensive sex ed is. To pressure a child or teenager to make a decision about their sex life and report on it, as often happens in abstinence-only classes, overreaches far more than telling a class of high schoolers that "condoms exist and here is how they are used." Yet abstinence advocates would have us believe that the opposite is true.

On the question of what sex ed *should* be, I—being somewhat of a contrarian—would be curious to see if a truly value-neutral sex ed curriculum could exist. However, I also know that sex ed, like everything humans have a hand in, does not exist in a vacuum. It exists now as a highly politicized topic with a long and complex history. We cannot start from scratch. And so, of course, I fully and vocally advocate for comprehensive sex ed for all.

On a practical level, I believe that the most important work to be done to improve sex ed in the United States is to cease funding abstinence education and to establish equity among state sex ed requirements. As I was finishing up this book, in a stroke of truly fortuitous timing (or not so fortuitous, if you are my long-suffering editor), I completed a comprehensive sex ed facilitator training so I can teach sex ed on the small island in Maine where I live. I am now certified to teach the youngest ages that this program provides lessons for, students in grades K to 2, and 4 to 6

This liberal CSE curriculum training was attendant to every aspect of, well, everything, falling over itself to be sensitive to minute details. I thought of those young people I would be teaching on Sundays at the local church ("But it's not religious!" all our literature screams, anticipating questions): mostly white kids whom I'll be giving a head start on the sex ed they will also receive in Maine public schools in a few short years. Then I thought of the young people in Texas, who—if they have sex ed in their school at all, and if their parents opt them into it—must be taught that "homosexuality is not an acceptable lifestyle to the general public."[2] Texas also has no standards about the medical accuracy of a school's curriculum.

This complete disparity is an equity issue. Providing all young people with the real sex education they need will take real and radical change. There are groups doing good work. AFY, SIECUS, and SIECUS's newly formed advocacy organization, EducateUS, all fight to actively support comprehensive sex education in the United States, and they all need, and deserve, our support. We could also work toward equity by restricting funding for abstinence-only programs and by implementing sensible, rational guidelines nationwide.

Unfortunately, however, it is hard to strike an overly optimistic tone that this change will, or even could, happen when our country has been hijacked by a political group that is unwilling to listen and learn and which is holding hostage not just sex ed but our entire school system and government.

How we truly make change in this modern era is one that has not been answered. But it does seem clear that the current political status quo will not solve the situation we find ourselves in—both in terms of sex ed and with myriad other social and political issues. How could it? It's what got us here.

At some point while I was writing this book, Margaret Mead's quote about how "a small group of thoughtful, committed citizens" being the only thing that has ever changed the world stopped being inspiring and started being ominous. I can only hope that "we"—an ambiguous term I will use for those of us committed to democracy, honesty, truth, bodily autonomy, liberty and justice for all, and so on and so forth, can muster some of the same activism that Republicans on the right have for so long—and to such productive ends. The stakes are higher than ever.

ACKNOWLEDGMENTS

In my first, unserious draft of these acknowledgments, I thanked every person I had ever met. This is only a slight overstatement, as this book would not exist without the many people in my life who helped bring it to reality, whether they know they did or not.

For shaping this book into the readable condition that it's in, and seeing what it could be when it was in proposal form, and for her endless patience in the face of emails asking for just a few more weeks, I am so grateful to Catherine Tung at Beacon Press, whose insightful edits made this book immeasurably better. Thanks also to Rachel Kim, who truly saw this project, from its very inception when we lived together in our Smith Street apartment while I was getting my MFA that led to the idea for this book, to holding my hand through many, many drafts of proposals, to the book's eventual sale. I am grateful for your keen eye and your faith in me.

There are so many people at Goucher College's MFA in Nonfiction Program to thank—all the mentors I worked with, or even just came to know during my time there—and in particular Suzannah Lessard, Diana Hume George, Porscha Burke, Maggie Messitt, Jesse Holland, and Jacob Levenson. Jacob crystalized this idea of the "history of sex ed" as a viable book topic, and for that I will be forever grateful. I met so many friends during my time at Goucher, all of whom made this project better by their critiques, kindness, and continued support of my work. I am especially grateful to Katie Gilbert, who asked the extremely sensible and extremely important question: "What is social hygiene?," during my first critique at Goucher, which in many ways set me off on this strange journey; to

Stephanie Gorton, whose work has ended up being intertwined with my own in important ways, and who responded to my last-minute request for research about condoms with joy and many sources; and to Jennie Burke, who has shown me how to be a more open, loving, and kind person and writer.

Then there are all the other professors and teachers I have had in my academic career. I am cheesy enough to think that all of you have had an impact on this book, and I thank you all. It is special to remain close with mentors after graduating, and I am exceptionally thankful for Dr. Gregory Spinner—my religion advisor at Skidmore College, who saw potential in me during my first year at Skidmore and whose wisdom and friendship has meant so much to me in the decade since I graduated; and to Dana Anderson, my favorite high school English teacher, who was probably the first teacher to make me believe I could be a "real writer," and whose continued support and friendship mean the world to me.

On the subject of school, I am also grateful for the US Department of Education's Office of Federal Student Aid, whose absurd lending practices allowed me to get not one, but two master's degrees in addition to my undergraduate degree, through loans I will almost certainly never be able to pay back. On that same note, I am thankful to several credit card companies who have provided me accounts—to you, also, I will be in literal debt for many years, but it is because of you that I could afford groceries and clothes. I highlight these institutions and my debt because in addition to the myriad difficulties of writing—the craft aspect, the finding-the-time aspect, the pitching and proposing and selling aspect— the financial aspect is extremely difficult.

I babysat and nannied my way through writing this book, and I am grateful to every family who welcomed me into their home, whose children I cared for, and whose coffee tables I turned into my office once their kids went to bed. You made this book possible too. Megan and David Lagueux were particularly lovely and supportive during the almost-final stretch of this work. While finishing my MFA and directly afterward, I was lucky to work at Books Are Magic in Brooklyn, where I worked with and met so many people who became important to the life of this book. I am grateful to Mike and Emma Fusco-Straub for their flexibility and understanding as I wrote, was in school, and worked; and who are always happy to see the people in their circles succeed. At Books Are Magic I met many lifelong pals whose support of this project has been crucial. Among them: Michael Chin, a true friend from day one; Maritza Montañez, whose laughter and wisdom got me through many closing shifts; Shira Erlichman, who has taught me so much about writing, life, love, and even poetry; and Colleen Callery—who will get more words later.

Also through Books Are Magic, I was lucky enough to meet Susannah Cahalan and her amazing group of "Sob Sisters"—the brain child of Cahalan, Abbott Kahler, and Ada Calhoun. What a gift to have strong, smart, accomplished female nonfiction writers to look up to! Speaking of strong, smart, accomplished female nonfiction writers: I owe so much to my friend Mira Ptacin (and her husband, Andy Jackson), who has only ever given me love and light and inspiration; and Hannah Matthews, who in addition to her friendship and genius and abortion work, also instructed me—through her writing—on better ways to think and talk about *Roe v. Wade*, and whose piece about the Supreme Court and the invention of the trimester system in pregnancy was well timed for the writing of this book.

Then there are the people who saw the vision for this book even when I temporarily misplaced it—and whose faith in me and this project sustained me just through their kindness, understanding, and positive regard for the whole thing. Rose Heithoff, who I met through the kismet of indie bookstores, has seen the vision since day one, and I am so beyond grateful for that. Peter Brannen has been a faithful sounding board through this whole process; I am thankful for your wisdom, insight, and in these last maddening months, the sense of not being so alone in this solitary work. Also, for remembering the word *establishment*.

So many people on Peaks Island have offered me genuine interest, care, and attention during the writing of this book, which sustained me whether you knew it or not. I'm thinking in particular of Jean and John Gulliver, Kate Gulliver and Sam Spirn, Tonya and Gigi Guyton-Thompson, Will Green and Tyler Schwaller, Cate and Ian Stevenson, Irv Williams, and Scott and Cara Dolan—but there are so many more of you.

Then there are those people whose lives were made less convenient by the writing of this book. I am so grateful for the patience and kindness shown to me by all the children, parents and caregivers, and staff at the

Peaks Island Children's Workshop, in particular Nettie Wood, Abby Knight, Etta Frederick, and Abby Annis. Your good humor, flexibility, talent, and skill while contending with a first-time boss who was also finishing a first book mean the world to me. I love you all.

My mom, Grace Houghton, never had anything but faith in me that I could do this (or, if she did, I never knew anything about it!). I am so grateful that you, and Dad, never let me think there was anything I couldn't do. This book also benefited from my mother's editorial eye during the first phase of the manuscript, as did so many of my high school essays. You improved this book significantly.

I can't thank all of my family members by name here, but I will mention Maggy Myers and Jon Epstein—I treasure the time spent at Salisbury Cove in 2020 with you, as we all set to work on our own projects. What a gift! My cousin Gretchen Blank has been an amazing scout for additions to my collection of sex ed materials and has opened her home to me whenever I needed it. Meagan and Lindsay Falls have also given me so much: always a place to spend the night, store my stuff, and a listening ear. To the rest of my family, all of you: my brother John, my grandmother, aunts, uncles, cousins, siblings of aunts and uncles, cousins of cousins—thank you for your curiosity, your patience, and your understanding as I lived, hermit-like, on my island for so long. I look forward to reemerging soon.

Those most acutely affected by the writing of this book have been my closest friends, who I am so profoundly thankful for. Fiona Owens and Emlyn Hilson (and Dillon too!)—you are my tried and true, my soulmates, the loves of my life. I have never once doubted your love and support for me, even when the fifteen-minute ferry ride to Portland was impossible for me to manage.

Matt "Yellow Shoes" Cohen—you have had more faith in me than I ever will. Thank you for always, always being there for me in all things. I could not have done this without you. I am also indebted to you for the photos you took of me for this book—something we dreamed of ten years ago.

Mariah Vitali is another of those always-there pals, who in addition to responding to every inane message I've ever sent, also answered all of my questions about the law, making this book far more comprehensible.

Colleen Callery, you are the closest thing I've ever had to a sister, and you've been right here with me for so much of this. You've responded to every text, answered every phone call (mostly), and listened to every thought I've had, even when they were truly absurd. I could not have done this without you, Birthday, Frank, or Len Crifo, who helped make our pandemic house a home.

And so now I have thanked, essentially, every person I have ever met. I am sure I am forgetting many of you who have helped in large and small ways. If you find yourself thinking you should be listed on these pages but are not, consider it my oversight (unless it wasn't. Ooh, intrigue!).

NOTES

PREFACE: THEN AND NOW

1. Howard Zinn, "Introduction: The American Creed," in *Postwar America: 1945–1971* (Chicago: Haymarket Books, 1973), xiii.

2. Robert Heinlein, "Cliff and the Calories," *The New Worlds of Robert A. Heinlein* (New York: Ace Books, 1980).

CHAPTER I: DR. PRINCE MORROW AND THE BIRTH OF SEXUAL HEALTH ADVOCACY IN AMERICA

1. Prince Morrow, "Translator's Preface," in Jean Alfred Fournier, *Syphilis and Marriage*, trans. Prince Morrow (New York: D. Appleton and Co., 1880).

2. John C. Burnham, "Morrow, Prince A., and the Social Hygiene Movement," in *Human Sexuality: An Encyclopedia* (New York: Routledge, 2014), 402.

3. "An English Member," *Preventive Hygiene: An Account of the Brussels International Conferences, 1899 and 1902*, 3rd ed. (London: Hazell, Watson, & Viney, 1909).

4. Abraham Flexner, *Prostitution in Europe* (New York: The Century Co., 1914).

5. "An English Member," *Preventive Hygiene*, 16.

6. Ludwig Weiss, "Venereal Prophylaxis That Is Feasible," *Journal of the American Medical Association* XL, no. 4 (Jan. 24, 1903): 232–40, https://doi.org/10.1001/jama.1903.92490040028001g.

7. Prince A. Morrow, "Report of the Committee of Seven of the Medical Society of the County of New York on the Prophylaxis of Venereal Disease in New York City," *New York Medical Journal* 74 (Dec. 21, 1901): 1146–50.

8. Morrow, "Report of the Committee," 1146.

9. Morrow, "Report of the Committee," 1146.

10. Morrow, "Report of the Committee," 1147.

11. Morrow, "Report of the Committee."

12. Morrow, "Report of the Committee," 1149.

13. B. H. Lerner, "New York City's Tuberculosis Control Efforts: The Historical Limitations of the 'War on Consumption,'" *American Journal of Public Health* 83, no. 5 (May 1993): 758–66.

14. Theresa Machemer, "When a Women-Led Campaign Made It Illegal to Spit in Public in New York City," *Smithsonian Magazine*, Feb. 10, 2020, https://

www.smithsonianmag.com/history/19th-century-public-health-campaign-made
-it-illegal-spit-public-new-york-city-180974023/.

15. Prince A. Morrow, "The Society of Sanitary and Moral Prophylaxis: Its Objects and Aims," *Transactions of the American Society of Sanitary and Moral Prophylaxis* 1 (1906): 26–38; 31.

16. "Report of the Committee of Seven on the Prophylaxis of Venereal Disease in New York City," *Therapeutic Gazette* xxviii, no. 4 (Apr. 15, 1902): 237–38.

17. Burnham, "Morrow, Prince A., and the Social Hygiene Movement."

18. Edward Bennet Bronson, "Dr. Morrow, the Physician," *Social Diseases* IV, no. 3 (July 1913): 105–12.

19. Prince A. Morrow, *Social Diseases and Marriage* (New York: Lea Brothers and Co., 1904).

20. Charles Stedman Bull, "Ophthalmia Neonatorum and Its Prophylaxis, from the Standpoint of the Ophthalmologist," *Transactions of the American Society of Sanitary and Moral Prophylaxis* III (1910): 63.

21. Prince A. Morrow, "The Prophylaxis of Venereal Diseases—Medical Aspects of the Social Evil," *Indian Medical Journal* 19, no. 11 (May 1901): 414–20.

22. Aine Collier, *The Humble Little Condom: A History* (Amherst, NY: Prometheus Books, 2010).

23. "The Comstock Law," 211 Criminal Code of 1909 § 211 (1873).

24. "Anthony Comstock's 'Chastity' Laws," from "The Pill," *American Experience*, PBS, https://www.pbs.org/wgbh/americanexperience/features/pill
-anthony-comstocks-chastity-laws/, accessed Oct. 1, 2024.

25. Bronson, "Dr. Morrow, the Physician."

26. Morrow, "The Society of Sanitary and Moral Prophylaxis."

27. Edith Houghton Hooker, "The Basic Argument Against Prophylaxis," *The Arbitrator* 2, no. 5 (Oct. 1919): 2–9.

28. Allan M. Brandt, *No Magic Bullet: A Social History of Venereal Disease in the United States Since 1880* (New York: Oxford University Press, 1987), 32.

29. Prince A. Morrow, "Should the Youth of This Country Be Instructed in a Knowledge of Sexual Physiology and Hygiene?" *Transactions of the American Society of Sanitary and Moral Prophylaxis* 1 (Oct. 12, 1905): 85–91.

30. E. L. Keyes, "If Education Upon Sexual Matters Is to Be Offered to Youth, What Should Be Its Nature and Scope, and at What Age Should It Commence?" *Transactions of the American Society of Sanitary and Moral Prophylaxis* (Oct. 12, 1905); 91–95; Burt G. Wilder, "The Desirability of Correct Instruction Before College Years, with Suggestions as to Specific Methods and Discussion," *Transactions of the American Society of Sanitary and Moral Prophylaxis* 2 (Dec. 13, 1906): 48–59.

31. "Stated Meeting, Held at the New York Academy of Medicine, Apr. 12, 1906," *Transactions of the American Society of Sanitary and Moral Prophylaxis* 1 (Apr. 12, 1906): 146–247.

32. Helen C. Putnam, "Instruction in the Physiology and Hygiene of Sex: Its Practicability as Demonstrated in Several Public Schools," *Transactions of the American Society of Sanitary and Moral Prophylaxis* 1 (Dec. 13, 1906): 35–48.

CHAPTER 2: ELLA FLAGG YOUNG AND THE FIRST SEX ED LECTURES IN AMERICAN PUBLIC SCHOOLS

1. Vice Commission of Chicago, *The Social Evil in Chicago: A Study of Existing Conditions with Recommendations by the Vice Commission of Chicago* (Chicago: Vice Commission of the City of Chicago, 1911), 36.

2. Vice Commission of Chicago, *The Social Evil in Chicago*, 36.

3. Prince A. Morrow, "Results of the Work Accomplished by the Society of Sanitary and Moral Prophylaxis," *Transactions of the American Society of Sanitary and Moral Prophylaxis* 2 (Oct. 10, 1907): 116–28.

4. Maurice A. Bigelow, "Biology in Relation to Sex Instruction in Schools and Colleges," *Social Diseases* II, no. 4 (Oct. 1911): 10–15.

5. Editors of Encyclopedia Britannica, "Ella Flagg Young: Chicago School Superintendent, Women's Rights Advocate," *Britannica*, https://www.britannica.com/biography/Ella-Flagg-Young, accessed Oct. 2, 2024.

6. "Pass Grant for Teaching Sex Hygiene in Schools," *Chicago Tribune*, Apr. 12, 1912.

7. "Chicago Parents to Hear of Sex Hygiene," *Inter Ocean*, June 5, 1912.

8. "Women Put Fingers in Their Ears at Sex Problem Talk," *Star-Gazette*, June 8, 1912.

9. "Women Put Fingers in Their Ears at Sex Problem Talk."

10. Thomas M. Balliet, Maurice A. Bigelow, and Prince A. Morrow, "Report of the Special Committee on the American Federation of Sex Hygiene," *Social Diseases* IV, no. 1 (Jan. 1913): 1–53.

11. Maurice Alpheus Bigelow, Thomas Minard Balliet, and Prince Albert Morrow, *Report of the Special Committee on the Matter and Methods of Sex Education: Presented Before the Subsection on Sex Hygiene of the Fifteenth International Congress on Hygiene and Demography Held in Washington, D.C. September Twenty-third to Twenty-Eighth Nineteen Hundred and Twelve* (United States: American Federation for Sex Hygiene, 1913); "Attack Eugenics for High Schools," *Chicago Tribune*, June 26, 1913.

12. "Attack Eugenics for High Schools," *Chicago Tribune*.

13. "No Sex Hygiene Teaching in Chicago Public School," *Buffalo Commercial*, June 27, 1913.

14. "Personal Purity Will Be Taught," *Hamilton Spectator*, July 10, 1913.

15. "Sex Hygiene Talks Heard by Students," *Inter Ocean*, Oct. 28, 1913.

16. "Only Two Miss Purity Lectures," *Chicago Tribune*, Oct. 31, 1913; "7 Hygiene Talks Delivered," *Inter Ocean*, Oct. 30, 1913.

17. "Brands Sex Hygiene Course as Futile," *Inter Ocean*, Oct. 29, 1913.

18. "Sex Hygiene Is Discussed," *Leader-Telegram*, Nov. 14, 1913.

19. Leslie Woodcock Tentler, "'The Abominable Crime of Onan': Catholic Pastoral Practice and Family Limitation, 1873–1919," in *Catholics and Contraception: An American History* (Ithaca, NY: Cornell University Press, 2019), 15–42.

20. Tentler, "'The Abominable Crime of Onan.'"

21. Tentler, "'The Abominable Crime of Onan.'"

22. Jeffrey P. Moran, "'Modernism Gone Mad': Sex Education Comes to Chicago, 1913," *Journal of American History* 83, no. 2 (Sept. 1996): 481, https://doi.org/10.2307/2944944.

23. "Sex Teachings Murder Child's Soul," *Town Talk*, Dec. 30, 1913.

24. "Sex Hygiene Talks Barred from Mails," *Inter Ocean*, Nov. 14, 1913.

25. "Sex Hygiene Talks Barred from Mails," *Inter Ocean*.

26. "Altruism in Chicago, Sex Hygiene, Mails Closed to Extracts from Sex Lectures," *Medical Freedom* III, no. 4 (Dec. 1913): 3–4.

27. "Loeb Defends Sex Lectures," *Chicago Tribune*, Nov. 16, 1913.

28. "U.S. Censorship on Mail Likened to That in Russia," *Chicago Tribune*, Nov. 21, 1913.

29. "Mrs. Young Names Carey and Kenna Book 'Influences,'" *Chicago Tribune*, May 29, 1913.

30. "Mrs. Young Quits; Women to Demand She Be Retained," *Chicago Tribune*, July 25, 1913.

31. "Mrs. Young to Stay as Head of Schools," *Inter Ocean*, July 31, 1913.

32. "Board Ousts Ella F. Young; John D. Shoop Heads Schools," *Chicago Tribune*, Dec. 11, 1913.

33. "Board Ousts Ella F. Young," *Chicago Tribune*.

34. "Board Ousts Ella F. Young," *Chicago Tribune*.

35. "Ousting of Ella Flagg Young May Have Far-Reaching Effect in Political Way," *Day Book*, Dec. 11, 1913.

36. "Board Ousts Ella F. Young," *Chicago Tribune*.

37. "Mayor Ousts Five Men from School Board," *Chicago Tribune*, Dec. 13, 1913.

38. "Typos Turn Fire on Sex Hygiene," *Chicago Tribune*, Dec. 29, 1913.

39. "Says Thousands of Kids Hear Sex Hygiene Talks," *Topeka Daily Capital*, Dec. 30, 1913.

40. "School Board Stops Teaching of Sex Hygiene," *Chicago Tribune*, Jan. 8, 1914.

41. "Vitality and Efficiency at Richmond," *Journal of Education* LXXIX, no. 11 (Mar. 12, 1914).

42. "Personal Purity Lectures Success," *Decatur Herald*, June 16, 1914.

43. E. L. Keyes, "Dr. Morrow, the Educator," *Social Diseases* IV, no. 3 (July 1913): 114.

CHAPTER 3: FIT TO FIGHT

1. "Induction Statistics," Selective Service System, https://www.sss.gov/history-and-records/induction-statistics/, accessed Oct. 5, 2024.

2. William C. Gorgas, "The Venereal Diseases and the War," *Social Hygiene* IV, no. 1 (Jan. 1918).

3. M. J. Exner, "Prostitution in Its Relation to the Army on the Mexican Border," *Social Hygiene* III, no. 2 (Apr. 1917): 205–21.

4. William F. Snow, "Social Hygiene and the War," *Social Hygiene* 3 (1917): 417–48.

5. Snow, "Social Hygiene and the War," 417–48.

6. Patricia Spain Ward, "The American Reception of Salvarsan," *Journal of the History of Medicine and Allied Sciences* XXXVI, no. 1 (Jan. 1981): 44–62.

7. Ward, "The American Reception of Salvarsan."

8. US Surgeon General's Office, *The Medical Department of the United States Army in the World War* (Washington, DC: US Government Printing Office, 1927).

9. US Surgeon General's Office, *The Venereal Diseases: An Outline of Their Management* (Chicago: American Medical Association, 1920).

10. Edith Houghton Hooker, "Criticism of Venereal Prophylaxis," *Journal of Social Hygiene* IV, no. 2 (Apr. 1918).

11. Allen M. Brandt, *No Magic Bullet: A Social History of Venereal Disease in the United States Since 1880* (New York: Oxford University Press, 1987).

12. Kimberley A. Reilly, "'A Perilous Venture for Democracy': Soldiers, Sexual Purity, and American Citizenship in the First World War," *Journal of the Gilded Age and Progressive Era* 13, no. 2 (2014): 223–55.

13. Brandt, *No Magic Bullet*, 109.

14. Reilly, "'A Perilous Venture for Democracy.'"

15. E. H. Beardsley, "Allied Against Sin: American and British Responses to Venereal Disease in World War I," *Medical History* 20, no. 2 (Apr. 1976): 189–202.

16. Beardsley, "Allied Against Sin."

17. Aine Collier, *The Humble Little Condom: A History* (Amherst, NY: Prometheus Books, 2010), 187.

18. M. W. Ireland, "Chapter VII: The Venereal Diseases," in *The Medical Department in the United States Army in the World War, Vol. IX: Communicable and Other Diseases* (Washington, DC: US Government Printing Office, 1928), 263.

19. "The Control of Venereal Diseases," *Public Health Reports (1896–1970)* 33, no. 1 (1918): 1–3.

20. Thomas A. Storey, "A Summary of the Work of the United States Interdepartmental Social Hygiene Board, 1919–1920," *Journal of Social Hygiene* VII, no. 1 (Jan. 1921): 76.

21. "Miss Amanda Landes Heads the W.C.T.U.," *Semi-Weekly New Era*, Aug. 31, 1918.

22. "Sex Education in Schools," *Education* XXXIX, no. 9 (May 1919).

23. E. F. Van Buskirk, "The Aim and Scope of Sex Education in the High School," in *Proceedings of Educational Congress: November 17 to 22, 1919* (Harrisburg, PA: J. L. L. Kuhn, Printer to the Commonwealth, 1920).

24. "Division of Venereal Diseases," in *Annual Report of the Surgeon General of the Public Health Service of the United States for the Fiscal Year 1919* (Washington, DC: Government Printing Office, 1919).

25. "Division of Venereal Diseases."

26. Newell W. Edson, *The Status of Sex Education in High Schools* (Washington, DC: US Public Health Service and US Bureau of Education, 1921).

27. "Public Instruction," *Department Reports of Pennsylvania* VI, no. 37 (Sept. 10, 1920): 2088.

28. Sina Stratton, "Racial Force—An Important Factor in the Development of the Child," in *Proceedings of Educational Congress*.

29. Garland E. Allen, "The Misuse of Biological Hierarchies: The American Eugenics Movement, 1900–1940," *History and Philosophy of the Life Sciences* 5, no. 2 (1983): 105–28.

30. Percy W. Toombs, "Parenthood and Race Culture," *Journal of Heredity* 14, no. 1 (Apr. 1923).

31. Stratton, "Racial Force."

32. "Says Sex Talks Are at Option of School Boards," *Evening News*, Dec. 16, 1921.

33. United News, "A Question of What Should Be Taught," *Morning News*, Dec. 29, 1921.

34. Ira S. Wile, "The Problem of Sex Instruction as Viewed by Boards of Education," *Journal of the Society of Sanitary and Moral Prophylaxis* VI, no. 4 (Oct. 1915): 141–48.

35. "Says Sex Talks," *Evening News*.

36. International News Services, "Put Restriction on Lecturers for the State," *Evening News*, Dec. 15, 1921.

37. "Dr. Stratton Defends Her Lectures on Sex," *Evening News*, Dec. 20, 1921.

38. "Dr. Stratton, of Philadelphia, Made Two Addresses Last Thursday to High School Students," *Wellsboro Gazette Combined with Mansfield Advertiser*, Feb. 15, 1922.

39. "Sex Education Is Banned Here by School Board," *Capital Times*, Jan. 17, 1923.

CHAPTER 4: THOMAS PARRAN AND THE "NEXT GREAT PLAGUE TO GO"

1. US Interdepartmental Social Hygiene Board Records, MS C 558, Archives and Modern Manuscripts Collections, National Library of Medicine.

2. US Interdepartmental Social Hygiene Board, *Report of the United States Interdepartmental Social Hygiene Board* (Washington, DC: US Government Printing Office, 1920), 16.

3. Michael Imber, "The First World War, Sex Education, and the American Social Hygiene Association's Campaign Against Venereal Disease," *Journal of Educational Administration and History* 16, no. 1 (Jan. 1984): 49, https://doi.org /10.1080/0022062840160106.

4. Imber, "The First World War, Sex Education, and the American Social Hygiene Association's Campaign Against Venereal Disease," 49.

5. Virginia Committee on Training Camp Activities, Virginia State Board of Charities and Corrections, *Virginia Laws for the Suppression of Vice* (Richmond, VA: Davis Bottom, Superintendent Public Printing, 1917).

6. Ennion G. Williams, "Social Hygiene," *The Virginia Journal of Education* 23, no. 4 (Dec. 1929).

7. *Report of the Bureau of Social Hygiene, July, 1925, to July, 1926*, Report of the State Commissioner of Health (Commonwealth of Virginia, 1926).

8. Fereba B. Croxton, *Report of the Bureau of Social Hygiene, July, 1926, to July, 1927*, Report of the State Commissioner of Health (Commonwealth of Virginia, 1927).

9. Croxton, *Report of the Bureau of Social Hygiene*.

10. Allen M. Brandt, *No Magic Bullet: A Social History of Venereal Disease in the United States Since 1880* (New York: Oxford University Press, 1987), 124; *Report of the Bureau of Social Hygiene, July 1925, to July 1926*.

11. "Appendix X," in *Report of State Board of Health and the State Health Commissioner to the Governor of Virginia for the Biennium Ending June 30, 1925* (Richmond, VA: Davis Bottom, Superintendent Public Printing, 1925).

12. George Elliott Howard, "Bad Marriage and Quick Divorce," *Journal of Applied Sociology* VI, no. 2 (Dec. 1921).

13. John M. Cooper, "Human Welfare and the Monogamous Ideal," *Social Hygiene* VI, no. 4 (Oct. 1920).

14. Maurice A. Bigelow, "The Established Points in Social Hygiene Education, 1905–1924," *Social Hygiene* X, no. 1 (Jan. 1924).

15. Benjamin C. Gruenberg, *High Schools and Sex Education: A Manual of Suggestions on Education Related to Sex* (Washington, DC: US Government Printing Office, 1922).

16. John D. Wolcott, "New Books in Education," *School Life* VIII, no. 4 (Dec. 1922): 91; "Sex Education," *Journal of Education* XCVI, no. 20 (Nov. 30, 1922): 551; "Recent and Periodical Literature," *Eugenics Review* XV (Apr. 1923): 441.

17. *Report of the State Department of Health and the State Health Commissioner to the Governor of Virginia* (Richmond, 1928).

18. Lida J. Usilton and Newell W. Edson, "The Status of Sex Education in the Senior High Schools of the United States in 1927," *V.D. Bulletin* (Washington, DC: Division of Venereal Diseases, 1928).

19. Usilton and Edson, "Status of Sex Education."

20. Ennion G. Williams, "Social Hygiene," *Virginia Journal of Education* 23, no. 4 (Dec. 1929), https://archive.org/details/sim_virginia-journal-of-education_1929-09_23_1/mode/2up.

21. Williams, "Social Hygiene."

22. "Social Hygiene," *Annual Report of the State Department of Health* (Commonwealth of Virginia, 1931).

23. Usilton and Edson, "The Status of Sex Education in the Senior High Schools."

24. Gruenberg, *High Schools and Sex Education*.

25. US Public Health Service Division of Venereal Diseases, *The National Venereal Disease Control Program* (Washington, DC: Federal Security Agency, Public Health Service, Division of Venereal Disease of the Bureau of State Services, 1951).

26. Brandt, *No Magic Bullet*, 129.

27. Brandt, *No Magic Bullet*, 133.

28. Thomas Parran, "Stamp Out Syphilis," *Survey Graphic*, July 1936.

29. "TIME Magazine Cover: Dr. Thomas Parran Jr.—Oct. 26, 1936," *Time*, https://content.time.com/time/covers/0,16641,19361026,00.html, accessed Oct. 6, 2024.

30. John J. Wright, "Venereal Disease Control," *Journal of the American Medical Association* 147, no. 15 (Dec. 8, 1951): 1408, https://doi.org/10.1001/jama.1951.03670320008004.

31. Brandt, *No Magic Bullet*, 146.

32. Brandt, *No Magic Bullet*, 147.

33. Maurice A. Bigelow, "Sex Education in America Today," *Journal of Social Hygiene* 24, no. 9 (Dec. 1938).

34. Bigelow, "Sex Education in America Today," 532.

35. "Sex Education Courses Opposed by Dr. Bigelow," *Press and Sun-Bulletin*, Nov. 9, 1939.

36. Brandt, *No Magic Bullet*, 158.

37. National Museum of American History, "Liquid Latex Prophylactic," https://americanhistory.si.edu/collections/nmah_892350, accessed Oct. 6, 2024; Joshua Gamson, "Rubber Wars: Struggles over the Condom in the United States," *Journal of the History of Sexuality* 1, no. 2 (1990): 262–82.

38. Maria T. Vullo, "People v. Sanger and the Birth of Family Planning Clinics in America," *Judicial Notice* (blog), n.d., https://history.nycourts.gov/people-v-sanger-birth-family-planning-clinics-in-america/.

39. Margaret Sanger, "Principles and Aims of the American Birth Control League," in *The Pivot of Civilization* (New York: Brentano's Publishers, 1922).

40. "Tracing One Package—The Case That Legalized Birth Control," *Margaret Sanger Papers Project Newsletter*, Winter 2011, https://sanger.hosting.nyu.edu/articles/tracing_one_package/.

41. "Tracing One Package"; Malladi Lakshmeeramya, "*United States v. One Package of Japanese Pessaries* (1936)," *Embryo Project Encyclopedia* (May 24, 2017), https://embryo.asu.edu/pages/united-states-v-one-package-japanese-pessaries-1936, ISSN: 1940-5030, https://hdl.handle.net/10776/11516.

42. "Tracing One Package."

43. "Tracing One Package."

44. Brandt, *No Magic Bullet*, 159.

45. H. H. Hazen et al., "The Chemical and Mechanical Prevention of Syphilis and Gonorrhea: Preliminary Statement by the Special Joint Committee Appointed by the American Social Hygiene Association and the United States Public Health Service," *Venereal Disease Information* 21 (1940): 311.

CHAPTER 5: ELLSWORTH BUCK'S DRIVE TO EDUCATE NEW YORK CITY

1. "Report in Reference to General Science Course of Study," *Journal of the Board of Education of the City of New York City* 2 (Nov. 9, 1938): 2467.

2. "Report in Reference to General Science Course of Study," 2467.

3. "Report in Reference to General Science Course of Study," 2469.

4. Eugene R. Canudo, *The Case for Rational Sex Instruction in New York City Schools: A Report to Ellsworth B. Buck* (1939), 5.

5. Canudo, *The Case for Rational Sex Instruction in New York City Schools*, 6.

6. Canudo, *The Case for Rational Sex Instruction in New York City Schools*, 16.

7. Carl Warren, "96 Unwed Mothers Under 16 Here in '38," *Daily News*, Jan. 31, 1939.

8. "Sex Education Up to Parents, Teachers Say," *Brooklyn Daily Eagle*, Feb. 21, 1939.

9. "From the Managing Editor's Desk," *The Tablet*, Mar. 4, 1939.

10. "From the Managing Editor's Desk."

11. "Sex Education Test Is Urged Over 3 Years," *Daily News*, Feb. 10, 1939.

12. "Parents Approve Sex Education," *Brooklyn Daily Eagle*, Mar. 8, 1939.

13. "Supports Sex Education in Junior High Schools," *Brooklyn Daily Eagle*, Mar. 28, 1939.

14. Ellsworth B. Buck, "Our Public Schools and Sex," *American Mercury*, May 1939.

15. "Schools Name 8 for Survey of Sex Course," *Daily News*, June 30, 1939.

16. "What Is Behind It?" *The Tablet*, July 8, 1939.

17. Ellsworth B. Buck, George J. Lent, and Francis S. Moseley, "Should Public Schools Teach the 'Facts of Life'? A Debate," *Forum and Century*, Oct. 1939.

18. William F. Snow, "Social Hygiene in Schools," *Report of the Subcommittee on Social Hygiene in Schools*, White House Conference on Child Health and Protection (New York: The Century Co., 1932), 14, available at https://babel .hathitrust.org/cgi/pt?id=uva.x004914756&view=1up&seq=21&skin=2021.

19. "Sex Education Held 'Dead Issue,'" *Daily News*, Nov. 29, 1939.

CHAPTER 6: WORLD WAR II

1. Walter Clarke, "Syphilis, Gonorrhea, and The National Defense Program," *Journal of Social Hygiene* 26, no. 8 (Nov. 1940): 341–52.

2. US Army and Navy, "The National Point of View Regarding the Control of Venereal Disease in Wartime," *Journal of Social Hygiene* 29, no. 4 (May 1943).

3. Allen M. Brandt, *No Magic Bullet: A Social History of Venereal Disease in the United States Since 1880* (New York: Oxford University Press, 1987), 164.

4. Brandt, *No Magic Bullet*, 164.

5. "The Annual Business Meeting," *Journal of Social Hygiene* 29, no. 3 (Mar. 1943): 179.

6. T. J. Carter, "New Patterns in Venereal Disease Control, as Seen by the Navy Medical Officer," *Journal of Social Hygiene* 29, no. 4 (Apr. 1943).

7. Carter, "New Patterns in Venereal Disease Control," 211.

8. "Teamwork in Venereal Disease Prevention," *Journal of Social Hygiene* 30, no. 3 (Mar. 1944): 3.

9. "Teamwork in Venereal Disease Prevention."

10. Winfred Overholser, "Who Are the Juvenile Delinquents?" *Journal of Social Hygiene* 30, no. 5 (May 1944): 5

11. Overholser, "Who Are the Juvenile Delinquents?" 5.

12. "Expansion of Sex Education in Schools Urged by PTA," *Los Angeles Times*, Sept. 25, 1942.

13. Maurice A. Bigelow, "Why Youth Should Know the Important Facts About Venereal Disease," *Journal of Social Hygiene* 29, no. 9 (Dec. 1943).

14. Bigelow, "Why Youth Should Know the Important Facts About Venereal Disease."

15. Richard A. Koch and Ray Lyman Wilbur, "Promiscuity as a Factor in the Spread of Venereal Disease," *Journal of Social Hygiene* 30, no. 9 (Dec. 1944).

16. J. R. Heller Jr., "Venereal Disease Control of Tomorrow," *Journal of Social Hygiene* 31, no. 1 (Jan. 1945).

17. John Parascandola, "John Mahoney and the Introduction of Penicillin to Treat Syphilis," *Pharmacy in History* 43, no. 1 (Jan. 2001): 3–13.

18. "Sex Education in D.C. Schools Under Review," *Washington Post*, Apr. 23, 1943.

19. "High School Sex Training Made Public," *Washington Post*, Apr. 25, 1943.

20. "School Board Member Objects to Teaching of Sex Education: Gannon Objects to Course in Sex Education," *Washington Post*, Apr. 22, 1943.

21. "Dr. Gannon's Sex Statement Is Criticized," *Washington Post*, Apr. 24, 1943.

22. "Educators Review Sex Study Today," *Washington Post*, Apr. 27, 1943.

23. "Sex Education," *Washington Post*, May 1, 1943.

24. Helene Champlain, "Simplified Sex Course Approved: Dr. J. A. Gannon Satisfied with New Plan Suggested for District Schools," *Washington Post*, May 20, 1943.

25. Champlain, "Simplified Sex Course Approved."

26. Cole E. Morgan, "Growing Delinquency in Capital Revealed," *San Francisco Examiner*, Nov. 26, 1943.

27. Morgan, "Growing Delinquency in Capital Revealed."

28. Paul Mallon, "Common Sense Teaching Is Back," *The Dispatch*, Sept. 8, 1944.

CHAPTER 7: THE BIRTH AND BOYCOTT OF THE SEX ED FILM

1. American Institute of Public Opinion, George Gallup, "The Gallup Poll: High School Courses in Sex Education Favored by Big Vote in National Survey," *Washington Post*, June 4, 1943.

2. Associated Press, "More, Better Sex Education Urged for Delinquent Youths," *Washington Post*, Dec. 2, 1943.

3. "Deficient Instruction in Biology in High Schools," *Journal of the American Medical Association* 125, no. 5 (June 3, 1944): 356–57, https://doi.org/10.1001/jama.1944.02850230036012.

4. "Notes on Recent State Activities Relating to Sex Education," *Journal of Social Hygiene* 31, no. 4 (Apr. 1945).

5. Dale L. Womble, "The E. C. Brown Foundation: A Pioneering Enterprise in Family Life and Sex Education," *Family Relations* 32, no. 2 (1983): 173–78, https://doi.org/10.2307/584675.

6. Elizabeth Peterson and Michael Aronson, "No Birds, No Bees, No Moralizing: Lester F. Beck, Progressive Educational Filmmaker," *Moving Image: The Journal of the Association of Moving Image Archivists* 14, no. 1 (2014): 49–70, https://doi.org/10.5749/movingimage.14.1.0049.

7. Peterson and Aronson, "No Birds, No Bees, No Moralizing," 49–70.

8. "Sex Education," *Life*, May 24, 1948.

9. "School Children Here to See Film on Sex Education," *Nevada State Journal*, May 2, 1948.

10. Associated Press, "Sex Education in High School Wins PTA Nod," *News-Review*, Mar. 22, 1949.

11. Associated Press, "Oregon Sex Film Popular," *Herald and News*, Oct. 7, 1949.

12. Evelyn Imel, "Association Goes to Bat on Sex Education," *Indianapolis Star*, Oct. 31, 1948.

13. Anna Jane Phillips, "Sex Education," *Pittsburgh Post-Gazette*, June 12, 1949.

14. "Sex Education in Schools Urged in Report by State Committee," *Central New Jersey Home News*, Apr. 1, 1948.

15. "State Agencies List Guide to Sex Education," *News-Palladium*, June 24, 1948.

16. "McGrath Favors Sex Education in School," *Casper Star-Tribune*, Mar. 18, 1949.

17. Juanita R. Krentzman, "92 Per Cent of Florida Students Want to Study About Marriage, Surveys Show," *Tampa Bay Times*, Feb. 23, 1948.

18. "Most Youths Want School to Provide Instruction in Sex," *Press and Sun-Bulletin*, Aug. 6, 1948.

19. Edyth Thomas Wallace, "Our Homes: Shall School Curriculum Include Sex Education?" *Daily Oklahoman*, Mar. 14, 1948.

20. "Most Voters Believe Teaching Methods in Iowa Have Improved," *Des Moines Register*, Apr. 11, 1948.

21. "Sex Education Has No Place in Grammar School, Declare Police Psychiratist [sic]," *La Grande Observer*, June 23, 1948.

22. "Communists Accused of Using Sex Education in Schools," *San Bernardino County Sun*, Mar. 5, 1951.

23. "Catholic Statement Condemns School Films on Sex Education," *Courier Journal*, Mar. 31, 1949.

24. "Catholic Statement Condemns School Films on Sex Education."

25. "Protect All Children," *Catholic Courier Journal*, Apr. 7, 1949.

26. "Catholics Demand State Drop School Sex Program," *Catholic Advance*, Oct. 21, 1949.

27. "Sex Education Will Continue," *Journal News*, Nov. 29, 1949.

28. "Bishop Assails School Film," *Daily News*, Dec. 5, 1949.

29. "Catholic Boycott of Sex Film Urged," *Evening Sun*, Dec. 10, 1949.

30. "Bars Catholic Children from Sex Education Classes," *Minneapolis Star*, Dec. 12, 1949.

31. "Bars Catholic Children from Sex Education Classes."

32. "Catholic Women Take Sex Education Stand," *Morning News*, Oct. 18, 1950.

33. "Catholic Bishops Denounce Sex Education in the Schools," *Boston Globe*, Nov. 19, 1950.

34. "Pope Condemns Sex Education," *Kane Republican*, Sept. 19, 1951.

35. W. H. Aufranc, "Are Venereal Diseases Disappearing?" *Journal of Social Hygiene* 36, no. 8 (Nov. 1950).

36. Wardell B. Pomeroy, "Masturbation," in *Foundations for Christian Family Policy: The Proceedings of the North American Conference on Church and Family* (New York: Dept. on Family Life, National Council of the Churches of Christ in the USA., 1961), http://archive.org/details/foundationsforch0000nort.

37. Pomeroy, "Masturbation."

38. Kinsey Institute, *75 Years: Kinsey Institute, Indiana University*, https://kinseyinstitute.org/pdf/75th_Anniversary_Historical_Review.pdf, accessed Aug. 31, 2024.

39. Francis Sill Wickware, "Report on Kinsey," *Life*, Aug. 2, 1948.

40. Wickware, "Report on Kinsey."

41. Alfred C. Kinsey, Wardell B. Pomeroy, and Clyde E. Martin, *Sexual Behavior in the Human Male* (Philadelphia: W. B. Saunders Co., 1949).

42. Kinsey, Pomeroy, and Martin, *Sexual Behavior in the Human Male*.

43. "Blasts Kinsey Report," *Wilmington Daily Press Journal*, Aug. 24, 1953.

44. "Sounds Like Red Plot," *News Journal*, Sept. 23, 1953.

45. "Sexual Behavior: How Shall We Define and Motivate What Is Acceptable?" *Journal of Social Hygiene* 36, no. 4 (Apr. 1950).

46. "Religion: Sex Before Marriage," *Time*, Feb. 13, 1950.

47. George Sokolsky, "More on Euthanasia," *Record American*, Feb. 9, 1950.

48. "Sex Anarchy," *America: National Catholic Weekly Review*, Feb. 25, 1950.

49. Lester A. Kirkendall, "Sound Attitudes Toward Sex," *Journal of Social Hygiene* 37, no. 6 (June 1951).

50. Kirkendall, "Sound Attitudes Toward Sex."

51. "Two Schools of Sexology," *Monroe News-Star,* Jan. 8, 1952.

CHAPTER 8: SEX ED AND FAMILY LIFE EDUCATION IN THE 1950S

1. "Improvident Thrift," *Journal of Social Hygiene* 40, no. 3 (Mar. 1954): 97–98.

2. "Improvident Thrift," 97–98.

3. Philip R. Mather, "The Job Ahead," *Journal of Social Hygiene* 40, no. 5 (May 1954): 162–63.

4. American Social Hygiene Association, "First Rise Seen in Eight Years," *Social Hygiene News* 32, no. 2 (Feb. 1957): 1–2.

5. Shirley Prince Kurlander, "Grade School-Aged Pupils Show Greatest Rise of VD," *Indianapolis Star,* Jan. 28, 1960.

6. Joan Beck, "The Shocking Facts About Teen-Age Sex: Tawdry Movies and Magazines, Timid Parents and Schools Are Keeping Our Youngsters in Ignorance—and Jeopardy," *Chicago Sunday Tribune Magazine*, May 22, 1960.

7. New York Times Service, "Schools Gun-Shy on 'Hot' Issue," *Detroit Free Press*, June 29, 1953.

8. Elena M. Sliepcevich, "VD Education in Schools," *Journal of Social Hygiene* 40, no. 7 (Oct. 1954): 259–65.

9. "Annual Joint Statement Notes National VD Increase—Spotlights Teenage Rise," *Social Health News* 35, no. 2 (Feb. 1960).

10. "Survey VD Teaching," *Social Hygiene News* 32, no. 8 (Oct. 1957).

11. "Teenage VD Study Scores Public Attitudes; Sex Taboos, Class Biases and Ignorance Cited as Factors Impeding VD Control," *Social Health News* 36, no. 6 (June 1961).

12. "Sex Education and VD," *Leaf-Chronicle*, June 28, 1961.

13. Nolan C. Kearney, "Sex Education in the Public Schools and Factors Affecting It," *Social Hygiene Papers: A Symposium on Sex Education*, Nov. 1957, https://archive.org/details/sim_social-health-news_1957-11_32/mode/2up?q=%22Sex+Education+In+The+Public+Schools+And+Factors+Affecting+It%22.

14. Judson T. Landis, "Community Responsibility in Family Life," *Journal of Social Hygiene* 37, no. 4 (Apr. 1951): 153–62.

15. Kearney, "Sex Education in the Public Schools and Factors Affecting It."

16. "Decision on Sex Education Course Deferred by Board," *The Missoulian*, Feb. 7, 1962.

17. "Decision on Sex Education Course Deferred by Board."

18. "Great Bend Teacher Loses Job Over Sex Education Material," *Olathe News*, Mar. 23, 1961.

19. "Great Bend Teacher Is Losing Job Because of Stand on Sex Education," *Emporia Gazette*, Mar. 22, 1961.

CHAPTER 9: THE FIRST NORTH AMERICAN CONFERENCE ON CHURCH AND FAMILY

1. North American Conference on Church and Family, *Foundations for Christian Family Policy: The Proceedings of the North American Conference on Church and Family* (New York: Dept. on Family Life, National Council of the Churches of Christ in the USA, 1961).

2. Evelyn M. Duvall and Sylvanus M. Duvall, *Sex Ways in Fact and Faith: Bases for Christian Family Policy* (New York: Association Press, 1961).

3. Harold T. Christensen, "Pregnant Brides—Record Linkage Studies," in Duvall and Duvall, *Sex Ways in Fact and Faith*, 101–17.

4. Evelyn Hooker, "Homosexuality," in North American Conference on Church and Family, *Foundations for Christian Family Policy*, 166–89.

5. David Mace, "The Services of Worship," in North American Conference on Church and Family, *Foundations for Christian Family Policy*, 1–19.

6. John Charles Wynn, "Where the Churches Speak and Where They Are Silent," in North American Conference on Church and Family, *Foundations for Christian Family Policy*, 1–19.

7. Ed Keister, "Is the Church Changing Its Mind About Sex?" *St. Louis Post-Dispatch*, Oct. 1, 1961.

8. *Year Book of the Michigan Congregational Christian Conference: With Minutes of the Annual Meeting Held in Together with and Statistics, 1963*, Michigan Congregational Christian Conference.

9. Walter R. Stokes, "Sex Education of Children," *Advances in Sex Research* 1 (1963): 48–60.

10. Edmund Willingham, "Church Aid Urged in Sex Education," *The Tennessean*, Mar. 2, 1963.

CHAPTER 10: THE BIRTH OF SIECUS

1. Ellen S. More, "A Sex Education Apprenticeship: Calderone and Planned Parenthood," in *The Transformation of American Sex Education: Mary Calderone and the Fight for Sexual Health* (New York: New York University Press, 2022), 66.

2. More, "A Sex Education Apprenticeship."

3. Committee, US Congress Senate Agriculture and Forestry, *Food for Freedom Program and Commodity Reserves: Hearings Before the Committee on Agriculture and Forestry S. 2157, S. 2826, S. 2932, June 15, 1966*, p. 456.

4. More, "A Sex Education Apprenticeship," 69.

5. Mary Steichen Calderone, "Illegal Abortion as a Public Health Problem," *American Journal of Public Health* 50, no. 7 (July 1960): 948–54, https://doi.org/10.2105/AJPH.50.7.948.

6. "Playboy Interview: Mary Calderone, MD," in *Sex, American Style*, ed. Frank M. Robinson and Nat Lehrman (Chicago: Playboy Press, 1971), 277–335.

7. Lester Kirkendall, interview, Feb. 19, 1984, College of Home Economics Oral Histories, Oregon State University, http://scarc.library.oregonstate.edu /omeka/exhibits/show/oralhistory/item/33761.

8. Lester A. Kirkendall and A. E. Gravatt, "Teen-Agers' Sex Attitudes and Behavior," in *Sex Ways in Fact and Faith: Bases for Christian Family Policy*, ed. Evelyn M. Duvall and Sylvanus M. Duvall (New York: Association Press, 1961), 1–19.

9. "1962–1969: Education. Education Division, General Sex Information and Education Council of the United States (SIECUS)," box 094, folder 08, Social Welfare History Archives, University of Minnesota Libraries, https:// umedia.lib.umn.edu/item/p16022coll223:160223, accessed Oct. 9, 2024.

10. "1962–1969: Education."

11. "Clergy, Educators, Social Workers Form New Sex Education Council," *Journal Times*, Jan. 9, 1965.

12. David Lam, "How the World Survived the Population Bomb: Lessons from 50 Years of Extraordinary Demographic History," *Demography* 48, no. 4 (Nov. 2011): 1231–62, https://doi.org/10.1007/s13524-011-0070-z.

13. Lam, "How the World Survived the Population Bomb."

14. John R. Wilmoth and Patrick Ball, "Arguments and Action in the Life of a Social Problem: A Case Study of 'Overpopulation,' 1946–1990," *Social Problems* 42, no. 3 (1995): 318–43, https://doi.org/10.2307/3096851.

15. Irwin Slesnick, "Population Expansion and Birth Control: An Appropriate Problem for High School Study," *American Biology Teacher* 26, no. 8 (Dec. 1, 1964): 581–84, https://doi.org/10.2307/4440761.

16. Slesnick, "Population Expansion and Birth Control," 581–84.

17. Harriet F. Pilpel, "New Policies," *SIECUS Newsletter* 1, no. 2 (Summer 1965): 1–2.

18. "Sex Education in Schools Is Given Backing," *Chicago Tribune*, Nov. 18, 1964.

19. Olga Curtis, Women's News Service, "Sex Education Fails to Tell Things Teens Need to Know," *Star Press*, Oct. 10, 1963.

20. *Population Crisis: Hearings Before the United States Senate Committee on Government Operations, Subcommittee on Foreign Aid Expenditures*, Eighty-Ninth Congress, first session, June 22, 1965, https://babel.hathitrust.org/cgi/pt?id=umn .31951d02135246t&view=1up&seq=33&q1=Mary+Calderone.

21. Mary S. Calderone, "SIECUS: Its Present and Its Future," *SIECUS Newsletter* 1, no. 2 (Summer 1965): 1–2.

22. Curtis E. Avery, "Sex Education Through Rose Colored Glasses," *Family Life Coordinator* 13, no. 4 (1964): 83–90, https://doi.org/10.2307/581534.

23. Avery, "Sex Education Through Rose Colored Glasses."

24. American Social Health Association, "Joint Statement on VD Recommends 14 Million Dollar Federal Appropriation," *Social Health News* 40, no. 3 (Mar. 1965): 1.

25. American Medical Association, "American Medical Association Opens Campaign Against VD; Called Nation's Most Urgent Communicable Disease Problem," *Social Health News* 40, no. 8 (Oct. 1965): 1.

26. Lester A. Kirkendall, "SIECUS Discussion Guide No. 1: Sex Education," SIECUS, 1965.

27. "Doctor Says Nation Needs Sex Education Program," *Gazette and Daily*, Apr. 14, 1965.

28. George Packer Berry, "The SIECUS Purpose: SIECUS 1967—Retrospect and Prospect," *SIECUS Newsletter* 2, no. 4 (Winter 1967): 1–2.

29. Berry, "The SIECUS Purpose," 1–2.

30. "U.S. Office of Education Support," *SIECUS Newsletter* 2, no. 4 (1967): 1–2.

31. "Playboy Interview: Mary Calderone, MD."

CHAPTER II: THE RELIGIOUS RIGHT COMES FOR SIECUS

1. "Couple Opposes School Sex Film," *Independent*, Aug. 1, 1962.

2. "Couple Opposes School Sex Film."

3. "Couple Opposes School Sex Film."

4. Sally R. Williams, "Family Life and Sex Education," *Bulletin of the National Association of Secondary School Principals* 52, no. 326 (Mar. 1, 1968): 49–55, https://doi.org/10.1177/019263656805232608.

5. "Let Homes Handle Sex Instruction," *Press-Telegram*, Sept. 14, 1962.

6. "Let Homes Handle Sex Instruction."

7. Anaheim Union High School District, "Family Life and Sex Education Course Outline: Grades Seven Through Twelve," Trinity College, June 1967, http://commons.trincoll.edu/edreform/files/2012/04/AnaheimSexEd1967.pdf.

8. "Citizens Group Names Leader," *Los Angeles Times*, Dec. 20, 1962.

9. "Sex Education Courses Recommended for AUHS," *Anaheim Gazette*, Mar. 5, 1964.

10. Anaheim Union High School District, "Family Life and Sex Education Course Outline."

11. Anaheim Union High School District, "Family Life and Sex Education Course Outline."

12. "Sex Education Courses Recommended."

13. "Sex Education Courses Recommended."

14. Anaheim Union High School District, "Family Life and Sex Education Course Outline."

15. "Suggested Content for the Ninth Grade," in Sally Williams and Esther D. Schulz, *Family Life and Sex Education: Curriculum and Instruction* (New York: Harcourt, Brace & World, 1968).

16. Anaheim Union High School District, "Family Life and Sex Education Course Outline," 24.

17. Vi Ehinger, "Sex Education in Anaheim Schools Gaining Acceptance," *Los Angeles Times*, Aug. 7, 1966.

18. Vi Smith, "Anaheim Considers Program Successful," *Los Angeles Times*, Nov. 26, 1967.

19. Smith, "Anaheim Considers Program Successful."

20. "Teen-Agers and VD," *Social Health News* 43, no. 5 (1968).

21. "1962–1969: Education. Education Division, General Sex Information and Education Council of the United States (SIECUS)," box 094, folder 08,

Social Welfare History Archives, University of Minnesota Libraries, https://umedia.lib.umn.edu/item/p16022coll223:160223, accessed Oct. 9, 2024.

22. Mary S. Calderone, "Foreword," in Williams and Schulz, *Family Life and Sex Education.*

23. Frances Breed and Mary S. Calderone, "Community Responsibility for Sex Education," *SIECUS Newsletter* 3, no. 1 (Spring 1967): 1–2.

24. Breed and Calderone, "Community Responsibility for Sex Education."

25. Derro Evans, "Committee to Map Plans for Sex Education Classes," *Austin American,* July 14, 1966.

26. "Sex Education Plan to Get Further Study," *The Argus,* July 14, 1966.

27. Brad O'Hearn, "Sex Education—Base for a Value System," *Morning Call,* July 21, 1966.

28. Lisa McGirr, *Suburban Warriors: The Origins of the New American Right* (Princeton, NJ: Princeton University Press, 2015).

29. "Benjamin R. Epstein and Arnold Forster, "The War Against Civil Rights," in *Report on the John Birch Society, 1966* (New York: Vintage Books, 1966).

30. McGirr, "Preface to the New Edition," in *Suburban Warriors.*

31. McGirr, "Introduction," in *Suburban Warriors,* 11.

32. Frank Capell, "A Look at Sex Education," *Herald of Freedom,* June 14, 1968.

33. Gordon V. Drake, *Is the Schoolhouse the Proper Place to Teach Raw Sex?* (Tulsa, OK: Christian Crusade Publications, 1968).

34. "On Teaching Children About Sex," *Time,* June 9, 1967.

35. "On Teaching Children About Sex."

36. William Stuart McBirnie, *The Truth About the New Sex Education in the Schools* (Glendale, CA: Center for American Research and Education, 1968), 31.

37. Mary Neiswender, "Teachers Divided on Sex Education," *Independent,* Dec. 16, 1969.

38. Jack Hyles, *Sex Education Program in Our Public Schools: What Is Behind It?* (Murfreesboro, TN: Sword of the Lord Publishers, 1969).

39. "Westchester Birchers Drive Against Sex Education," *Mount Vernon Argus,* Apr. 2, 1969.

40. Hal Lancaster, "Birch Society Emphasizes MOTOREDE—Movement to Restore Decency," *News-Pilot,* May 14, 1969.

41. "Sex Education Foes to Meet," *Capital Times,* Aug. 4, 1969.

42. Mary S. Calderone, "Sex Education and the American Democratic Process," *SIECUS Newsletter* 4, no. 4 (1969).

43. "Support for Schools' Program," *San Luis Obispo County Telegram-Tribune,* Mar. 12, 1968.

44. "Support for Schools' Program."

45. Gilbert Moore, "Board Compromises on Sex Education," *San Luis Obispo County Telegram-Tribune,* May 1, 1968.

46. "Sex Education Program by Mrs. Joseph Sarullo," *The Tribune,* Nov. 25, 1968.

47. Jack Magee, "Parents' Suit Asks Halt to Sex Education Classes," *The Tribune,* Sept. 13, 1968.

48. "Parents Debate Sex in Tustin Schools Issue," *Tustin News*, Mar. 21, 1968.

49. "Adverse Side of Sex Class Given Council," *Tustin News*, Mar. 28, 1968.

50. "Mother's Group to Oppose Sex Education in Schools," *Pasadena Independent*, May 9, 1968.

51. Sharon Hoagland, "Sex Education Foes Hit Lax Moral Instruction," *Tustin News*, May 23, 1968.

52. Hoagland, "Sex Education Foes Hit Lax Moral Instruction."

53. "Legislator Asks Probe of Sex Ed," *Courier-News*, Mar. 19, 1969.

54. "Sex Education in Parsippany: Noncontroversial, of Course," *Herald-News*, Apr. 12, 1968.

55. "Opposition to Sex Education Seen Mounting in Parsippany," *Herald-News*, Apr. 29, 1968.

56. "Opposition to Sex Education Seen Mounting in Parsippany."

57. Lee Hickling, "Schools Face Sex Education Protests," *Courier-News*, June 23, 1969.

58. "Sex Education Near in Parsippany," *The News*, July 8, 1969.

59. "Sex Education Near in Parsippany."

60. "Rally Set by Group," *Orlando Evening Star*, May 5, 1969.

61. Eric Sharp, "Orlando Forges Out Sex Course," *Miami News*, Sept. 30, 1969.

62. Eric Sharp, "Sex Education Plan Caused a Bitter Fight," *Miami Herald*, Oct. 6, 1969.

63. Charlie Jean, "Foes of Sex Education Pledge 12,000 for Suit," *Orlando Sentinel*, Nov. 3, 1969.

64. "Sex Classes Bill Cleared for Hearing," *Shreveport Times*, May 13, 1969.

65. Edgar P. Coltharp, "Committee Approves Bill Curbing Sex Education," *Shreveport Times*, May 21, 1969.

66. Harry Taylor, "Sex Education Neither Sexy, Popular," *Shreveport Journal*, May 21, 1969; Edgar Coltharp, "Sex Teaching Bill Passes House Vote," *Shreveport Times*, May 29, 1969.

67. "Sex Classes Bill Cleared for Hearing."

68. "Sex Classes Bill Cleared for Hearing."

69. James Bow, "State School Board OKs Sex Education," *San Bernardino County Sun*, Apr. 11, 1969.

70. Bow, "State School Board OKs Sex Education."

71. "State Roundup by Senator John Schmit," *Tustin News*, Feb. 27, 1969.

72. "State Roundup by Senator John Schmit."

73. "Bill Filed to Ban Compulsory Sex Education (CNS)," *Tracy Press*, Mar. 5, 1969.

74. Tom Arden, "Senate Group Urges 'Freeze' on Sex Education," *Sacramento Bee*, Apr. 17, 1969.

75. Arden, "Senate Group Urges 'Freeze' on Sex Education."

76. "Sen. Schmitz Measure Urges Existing Sex Education Remain Voluntary," *Sacramento Bee*, May 7, 1969.

77. "Sex Class Choice Bill Is Passed by Assembly," *Sacramento Bee*, July 31, 1969.

78. UPI, "Parents Given Option Over Sex Education," *Progress Bulletin*, Aug. 30, 1969.

79. Warren Groshong, "Sex Education Course; School Board Says 'Go,'" *The Tribune*, Feb. 19, 1969.

80. Groshong, "Sex Education Course; School Board Says 'Go.'"

81. Jack Magee, "Sex Class Opponents File Appeal," *The Tribune*, Mar. 26, 1969.

82. "Sex Ed Group's Chairman Quits," *Tustin News*, Aug. 29, 1968.

83. "Sex Ed Group's Chairman Quits."

84. "Sex Class Dropped, Narcotics Study Undertaken by Committee," *Tustin News*, Oct. 31, 1968.

85. "Sex Class Dropped."

86. "Legislator Asks Probe of Sex Ed," *Courier-News*, Mar. 19, 1969.

87. "Legislator Asks Probe of Sex Ed."

88. Michael Stoddard, "Senate Delays Beginning of Sex Education Programs in Schools," *Herald-News*, July 3, 1969.

89. "Baptist Pastor Set to Oppose Sex Education," *Herald-News*, Aug. 1, 1969.

90. "Parents Protest Sex Instruction," *Asbury Park Press*, Aug. 15, 1969.

91. Doris Kulman, "Probers May Ask Curb on Sex Study Content," *Daily Register*, Aug. 15, 1969.

92. Richard Benfield, "Sex-Ed Foes Twist Truth, State Told," *Morning Call*, Sept. 16, 1969.

93. Doris Kulman, "He Links Sex Education to Talmud," *Daily Register*, Sept. 16, 1969.

94. "Sex Ed Hearings Concluded," *Central New Jersey Home News*, Dec. 18, 1969.

95. Herb Gage, "Parsippany Board Adopts Sex Course," *Herald-News*, Oct. 17, 1969.

96. "Committee Urges Changes," *Herald-News*, Apr. 14, 1970.

97. "Committee Urges Changes."

98. "Committee Urges Changes."

99. "Committee Urges Changes."

100. Vernon A. Guidry Jr., "Senate Votes Sex Teaching Study Panel," *Shreveport Times*, May 30, 1969.

101. Associated Press, "Senate Votes to Ban School Sex Education," *Shreveport Times*, June 6, 1969.

102. "Sex Education Resolution Is Approved," *Shreveport Times*, June 11, 1969.

103. "Sex Course Defended by Anaheim Trustee," *Los Angeles Times*, Jan. 12, 1969.

104. Associated Press, "Sex Education Ending Under Pressure from Conservatives."

105. Herman Wong, "High School Sex Education Defended at Anaheim Forum," *Los Angeles Times*, Jan. 17, 1969.

106. Associated Press, "Anaheim Sex Education Foes Claim Victory," *San Francisco Examiner*, Sept. 27, 1969.

107. Jack Boettner, "Sex Education Opponent Hails Program Change," *Los Angeles Times*, Sept. 27, 1969.

108. "Anaheim Schools Chief Quits Post," *Los Angeles Times*, Oct. 24, 1969.

109. Associated Press, "Sex Education Ending Under Pressure from Conservatives," *Gazette and Daily*, Mar. 30, 1970.

110. "Revised Sex Studies Show Enrollment Drop," *Los Angeles Times*, Feb. 7, 1970.

111. Associated Press, "Sex Education Ending Under Pressure from Conservatives."

112. Associated Press, "Sex Education Ending Under Pressure from Conservatives."

CHAPTER 12: THE NEW BATTLES OF THE 1970S

1. Joyce Krieg, "Sex Education Rarely Raises Parental Ire," *Palo Alto Times*, Aug. 10, 1971.

2. "What Are We Really Teaching in Sex Education?" *SIECUS Newsletter* VII, no. 3 (Feb. 1972), http://archive.org/details/sim_siecus-newsletter_1972 -02_7_3.

3. "What Are We Really Teaching in Sex Education?"

4. "What Are We Really Teaching in Sex Education?"

5. "What Are We Really Teaching in Sex Education?"

6. Louis Maslinoff, "Sex Education Films: A Content Analysis," *Family Coordinator* 22, no. 4 (1973): 405–11, https://doi.org/10.2307/583311.

7. Maslinoff, "Sex Education Films."

8. Frederick E. Bidgood, "The Effects of Sex Education: A Summary of the Literature," *SIECUS Report* 1, no. 4 (Mar. 1973).

9. Bidgood, "The Effects of Sex Education."

10. Bidgood, "The Effects of Sex Education."

11. Bidgood, "The Effects of Sex Education."

12. Bidgood, "The Effects of Sex Education."

13. Bidgood, "The Effects of Sex Education."

14. Barbara A. Chandler, "The White House Conference on Children: A 1970 Happening," *Family Coordinator* 20, no. 3 (1971): 195–207, https://doi.org /10.2307/582065.

15. "Education Called Only Way to Halt VD Rise," *Los Angeles Times*, Oct. 14, 1971.

16. "Role of the School in S-X," *Press-Telegram*, Apr. 23, 1971.

17. "Education Called Only Way to Halt VD Rise."

18. "Lack of VD Instruction in Schools Hit," *Los Angeles Times*, Sept. 2, 1971.

19. "Bill Seeks Mandatory VD Classes," *News-Pilot*, Mar. 18, 1971.

20. "Role of the School in S-X."

21. "Bill Allowing VD Instruction Gaining," *Independent*, Apr. 28, 1971.

22. "V.D. Instruction, Like It or Not," *The Signal*, May 12, 1971.

23. "VD in the Schools," editorial, *Los Angeles Times*, Oct. 18, 1971.

24. "Bill on VD Classes OKd in Senate," *Independent*, Sept. 16, 1971.

25. "Reagan Vetoes VD Bill," *The Signal*, Oct. 8, 1971.

26. "Reagan-Supported VD Education Bill Gains in Assembly," *Independent*, Mar. 8, 1972.

27. Joe Brooks, "Reagan Signs VD Bills," *News-Pilot*, Aug. 3, 1972.

28. "California Lifts Restrictions Against SIECUS Materials," *SIECUS Report* 1, no. 5 (May 1973): 5.

29. Gordon V. Drake, *SIECUS: Corrupter of Youth* (Tulsa, OK: Christian Crusade Publications, 1969), https://archive.org/details/siecuscorrupter00drak/page/n2/mode/1up.

30. "Wanted: Sex Teacher Who'll Face Lawsuit," *Daily News*, Feb. 5, 1970.

31. Evalyn S. Gendel, "Sex Education Lawsuit in Kansas—Impressions and Implications," *SIECUS Newsletter* 6, no. 1 (Oct. 1970), https://archive.org/details/sim_siecus-newsletter_1970-10_6_1/mode/1up.

32. Gendel, "Sex Education Lawsuit in Kansas."

33. Harriet F. Pilpel, "From the President: Harold I. Lief, M.D.," *SIECUS Newsletter* 6, no. 1 (1970), https://archive.org/details/sim_siecus-newsletter_1970-10_6_1/mode/1up.

34. Jan Gugliotti, "Howell Parents Would Bar Sex Education in Schools," *Lansing State Journal*, Apr. 9, 1970.

35. Gugliotti, "Howell Parents Would Bar Sex Education in Schools."

36. Gugliotti, "Howell Parents Would Bar Sex Education in Schools."

37. "New Lawyer, DOER in Sex Ed Fight," *Livingston County Daily Press and Argus*, Dec. 27, 1972.

38. Bill Gail, "Howell Pair Seeks Aid in Sex Education Fight," *Lansing State Journal*, Dec. 31, 1972.

39. Gail, "Howell Pair Seeks Aid in Sex Education Fight."

40. "Chapter 2: Freedom of Religion in Education," in John J. Cleary, *Classroom Sex Education: Cancel It—For Keeps! And Give Us Back Freedom of Religion* (Staten Island, NY: St. Mary's School of Religion for Adults, 1975), 44.

41. American Humanist Association, "Our History," Sept. 16, 2024, https://americanhumanist.org/about/our-history/.

42. James E. Wood, "Editorial: Religious Fundamentalism and the Public Schools," *Journal of Church and State* 29, no. 1 (1987): 7–17.

43. "Chapter 2: Freedom of Religion in Education."

44. "Sex Education Law Upheld," *Herald-Palladium*, May 1, 1974.

45. "Howell Sex Ed Case Awaits Supreme Court," *Livingston County Daily Press and Argus*, July 17, 1974.

46. "Supreme Court Upholds Sex Education Decision," *Livingston County Daily Press and Argus*, Sept. 18, 1974.

47. "Sex Ed Fighters Close Down Shop," *Livingston County Daily Press and Argus*, Nov. 20, 1974.

48. "Sex Ed Fighters Close Down Shop."

49. Gendel, "Sex Education Lawsuit in Kansas."

50. Paul M. Kinsie, "Notes on Laws and Their Administration," *Journal of Social Hygiene* 35, no. 7 (Oct. 1949): 345–46.

51. Kinsie, "Notes on Laws and Their Administration."

52. Kinsie, "Notes on Laws and Their Administration."

53. Guy S. Parcel and Diana L. Kenepp, "The Status of State Policies Concerning Birth Control Education," *Journal of School Health* 42, no. 10 (1972): 614–17, https://doi.org/10.1111/j.1746-1561.1972.tb01805.x.

54. H. S. Hoyman, "Should We Teach About Birth Control in High School Sex Education," *Journal of School Health* 38, no. 9 (Nov. 1968): 545–56, https://doi.org/10.1111/j.1746-1561.1968.tb04273.x.

55. "A Timeline of Contraception," "The Pill," *American Experience*, PBS, https://www.pbs.org/wgbh/americanexperience/features/pill-timeline/, accessed Sept. 20, 2024.

56. Griswold v. Connecticut, 381 U.S. 479 (1965), Justia Law, https://supreme.justia.com/cases/federal/us/381/479/, accessed Sept. 20, 2024.

57. "*Griswold v. Connecticut* (1965)," *The Supreme Court*, Thirteen PBS, 2006, https://www.thirteen.org/wnet/supremecourt/rights/landmark_griswold.html, accessed Sept. 20, 2024.

58. "Griswold v. Connecticut (1965)."

59. Griswold v. Connecticut, Oyez, https://www.oyez.org/cases/1964/496, accessed Sept. 20, 2024.

60. Griswold v. Connecticut, Oyez.

61. "Eisenstadt v. Baird," Oyez, https://www.oyez.org/cases/1971/70-17, accessed Sept. 20, 2024.

62. National Family Planning & Reproductive Health Association, "Eisenstadt v. Baird," https://www.nationalfamilyplanning.org/pages/issues/eisenstadtvbairdmain, accessed Sept. 20, 2024.

63. "Eisenstadt v. Baird," Oyez.

64. National Family Planning & Reproductive Health Association, "Eisenstadt v. Baird."

65. "Eisenstadt v. Baird," Oyez.

66. Louis Heldeman, "Pair Challenge Ban on Teaching of Birth Control," *Detroit Free Press*, Mar. 23, 1974.

67. Heldeman, "Pair Challenge Ban on Teaching of Birth Control."

68. Heldeman, "Pair Challenge Ban on Teaching of Birth Control."

69. Heldeman, "Pair Challenge Ban on Teaching of Birth Control."

70. Heldeman, "Pair Challenge Ban on Teaching of Birth Control."

71. Rone Tempest, "Court Skips Test of Sex Education," *Detroit Free Press*, July 19, 1974.

72. Tempest, "Court Skips Test of Sex Education."

73. Mary Scheier, "Changing Birth Control Law Is Legislative Job," *Herald-Palladium*, Jan. 4, 1975.

74. "Birth Control Bill Entered in Lansing," *Ironwood Daily Globe*, Mar. 6, 1975.

75. "Birth Control Bill Entered in Lansing," *Ironwood Daily Globe*.

76. "Birth Control Fight Builds," *Hillsdale Daily News*, July 11, 1975.

77. "Birth Control Fight Builds," *Hillsdale Daily News*.

78. Phyllis Schlafly, "What's Wrong with 'Equal Rights' for Women?" *Phyllis Schlafly Report* 5, no. 7 (Feb. 1972), https://awpc.cattcenter.iastate.edu/2016/02/02/whats-wrong-with-equal-rights-for-women-1972/.

79. Geraldine Strozier, "Sex Education Fight Burns Nearer to Vote," *Detroit Free Press*, Sept. 22, 1975.

80. Strozier, "Sex Education Fight Burns Nearer to Vote."

81. William J. Holstein, "VD Education Is Killed," *Detroit Free Press*, July 18, 1975.

82. Malcolm Johnson, "Controversial Sex Education Bill Defeated in Senate," *Herald-Palladium*, July 18, 1975.

83. Roger Srigley, "Senate to Reconsider Sex Education Bill Tomorrow," *Petoskey News-Review*, July 21, 1975.

84. "Senate Tables Birth Curb Bill," *Detroit Free Press*, July 30, 1975.

85. "Delay Vote on Sex Education," *Holland Evening Sentinel*, Nov. 7, 1975.

86. Paul Varian, "Senate Kills Watered Down Sex Education Bill," *Petoskey News-Review*, Nov. 13, 1975.

87. Varian, "Senate Kills Watered Down Sex Education Bill."

88. Paula Holmes, "Area VD Increase Explained by Health Chief," *Petoskey News-Review*, Feb. 23, 1976.

89. Millicent Lane, "VD Education Still Required," *Lansing State Journal*, Mar. 10, 1976.

90. Lane, "VD Education Still Required."

91. Lane, "VD Education Still Required."

92. Lane, "VD Education Still Required."

93. Birth Control Lessons Sought," *Lansing State Journal*, Apr. 28, 1977.

94. Donald Woutat, "House Repeals Ban on Teaching Birth Control," *Times Herald*, July 6, 1977.

95. James V. Higgins, "Sex-Ed Bill Is Ready for Senate Debate," *Petoskey News-Review*, Oct. 20, 1977.

96. Malcolm Johnson, "Sex Education Bill Passed by Senate," *Herald-Palladium*, Nov. 4, 1977.

97. "Milliken Signs Law Allowing Birth Control Classes in Schools," *Battle Creek Enquirer*, Dec. 1, 1977.

98. "Sex Teaching Under Study by Committee," *Morning World*, Apr. 29, 1970.

99. "Legislature OKs Ban on Sex Education," *Shreveport Journal*, June 16, 1970.

100. "ERA, Sex Education to Be Emotional Topics in Session," *Shreveport Journal*, May 8, 1974.

101. John Hill, "Battle on Sex Education Starts Today in Capital," *Shreveport Times*, May 29, 1974.

102. Associated Press, "Former State Rep. Alphonse Jackson Dead at 87," *Shreveport Times*, Dec. 25, 2014, https://www.shreveporttimes.com/story/news/local/louisiana/2014/12/25/alphonse-jackson-dead-at-87/20889707/.

103. "Alphonse Jackson Obituary (2014)—Baton Rouge, LA—The Advocate," Legacy.com, https://obits.theadvocate.com/us/obituaries/theadvocate/name/alphonse-jackson-obituary?id=19140210.

104. "House OKs $9.3 Million Deficit Spending Bill," *Shreveport Times*, May 21, 1974.

105. John Hill, "Sex Education Hearing to Continue Friday," *Shreveport Times*, May 30, 1974.

106. "Proposal Opposed in Catahoula," *Shreveport Times*, June 6, 1974.

107. John Hill, "House OKs Sex Education Survey," *Shreveport Times*, June 3, 1974.

108. John Hill, "Sex Education Question Is Facing Solons Again," *Shreveport Times*, Apr. 20, 1975.

109. Jua Nyla Hutcheson, "Panel Kills Sex Education Bills," *Shreveport Journal*, May 14, 1975.

110. Hutcheson, "Panel Kills Sex Education Bills."

111. Marsha Shuler, "Panel Appointed on Sex Education," *Shreveport Times*, May 13, 1975.

112. Shuler, "Panel Appointed on Sex Education."

113. Hutcheson, "Panel Kills Sex Education Bills."

114. Guy Coates, "Sex Education Debate: Is It Learning or Lust?" *Town Talk*, May 13, 1975.

115. Guy Coates, "Bill to End Sex Education Ban Aborted," *Town Talk*, May 14, 1975.

116. "Sex Education Bill Is Defeated by House Panel," *Shreveport Times*, July 14, 1976.

117. "Jackson Bill Would Allow Sex Education," *Shreveport Journal*, May 12, 1976.

118. "Sex Education Bill Voted Down," *Shreveport Journal*, July 14, 1976.

119. "Sex Education Proposal Again Fails in La. House," *Town Talk*, May 27, 1977.

120. "Sex Education Proposal Again Fails," *Town Talk*.

121. Jim Hammett, "Family Living Course Option Killed in House," *Shreveport Times*, May 27, 1977.

122. Ronni Patriquin, "Committee Okays Parish-Option Sex Education," *Shreveport Journal*, June 22, 1978.

123. John Hill, "Sex Education Measure Gets Senate's Approval," *Shreveport Times*, June 27, 1978.

124. "Senate Approves Bill to Allow Sex Education in State's Public Schools," *Shreveport Journal*, June 27, 1978.

125. "House Panel Takes Up Emotional Issue of Sex Education Today," *Shreveport Journal*, June 29, 1978.

126. Ronni Patriquin, "Vote Kills Bill on Sex Education," *Shreveport Journal*, June 29, 1978.

127. Ronni Patriquin, "Sex Education Battle Is Not Ended," *Shreveport Journal*, June 30, 1978.

128. Patriquin, "Sex Education Battle Is Not Ended."

129. "Disappointing Defeat for Sex Education," *Shreveport Journal*, July 3, 1978; "Editorial: Sex Education Bill," *Shreveport Times*, July 1, 1978; Steve Swartz, "Groping Through the Dark Ages," *Town Talk*, July 2, 1978.

130. Ronni Patriquin, "Some Senators Get 'Hate Mail' for Support of Sex Education," *Shreveport Journal*, July 6, 1978.

131. Ronni Patriquin, "Senate Move Forces House Debate, Action on Sex Education Proposal," *Shreveport Journal*, July 7, 1978.

132. Marsha Shuler, "Sex Education Issue Sent to House Floor," *Shreveport Times*, July 7, 1978.

133. Shuler, "Sex Education Issue Sent to House Floor."

134. "Sex-Course Debate Set in La. House," *Town Talk*, July 7, 1978.

135. Ronni Patriquin, "House Kills Sex Education Again," *Shreveport Journal*, July 8, 1978.

136. Patriquin, "House Kills Sex Education Again."

137. "Local Option Sex Ed Bill Again Sent to La. House," *Town Talk*, July 10, 1978.

138. "Sex Education Bill Killed for Year," *Town Talk*, July 11, 1978.

139. John Hill, "Jackson Presents Sex Education Bill," *Shreveport Times*, Apr. 19, 1979.

140. Hill, "Jackson Presents Sex Education Bill."

141. John Hill, "New Sex Education Bill Is Introduced," *Shreveport Times*, Apr. 20, 1979.

142. "Sexual Ignorance Is Too Great a Burden," *Shreveport Journal* Apr. 25, 1979.

143. John Hill, "Panel OKs Measure on Sex Education," *Shreveport Times*, Apr. 27, 1979.

144. "Editorial: The House Can't Hide," *Shreveport Times*, Apr. 29, 1979.

145. "Rally Held," *Shreveport Times*, May 1, 1979.

146. Ronni Patriquin, "50 Persons Attend Anti-Sex Education Rally," *Shreveport Journal*, Apr. 30, 1979.

147. "Ironic Justice Favors Sex-Education Debate," *Shreveport Journal*, May 1, 1979.

148. "Baptists Protest Sex-Ed Bill," *Shreveport Times*, May 11, 1979.

149. "Baptists Protest Sex-Ed Bill," *Shreveport Times*.

150. Randy Griffith, "The Man in the Anti-Sex Education Spotlight Reluctant, But Compelled," *Shreveport Journal*, May 18, 1979.

151. Patriquin, "House Kills Sex Education Again."

152. John M. Hill, "House Votes to Kill Bill on Sex Education," *Shreveport Times*, May 15, 1979.

153. John LaPlante, "Legislators Adopt Local-Option Plan on Sex Education," *Town Talk*, July 3, 1979.

154. "Sex Ed Pay Hike Among Bills Passed," *Shreveport Journal*, July 13, 1979.

CHAPTER 13: A DECADE OF FEDERAL ACTION

1. Mary Ann Lee, "Attitudes Have Changed over the Years," *Daily News-Post*, Apr. 20, 1970.

2. Al Pagel, "Teenage Pregnancy Rate Is Climbing," *Miami Herald*, Feb. 8, 1970.

3. Ursula Vils, "Sweeping Plan Urged to Aid Pregnant Teens," *Los Angeles Times*, Aug. 2, 1972.

4. Center for Disease Control, *Abortion Surveillance: Annual Summary 1972* (Atlanta: US Department of Health, Education, and Welfare, Public Health Service, Apr. 1974).

5. Center for Disease Control, *Abortion Surveillance*.

6. Center for Disease Control, *Abortion Surveillance*.

7. "Roe v. Wade Case Summary: What You Need to Know," FindLaw, https://supreme.findlaw.com/supreme-court-insights/roe-v--wade-case-summary--what-you-need-to-know.html, accessed Sept. 19, 2024.

8. Center for Disease Control, *Abortion Surveillance*.

9. Frederick S. Jaffe and Joy G. Dryfoos, "Fertility Control Services for Adolescents: Access and Utilization," *Family Planning Perspectives* 8, no. 4 (1976): 167–75, https://doi.org/10.2307/2134202.

10. Patsy Ciardullo, Wagoner, Nevada, "Title X Family Planning Program (1970–1977)," Embryo Project Encyclopedia (2016–10–21), ISSN: 1940–5030, https://hdl.handle.net/10776/11368.

11. Ciardullo, "Title X Family Planning Program (1970–1977)."

12. Frederick S. Jaffe, Joy G. Dryfoos, and Marsha Corey, "Organized Family Planning Programs in the United States: 1968–1972," *Family Planning Perspectives* 5, no. 2 (1973): 73–79, https://doi.org/10.2307/2133759.

13. Ciardullo, "Title X Family Planning Program (1970–1977)," 8.

14. Jaffe, Dryfoos, and Corey, "Organized Family Planning Programs in the United States," 73–79.

15. Diane S. Fordney Settlage, Sheldon Baroff, and Donna Cooper, "Sexual Experience of Younger Teenage Girls Seeking Contraceptive Assistance for the First Time," *Family Planning Perspectives* 5, no. 4 (1973): 223–26, https://doi.org/10.2307/2133973.

16. Farida Shah, Melvin Zelnik, and John F. Kantner, "Unprotected Intercourse Among Unwed Teenagers," *Family Planning Perspectives* 7, no. 1 (1975): 39–44, https://doi.org/10.2307/2134113.

17. Shah, Zelnik, and Kantner, "Unprotected Intercourse Among Unwed Teenagers," 39–44.

18. Shah, Zelnik, and Kantner, "Unprotected Intercourse Among Unwed Teenagers," 39–44.

19. Early Legal Access: Laws and Policies Governing Contraceptive Access, 1960–1980 https://websites.umich.edu/~baileymj/ELA_laws.pdf.

20. Aine Collier, *The Humble Little Condom: A History* (Amherst, NY: Prometheus Books, 2010).

21. Jaffe and Dryfoos, "Fertility Control Services for Adolescents."

22. Shah, Zelnik, and Kantner, "Unprotected Intercourse Among Unwed Teenagers," 39–44.

23. Patrick Riordan, "Religious Right Becoming Potent Political Force," *Orlando Sentinel*, May 8, 1980.

24. Riordan, "Religious Right Becoming Potent Political Force."

25. Daniel K. Williams, *God's Own Party: The Making of the Christian Right* (Oxford: Oxford University Press, 2010), 179.

26. Williams, *God's Own Party*.

27. Williams, *God's Own Party*, 188.

28. Williams, *God's Own Party*, 185.

29. Williams, *God's Own Party*, 191.

30. "Marching Right," *Winston-Salem Journal*. Sept. 28, 1980.

31. Brian Kates, "Targets of the Brimstone Brigade," *Daily News*, Sept. 9, 1980.

32. Kates, "Targets of the Brimstone Brigade."

33. Kates, "Targets of the Brimstone Brigade."

34. Louis Harris, "Moral Majority Gave Reagan Support He Needed at Polls," *Asbury Park Press*, Nov. 13, 1980.

35. HEW Cites 'Quiet' Sex Education," *Press-Telegram*, Jan. 17, 1973.

36. "Sex Education a U.S. Duty—Califano," *Los Angeles Times*, June 26, 1977.

37. Peter Scales, "Sex Education in the '70s and '80s: Accomplishments, Obstacles and Emerging Issues," *Family Relations* 30, no. 4 (Oct. 1981): 557–66, https://doi.org/10.2307/584345.

38. "Carter Budget: Few $ to Prevent Teen Pregnancy; Most Earmarked for Teenagers Already Pregnant," *Family Planning Perspectives* 10, no. 2 (1978): 114–15, https://doi.org/10.2307/2134333.

39. Maxwell Glen and Cody Shearer, "Government Tries to Sell Supply-Side Chastity," *Miami News*, Aug. 15, 1981.

40. Nicholas von Hoffman, "The New Chastity's Goals," *Daily Register*, Apr. 5, 1981.

41. Jack Fischer, "Sex Education Courses to Be Expanded in Area Schools," *The News*, Feb. 12, 1980.

42. "State Board Considering Sex Education Question," *Daily Register*, Apr. 7, 1980.

43. Mary Ellen Schoonmaker, "North Jersey Is Cool to Mandate on Sex Education," *The Record*, Apr. 10, 1980.

44. Fischer, "Sex Education Courses to Be Expanded in Area Schools."

45. Fischer, "Sex Education Courses to Be Expanded in Area Schools."

46. Mark Magyar, "State Approves Sex Education," *Daily Register*, Apr. 9, 1980.

47. Mary Ellen Schoonmaker, "State Mandates Sex Education in Public Schools," *The Record*, Apr. 9, 1980.

48. Schoonmaker, "State Mandates Sex Education in Public Schools."

49. Pamela Brownstein, "State Board Revises Sex Ed Requirements," *The News*, Aug. 7, 1980.

50. "Four Groups Seek to Bar Mandating of Sex Education," *Asbury Park Press*, Nov. 19, 1980.

51. "Sex Ed Uncertainties," *Press of Atlantic City*, Feb. 26, 1981.

52. Janet Thompson, "New Sex Education Guidelines Optional," *Courier-News*, Apr. 3, 1981.

53. Thompson, "New Sex Education Guidelines Optional."

54. "Schlafly to Speak," *Madison Eagle*, May 21, 1981.

55. Linda Fowler, "Sex Education Will Lead to Promiscuity, Schlafly Says," *Daily Record*, June 9, 1981.

56. Fowler, "Sex Education Will Lead to Promiscuity, Schlafly Says."

57. Mark Fitzgerald, "Peril Seen in Sex Ed by Schlafly" *The Herald-News,* June 9, 1981.

58. Douglas Kirby, Judith Alter, and Peter Scales, *An Analysis of U.S. Sex Education Programs and Evaluation Methods: Volume I,* US Department of Health, Education, and Welfare, July 1979, https://files.eric.ed.gov/fulltext /ED188981.pdf.

59. Kirby, Alter, and Scales, *An Analysis of U.S. Sex Education Programs and Evaluation Methods.*

60. Frank Morring Jr., "Funds Hearing Airs Complaints," *Birmingham Post-Herald,* Apr. 1, 1981.

61. "Mormons Fight U.S. Funds for Family-Planning Clinics," *Miami Herald,* Feb. 21, 1980.

62. Sylvia Townsend, "Parents Group Takes Planned Parenthood to Task," *Santa Cruz Sentinel,* Dec. 2, 1980.

63. Townsend, "Planned Parenthood Defends."

64. Townsend, "Planned Parenthood Defends."

65. Karen DeMasters, "Planned Parenthood Cut Follows Abortion Tempest," *Asbury Park Press,* Apr. 10, 1981.

66. DeMasters, "Planned Parenthood Cut Follows Abortion Tempest."

67. "Senate Committee Weighs Teen-Age Chastity Program," *The Record,* May 6, 1981.

68. "Promote Teen Chastity, Not Pill, Senators Urge," *Miami News,* May 6, 1981.

69. Frank Morring Jr., "Denton Bill Would Promote Teen Chastity," *Birmingham Post-Herald,* May 7, 1981.

70. "Giving Chastity a Bad Name," *Los Angeles Times,* May 11, 1981.

71. "'Chastity Bill' Is Simplistic," *Boca Raton News,* May 8, 1981.

72. James J. Kilpatrick, "Chastity Is a Private Issue," *Charlotte Observer,* July 17, 1981.

73. Kilpatrick, "Chastity Is a Private Issue."

74. Kilpatrick, "Chastity Is a Private Issue."

75. David Lightman, "Kennedy, Denton Reach Accord on Teenage Pregnancy Measure," *Hartford Courant,* June 23, 1981.

76. "Senate Unit OK's 'Chastity' Bill," *Spokane Chronicle,* June 24, 1981.

77. Rebekah Saul, "Whatever Happened to the Adolescent Family Life Act?" *Guttmacher Report on Public Policy* 1, no. 2 (Apr. 1998).

78. Saul, "Whatever Happened to the Adolescent Family Life Act?"

CHAPTER 14: CURRICULA WARS

1. "EWHSA Federal Funds Legal Notice," *Spokane Chronicle,* June 22, 1982.

2. Frances Huessy, "Sex Ed: Permission or Prevention," *Spokane Chronicle,* Apr. 19, 1982.

3. Frances Huessy, "Funds Backed for Teen-Age Chastity Program," *Spokane Chronicle,* July 7, 1982.

4. Frances Huessy, "Pasco-Based Group Battling Youthful Promiscuity," *Spokane Chronicle,* Jan. 27, 1983.

5. "Celibacy Group Expands," *Longview Daily News*, Jan. 27, 1983.

6. "Teen Group Tells Youth to Say 'No' to Temptation," *Pensacola News Journal*, July 22, 1983.

7. Beverly Jacobsen, "Coach Challenges Teens to Lead Celibate Lives," *Tri-City Herald*, May 24, 1983.

8. Teresa Hill, "Alternative Sex-Education Programs Shown to Public," *Island Packet*, Aug. 8, 1986.

9. "Crusade Arouses Teens to Notion: Saying No to Sex," *St. Louis Post-Dispatch*, Feb. 6, 1986.

10. Coleen Kelly Mast, *Sex Respect: The Option of True Sexual Freedom; A Public Health Manual for Teachers* (Bradley, IL: Respect for Sexuality, 1986).

11. Lois Norder, "Sex Education Subcommittee: 'Say No' Advocate Says 'No' to Invitation," *Shreveport Journal*, July 11, 1986.

12. Aileen Mulhern, "Sex Education Decision Expected Soon," *Beaufort Gazette*, June 13, 1986.

13. Mulhern, "Sex Education Decision Expected Soon."

14. Teresa Hill, "Salisbury Picks Sex Education Program," *Island Packet*, June 18, 1986.

15. Hill, "Salisbury Picks Sex Education Program."

16. Aileen Mulhern, "Sex Ed Plan Moves Back to Committee," *Beaufort Gazette*, June 25, 1986.

17. "Pamphlet Cites '3 R' Reference Books," *Island Packet*. July 10, 1986.

18. "Pamphlet Cites '3 R' Reference Books," *Island Packet*, July 10, 1986.

19. "Sex-Ed Program Draws Fire at Hearing," *Island Packet*, Aug. 5, 1986.

20. "Sex-Ed Program Draws Fire," *Island Packet*.

21. Teresa Hill, "School Board Member Suggests Sex-Ed Option," *Beaufort Gazette*, July 23, 1986.

22. Teresa Hill, "Board Members Clash Over Sex-Ed Program," *Island Packet*, July 16, 1986.

23. Aileen Mulhern, "Board Delays Sex-Ed Decision; to Poll Parents," *Beaufort Gazette*, Aug. 27, 1986.

24. Mulhern, "Board Delays Sex-Ed Decision."

25. Mulhern, "Board Delays Sex-Ed Decision."

26. Teresa Hill, "Divided Board Votes to Adopt 'Teen-Ad' Sex-Education Program," *Island Packet*, Oct. 1, 1986.

27. Hill, "Divided Board Votes to Adopt 'Teen-Ad' Sex-Education Program."

28. Laura E. Edwards et al., "Adolescent Pregnancy Prevention Services in High School Clinics," *Family Planning Perspectives* 12, no. 1 (Feb. 1980): 6–14, https://doi.org/10.2307/2134673.

29. Edwards et al., "Adolescent Pregnancy Prevention Services in High School Clinics," 6–14.

30. Edwards et al., "Adolescent Pregnancy Prevention Services in High School Clinics," 6–14.

31. I. R. Alton, "Nutrition Services for Pregnant Adolescents Within a Public High School," *Journal of the American Dietetic Association* 74, no. 6 (June 1979): 667–69.

32. Edwards et al., "Adolescent Pregnancy Prevention Services in High School Clinics," 6–14.

33. Edwards et al., "Adolescent Pregnancy Prevention Services in High School Clinics," 6–14.

34. Joy Dryfoos, "School-Based Health Clinics: A New Approach to Preventing Adolescent Pregnancy?" *Family Planning Perspectives* 17, no. 2 (1985): 70–75, https://doi.org/10.2307/2135263.

35. Dryfoos, "School-Based Health Clinics," 70–75.

36. Dryfoos, "School-Based Health Clinics," 70–75.

37. Dryfoos, "School-Based Health Clinics," 70–75.

38. Dryfoos, "School-Based Health Clinics," 70–75.

39. E. R. Shipp, "Sex and School Clinic: A City at Odds," *New York Times*, Sept. 22, 1985, https://www.nytimes.com/1985/09/22/us/sex-and-school-clinic-a-city-at-odds.html.

40. Shipp, "Sex and School Clinic."

41. Associated Press, "And Now, Birth Control 101," *Syracuse Herald-Journal*, Sept. 26, 1985.

42. Shipp, "Sex and School Clinic."

43. Associated Press, "And Now, Birth Control 101."

44. Associated Press, "And Now, Birth Control 101."

45. Associated Press, "School Clinic Faces Birth Control Furor," *Southern Illinoisan*, Sept. 26, 1985.

46. Walter E. Williams, "Poor Blacks Disguise Agenda," *Herald-Sun*, Jan. 19, 1986.

47. "Health Clinics in Public Schools: Two Views," *Evansville Press*, Apr. 30, 1986.

48. Faye Wattleton, "Pro: Adolescents Gain from Information," *Evansville Press*, Apr. 30, 1986.

49. Ann McFeatters, "Measures Suggested to Stem Teen Pregnancies," *Commercial Appeal*, Feb. 10, 1986.

50. McFeatters, "Measures Suggested to Stem Teen Pregnancies."

51. McFeatters, "Measures Suggested to Stem Teen Pregnancies."

CHAPTER 15: AIDS

1. Karin A. Bosh, "Estimated Annual Number of HIV Infections—United States, 1981–2019," *MMWR (Morbidity and Mortality Weekly Report)* 70 (2021), https://doi.org/10.15585/mmwr.mm7022a1.

2. US Department of Health and Human Services, "Timeline of The HIV and AIDS Epidemic," HIV.gov, https://www.hiv.gov/hiv-basics/overview/history/hiv-and-aids-timeline, accessed September 23, 2024.

3. Mark R. Kowalewski, "Religious Constructions of the AIDS Crisis," *Sociological Analysis* 51, no. 1 (1990): 91, https://doi.org/10.2307/3711343.

4. "Teach Kids About AIDS, Surgeon General Suggests," *Miami Herald*, Oct. 22, 1986.

5. Marlene Cimons, "Koop Urges AIDS Education, Not Tests," *Boca Raton News*, Oct. 22, 1986.

6. "Nation's Doctor Gives Sound Advice on AIDS," *Tampa Tribune*, Oct. 29, 1986.

7. Ellen Goodman, "Fears About AIDS Spark Changes in Attitudes Sex Education," *Miami Herald*, Oct. 28, 1986.

8. "Schools Take Surgeon General's Advice on Sex Education, AIDS," *Daily Spectrum*, Dec. 7, 1986.

9. "Koop Says He's Target of Hate-Mail Barrage," *Miami Herald*, Feb. 6, 1987.

10. Lynda R. Page, "AIDS Talks in Schools Opposed," *Palm Beach Post*, October 23, 1986.

11. "Sex Education Is Cautiously Backed," *Boca Raton News*, Oct. 24, 1986.

12. "Surgeon General Has Reasons for Increasing Sex Education," *Salt Lake Tribune* Oct. 29, 1986.

13. "U.S. Awards AIDS Funds for Schools," *Miami Herald*, Nov. 10, 1986.

14. Elise F. Jones et al., "Teenage Pregnancy in Developed Countries: Determinants and Policy Implications," *Family Planning Perspectives* 17, no. 2 (1985): 53–63, https://doi.org/10.2307/2135261.

15. Jones et al., "Teenage Pregnancy in Developed Countries," 53–63.

16. Jones et al., "Teenage Pregnancy in Developed Countries."

17. Jones et al., "Teenage Pregnancy in Developed Countries."

18. Jones et al., "Teenage Pregnancy in Developed Countries."

19. "Schools Should Distribute Contraceptives, Panel Says," *Miami Herald*, Dec. 10, 1986.

20. "Schools Should Distribute Contraceptives, Panel Says," *Miami Herald*.

21. "Reagan Backs AIDS War, Calls for Education," *San Francisco Examiner*, Apr. 1, 1987.

22. David Voreacos, "17 States Require AIDS Education, Survey Finds," *Los Angeles Times*, Dec. 4, 1987.

23. Carl Ingram and Tillie Fong, "Senate Decides to Emphasize Abstinence in AIDS Classes," *Los Angeles Times*, Feb. 27, 1987.

24. Christopher P. Holly, "Debate Set on Two S.C. Bills That Call for Sex Education," *The Herald*, Jan. 26, 1988.

25. "Health Education Bill Has Slow Start," *Anderson Independent-Mail*, Jan. 29, 1988.

26. Clif LeBlanc, "Senator Says Foes Distorting Sex Study Bill," *The State*, Jan. 29, 1988.

27. LeBlanc, "Senator Says Foes Distorting Sex Study Bill."

28. "Opinion: Sex Education Crucial," *The Herald*. Jan. 31, 1988.

29. "Senators OK Sex Education," *The State*, Feb. 4, 1988.

30. Tim Flach, "Legislative Panel Starts Work on Final Version of Sex Education Bill," *Greenville News*, Mar. 9, 1988.

31. Clif LeBlanc, "Panel Finds Compromise," *The State*, Mar. 24, 1988.

32. "Code of Laws—Title 16—Chapter 15—Offenses Against Morality and Decency," South Carolina Legislature, https://www.scstatehouse.gov/code/t16c015.php, accessed Sept. 24, 2024.

33. Clif LeBlanc, "Classes on Sex Passed," *The State*, Apr. 7, 1988.

34. Lisa Buie, "Petition Calls for Guidelines on Sex Ed," *The Herald*, May 24, 1988.

35. Beth Harrison, "Teens Speak Out on the Teaching of Sex Education," *The Herald*, June 5, 1988.

36. Lisa Buie, "School Board Names 13 to Oversee Sex Ed Changes," *The Herald*, July 26, 1988.

37. Lisa Buie, "Sex Ed Curriculum Too Explicit, Rock Hill Parents Complain," *The Herald*, Nov. 27, 1988.

38. Lisa Buie, "School Board to Hear from Parents About Sex Ed," *The Herald*, Nov. 29, 1988.

39. Lisa Buie, "Rock Hill Board Votes to Teach About Contraceptives," *The Herald*, Dec. 13, 1988.

40. Sarah Glazer, "Sex Education: How Well Does It Work?" *Tulsa World*, July 2, 1989.

CHAPTER 16: THE RISE OF COMPREHENSIVE SEX ED

1. National Commission on Excellence in Education, *A Nation at Risk*, Apr. 1983. https://edreform.com/wp-content/uploads/2013/02/A_Nation_At_Risk_1983.pdf.

2. National Commission on Excellence in Education, *A Nation at Risk*.

3. National Commission on Excellence in Education, *A Nation at Risk*.

4. Diane Ravitch, "Education in the 1980's: A Concern for 'Quality,'" *Education Week*, Jan. 10, 1990, https://www.edweek.org/policy-politics/opinion-education-in-the-1980s-a-concern-for-quality/1990/01.

5. Ravitch, "Education in the 1980's."

6. Laura S. Hamilton, Brian M. Stecher, and Kun Yuan, "Standards-Based Reform in the United States: History, Research, and Future Directions," Rand Corporation, paper commissioned by the Center on Education Policy, Washington, DC, Dec. 2008.

7. Hamilton, Stecher, and Yuan, "Standards-Based Reform in the United States."

8. Diane de Mauro, "A Review of State Sexuality and AIDS Education Curricula," *SIECUS Report* 18, no. 2 (Dec. 1989).

9. Jacqueline Darroch Forrest and Jane Silverman, "What Public School Teachers Teach About Preventing Pregnancy, AIDS and Sexually Transmitted Diseases," *Family Planning Perspectives* 21, no. 2 (Mar. 1989): 65, https://doi.org/10.2307/2135556.

10. Asta M. Kenney, Sandra Guardado, and Lisanne Brown, "Sex Education and AIDS Education in the Schools: What States and Large School Districts Are Doing," *Family Planning Perspectives* 21, no. 2 (1989): 56–64, https://doi.org/10.2307/2135555.

11. Forrest and Silverman, "What Public School Teachers Teach About Preventing Pregnancy, AIDS and Sexually Transmitted Diseases," 65.

12. Mauro, "A Review of State Sexuality and AIDS Education Curricula."

13. Mauro, "A Review of State Sexuality and AIDS Education Curricula."

14. Douglas Kirby, "Research on Effectiveness of Sex Education Programs," *Theory into Practice* 28, no. 3 (1989): 165–71.

15. Kirby, "Research on Effectiveness of Sex Education Programs," 165–71.

16. Kirby, "Research on Effectiveness of Sex Education Programs," 165–71.

17. Mark W. Roosa and F. Scott Christopher, "Evaluation of an Abstinence-Only Adolescent Pregnancy Prevention Program: A Replication," *Family Relations* 39, no. 4 (1990): 363–67, https://doi.org/10.2307/585214.

18. Kendrick v. Sullivan, 766 F. Supp. 1180 (D.D.C. 1991), Justia Law, https://law.justia.com/cases/federal/district-courts/FSupp/766/1180/1646696/.

19. Janet Benshoof, "The Chastity Act: Government Manipulation of Abortion Information and the First Amendment," *Harvard Law Review* 101, no. 8 (1988): 1916–37, https://doi.org/10.2307/1341442.

20. Bowen v. Kendrick, 487 U.S. 589 (1988), Justia Law, https://supreme.justia.com/cases/federal/us/487/589.

21. *Bowen v. Kendrick.*

22. *Kendrick v. Sullivan.*

23. *Kendrick v. Sullivan.*

24. Civil Liberties in the United States, "Adolescent Family Life Act," July 5, 2014, http://uscivilliberties.org/legislation-and-legislative-action/3042-adolescent-family-life-act.html.

25. Nicole Aydt Klein et al., "Evaluation of Sex Education Curricula: Measuring Up to the SIECUS Guidelines," *Journal of School Health* 64, no. 8 (Oct. 1994): 328–33, https://doi.org/10.1111/j.1746-1561.1994.tb03322.x.

26. "Planned Parenthood Sues Over Sex Ed," *Stuart News*, Apr. 25, 1992.

27. "Florida Study Finds Fault with Teen-Aid Program," *Spokesman-Review*, Apr. 29, 1992.

28. "Sex-Education Showdown Brewing in Florida County," *Shreveport Times*, Oct. 6, 1992.

29. "Religion, Law Expert Will Defend Sex-Ed Curriculum," *Miami Herald*, May 15, 1992.

30. Susan Drumheller, "Teen-Aid Chief Reports Lawsuit Has Hurt Sales," *Spokesman-Review*, June 21, 1992.

31. "Judge: Settle Teen-Aid Sex Program Lawsuit," *Miami Herald*, Nov. 15, 1992.

32. "Board Bars Mediation in Sex-Education Suit," *Miami Herald*, Nov. 19, 1992.

33. "County Sues Over Teen-Aid Curriculum," *South Idaho Press*, Oct. 13, 1993.

34. "A Meeting of Minds on Sex-Ed," *Miami Herald*, Apr. 9, 1996.

35. Ron Word, "Group Wants to Drop Sex-Ed Suit," *Tallahassee Democrat*, Apr. 9, 1996.

36. Penny Brown Roberts, "'Sex Respect' Message: There Is No 'Safe Sex,'" *Shreveport Times*, Nov. 22, 1991.

37. "Schools Change Sex Ed Course," *Shreveport Times*, Nov. 21, 1991.

38. "Childhood Lost," *Shreveport Times*, Aug. 18, 1991.

39. Penny Brown Roberts and Thao Hua, "Abstinence Vote Splits Caddo," *Shreveport Times*, Nov. 22, 1991.

40. Penny Brown Roberts, "Board Delays 'Sex Respect' a Year," *Shreveport Times*, Dec. 12, 1991.

41. Diana Murphy, "Panel Wants Public Input on Sex Ed," *Shreveport Times*, Sept. 12, 1992.

42. Diana Murphy, "Caddo OKs Sex Ed Plans," *Shreveport Times*, Sept. 24, 1992.

43. "Follow the Law" *Shreveport Times*, Sept. 17, 1992.

44. Murphy, "Caddo OKs Sex Ed Plans."

45. Murphy, "Caddo OKs Sex Ed Plans."

46. Richard Whitmore, "Sex-Ed Ruling Called Significant," *Democrat and Chronicle*, Mar. 20, 1993.

47. Whitmore, "Sex-Ed Ruling Called Significant."

48. Anne Newman and Dinah Richard, *Healthy Sex Education in Your Schools: A Parents' Handbook* (Pomona, CA: Focus on the Family Publishing, 1990).

49. Dinah Richard, *Has Sex Education Failed Our Teenagers? A Research Report* (Colorado Springs, CO: Focus on the Family Publishing, 1990).

50. Mike McManus, "Sexual Abstinence Can Be Taught," *Indiana Gazette*, July 24, 1991.

51. Jim Sedlak, "Classroom Sex Education Doesn't Work, So Let's Stop It," *News and Record*, Apr. 10, 1994.

52. Jacqueline R. Kasun "Condom Nation: Government Sex Education Promotes Teen Pregnancy," *Policy Review*, no. 68 (Spring 1994): 79–82.

53. Jacqueline R. Kasun, "The Case Against Sex Education in the Nation's Schools," *Dothan Eagle*, June 5, 1994.

54. Trish Moyan Torruella, "Real Sex Education Works," *Evansville Courier and Press*, May 28, 1994.

55. Torruella, "Real Sex Education Works."

56. SIECUS, *Unfinished Business: A SIECUS Assessment of State Sexuality Education Programs*, Sept. 1993, https://archive.org/details/ERIC_ED364513/page/n4/mode/1up.

57. Barbara Dafoe Whitehead, "The Failure of Sex Education," *The Atlantic*, Oct. 1994, https://www.theatlantic.com/past/docs/politics/family/failure.htm.

58. Whitehead, "The Failure of Sex Education."

59. Cal Thomas, "'Comprehensive Sex Education' Has Failed Children, Society," *Advocate-Messenger*, Sept. 30, 1994.

60. F. Scott Christopher, "Adolescent Pregnancy Prevention," *Family Relations* 44, no. 4 (Oct. 1995): 384–91, https://doi.org/10.2307/584994.

CHAPTER 17: THE A-H DEFINITION

1. Andrew Glass, "Clinton Signs 'Welfare to Work' Bill, Aug. 22, 1996," *Politico*, Aug. 22, 2018, https://www.politico.com/story/2018/08/22/clinton-signs-welfare-to-work-bill-aug-22–1996-790321.

2. Glass, "Clinton Signs 'Welfare to Work' Bill."

3. 42 USC 710: Separate Program for Abstinence Education.

4. Daniel Daley, "Exclusive Purpose: Abstinence-Only Proponent Create Federal Entitlement in Welfare Reform," *SIECUS Report* 25, no. 4 (May 1997).

5. Tamar Lewin, "States Slow to Take U.S. Aid to Teach Sexual Abstinence," *New York Times*, May 8, 1997, https://www.nytimes.com/1997/05/08/us/states-slow-to-take-us-aid-to-teach-sexual-abstinence.html.

6. Melody Petersen, "Teaching Abstinence: The Price of Federal Money for Sex Education," *New York Times*, July 27, 1997, https://www.nytimes.com/1997/07/27/nyregion/teaching-abstinence-the-price-of-federal-money-for-sex-education.html.

7. Petersen, "Teaching Abstinence."

8. Abby Goodnough, "Sex Education Classes Will Get Federal Aid," *New York Times*, Jan. 27, 1998, https://www.nytimes.com/1998/01/27/nyregion/sex-education-classes-will-get-federal-aid.html.

9. Associated Press, "Bliley Wants Sex Ed Funds Spent Right," *Richmond Times-Dispatch*, Jan. 6, 1998.

10. Joan Lowry, "Federal Funds Cause Friction," *Birmingham Post-Herald*, Mar. 22, 1999.

11. David J. Landry, Lisa Kaeser, and Cory L. Richards, "Abstinence Promotion and the Provision of Information About Contraception in Public School District Sexuality Education Policies," *Family Planning Perspectives* 31, no. 6 (1999): 280–86, https://doi.org/10.2307/2991538.

12. Yomi Wronge and Lisa Fernandez, "Experts: Teens Missing Key Part of Message," *Sun-News*, Jan. 6, 2001.

13. "Bush and Gore on Abstinence Ed," *The Item*, Nov. 5, 2000.

14. Carmen Solomon-Fears, *Reducing Teen Pregnancy: Adolescent Family Life and Abstinence Education Programs*, CRS Report for Congress, updated July 22, 2008, https://digital.library.unt.edu/ark:/67531/metadc807494/.

15. Diana Jean Schemo, "Surgeon General Calls for Accuracy in Sex Education," *Miami Herald*, June 29, 2001.

16. Karen Brandon, "Critics See Muddled Message in Abstinence Education," *Santa Fe New Mexican*, Aug. 12, 2001.

17. James W. Brosnan, "Free-Thinking Satcher Out of Step with Conservatives," *Commercial Appeal*, Aug. 26, 2001.

18. Brosnan, "Free-Thinking Satcher Out of Step with Conservatives."

19. Brandon, "Critics See Muddled Message in Abstinence Education."

20. Barbara Santee, "Abstinence-Only Programs Shown to Be Ineffective," *Tulsa World*, Sept. 2, 2001.

21. Amy Bleakley, Michael Hennessy, and Martin Fishbein, "Public Opinion on Sex Education in US Schools," *Archives of Pediatrics and Adolescent Medicine* 160 (2006).

22. National Coalition Against Censorship, "Timeline of Abstinence-Only Education in U.S. Classrooms," https://ncac.org/resource/timeline-of-abstinence-only-education-in-u-s-classrooms, accessed Sept. 28, 2024.

23. John S. Santelli, "Abstinence-Only Education: Politics, Science, and Ethics," *Social Research* 73, no. 3 (2006): 835–58.

24. Ryan J. Foley, "New Law: State Sex Education Classes Must Stress Abstinence," *Wausau Daily Herald*, May 24, 2006.

25. Cara Fitzpatrick, "Sex Ed Foes Picket Board Member's Home," *Palm Beach Post*, Nov. 28, 2007.

26. National Coalition Against Censorship, "Timeline of Abstinence-Only Education in U.S. Classrooms."

27. Rachel La Corte, "Legislature OKs Accurate Sex Ed Bill," *The Olympian*, Apr. 12, 2007.

28. Fran Eaton, "Obama's Insistence on Sex-Ed Leaves America's Youth Unprotected," *Southtown Star*, Apr. 5, 2008.

29. Eaton, "Obama's Insistence on Sex-Ed Leaves America's Youth Unprotected."

30. Eaton, "Obama's Insistence on Sex-Ed Leaves America's Youth Unprotected."

31. Laura Bischoff, "McCain's 'Education' Ad," *Dayton Daily News*, Sept. 12, 2008.

32. Larry Rohter, "Ad on Sex Education Distorts Obama Policy," *New York Times*, Sept. 11, 2008, https://www.nytimes.com/2008/09/11/us/politics/11checkpoint.html.

33. Rohter, "Ad on Sex Education Distorts Obama Policy."

34. Solomon-Fears, *Reducing Teen Pregnancy*.

35. "Obama Budget Shifts Money," *USA Today*.

36. "Obama Budget Shifts Money," *USA Today*.

37. Adam Wise, "Sex Education Changes Focus," *Daily Tribune*, Feb. 27, 2010.

38. "'Age Appropriate' Sex Ed Plan Fails in State Senate," *The Dispatch*, May 4, 2011.

39. "Most S.C. Schools Fail to Comply with Sex Ed Law, Report Finds," *The Herald*, Jan. 31, 2013.

40. Sarah H. Kershner et al., "Support for Comprehensive Sexuality Education and Adolescent Access to Condoms and Contraception in South Carolina," *American Journal of Sexuality Education* 12, no. 3 (July 3, 2017): 297–314, https://doi.org/10.1080/15546128.2017.1359803.

41. Mike Stobbe, "U.S. Teen Birth Rate Still Far Higher Than in Western Europe," *Press Enterprise*, Jan. 4, 2011.

42. Karen Kaplan, "Doctors Advised to Talk More to Teenage Patients About Sex," *Orlando Sentinel*, Jan. 28, 2014.

43. Ann Ramsdell, "Sex Education Is Overdue; Just Ask My Med Students," *The State*, Mar. 23, 2015.

44. Mary Kate McGowan, "Sex Talk," *Index-Journal*, Aug. 31, 2015.

45. "Comprehensive Health Education, South Carolina," H. 3447, 121st session (2015), https://www.scstatehouse.gov/billsearch.php?billnumbers=3447&session=121&summary=B.

46. Anna M. Tinsley, "Local Lawmaker Seeks to Revamp Sex Ed in Texas," *Fort Worth Star-Telegram*, Feb. 27, 2015.

47. "Relating to Health Education Curriculum and Instruction in Public Schools," Texas H.B. 1351, 84th Legislature (2015), LegiScan, https://legiscan.com/TX/text/HB1351/id/1121393.

48. Erin Duffy, "Parents Weigh In on Sex Ed Overhaul 1," *Omaha World-Herald*, Apr. 8, 2015.

49. Duffy, "Parents Weigh In on Sex Ed Overhaul 1."

50. Erin Duffy, "Omaha Schools Sex Education Meeting Gets Heated, Physical," *Kearney Hub*, Oct. 21, 2015.

51. Erin Duffy, "OPS Ponders Next Step After Rowdy Meeting," *Omaha World-Herald*, Oct. 21, 2015.

52. Erin Duffy, "Sex Ed Attracts Another Big OPS Crowd," *Kearney Hub*, Nov. 17, 2015.

53. Erin Duffy, "Sounding Off on Sex Ed," *Omaha World-Herald*, Jan. 5, 2016.

54. Duffy, "Sounding Off on Sex Ed."

55. "93% of Omaha Public School Parents Support Comprehensive Sex Education," *Omaha World-Herald*, Jan. 3, 2016.

56. "Opponents of Sex Ed Update Will Host Psychiatrist Talk," *Omaha World-Herald*, Jan. 13, 2016.

57. Duffy, "After 30 Years."

58. Erin Duffy, "Teachers, Parents Can Review Sex Ed Options," *Omaha World-Herald*, Feb. 18, 2016.

59. Erin Duffy, "Community Gets a Sneak Peek at Sex Ed Materials," *Omaha World-Herald*, Feb. 26, 2016.

60. "Some Want More Time on Sex Ed Books," *Omaha World-Herald*, May 3, 2016.

61. Erin Duffy and Joe Dejka, "Psst," *Omaha World-Herald*, Feb. 12, 2017.

62. "Some Want More Time on Sex Ed Books."

63. Advocates for Youth, "Our Legacy," https://www.advocatesforyouth.org/about/our-legacy/, accessed Sept. 28, 2024.

64. Joe Dejka, "'3Rs' Lessons Generated Controversy," *Omaha World-Herald*, Feb. 12, 2017.

65. Dejka, "'3Rs' Lessons Generated Controversy."

CHAPTER 18: TRUMP, BIDEN, AND TODAY

1. Democracy Forward, "Behind the Scenes: An Abstinence-Only Ideologue at HHS," https://democracyforward.org/lawsuits/bts-valerie-huber-abstinence-ideologue/, accessed Nov. 4, 2023.

2. David Crary, "Trump Appoints Advocate of Abstinence-Only Sex Education to a Top Health and Human Services Post," *Business Insider*, June 7, 2017, https://www.businessinsider.com/ap-advocate-of-abstinence-only-sex-education-gets-high-hhs-post-2017-6.

3. Jennifer Haberkorn, "Abstinence Advocate Gets Final Say on Family Planning Dollars," *Politico*, Mar. 7, 2018, https://www.politico.com/story/2018/03/06/abstinence-advocate-family-planning-dollars-389453.

4. "Teen Pregnancy Grants Cut," *Austin American-Statesman*, July 24, 2017.

5. "Programs to Prevent Teen Pregnancy See Funds Cut," *Arizona Daily Star*, Oct. 2, 2017.

6. Editorial Board, "An Assault on Efforts to Prevent Teenage Pregnancy," *New York Times*, Aug. 12, 2017, https://www.nytimes.com/2017/08/11/opinion/health-teenage-pregnancy-prevention.html.

7. Haberkorn, "Abstinence Advocate Gets Final Say on Family Planning Dollars."

8. Jessie Hellmann, "Abstinence-Only Education Making a Comeback Under Trump," *The Hill*, Mar. 8, 2018, https://thehill.com/policy/healthcare /377304-abstinence-only-education-making-a-comeback-under-trump/.

9. "Trump Remaking Policy on Women's Reproductive Health," *News and Record*, May 31, 2018.

10. "Sex Education Should Cover Consent," *The Olympian*, Jan. 4, 2018.

11. Maryclaire Dale, "States Debate Teaching Consent to Kids," *Idaho Statesman*, May 26, 2019.

12. Howard Fischer, "New School Chief Seeks Repeal of Law About Gay Lifestyle," *Arizona Daily Star*, Feb. 5, 2019.

13. Lily Altavena, "Legislation Advances to Repeal Arizona Sex-Ed Law Seen as Anti-LGBTQ," *Arizona Republic*, Apr. 11, 2019.

14. Lily Altavena, "Legislation Advances to Release Arizona Sex-Ed Law Seen as Anti-LGBTQ," *Arizona Republic*, Apr. 11, 2019; Lily Altavena, "State Repeals Controversial Law on Sex Education," *Arizona Republic*, Apr. 12, 2019. Lily Altavena, "State Repeals Controversial Law on Sex Education," *Arizona Republic*, Apr. 12, 2019.

15. Neal Morton, "Wash. May Mandate 'Comprehensive' Sex Education in Public Schools," *Bellingham Herald*, Jan. 21, 2020.

16. Associated Press, "Contentious Sex-Ed Bill Passes House, Changes Force Another Senate Vote," *Spokesman-Review*, Mar. 6, 2020.

17. Jared Brown, "Protesters Hope for Veto by Governor," *Spokesman-Review*, Mar. 12, 2020.

18. Jim Camden, "Sex Ed Bill Signed, May Face Challenge," *Spokesman-Review*, Mar. 28, 2020.

19. Julia Ditto, "We Don't Need This Type of Sex Education," *Spokesman-Review*, May 25, 2020.

20. Joseph O'Sullivan, "New Sex Education Law Could Go to Ballot as Referendum," *Tri-City Herald*, June 12, 2020.

21. Laurel Demkovich, "Truth, Fiction and the New Sex Ed Law," *Spokesman-Review*, Oct. 17, 2020.

22. Sara Gentzler, "Washington Voters Approved Comprehensive Sex Ed in Schools," *Tri-City Herald*, Dec. 1, 2020.

23. "SIECUS Applauds the Biden Administration on the Release of a Progressive Budget for FY22," SIECUS, May 28, 2021, https://siecus.org/siecus -applauds-the-biden-administration-on-the-release-of-a-progressive-budget -for-fy22/.

24. Eva S. Goldfarb and Lisa D. Lieberman, "Three Decades of Research: The Case for Comprehensive Sex Education," *Journal of Adolescent Health* 68, no. 1 (Jan. 2021): 13–27, https://doi.org/10.1016/j.jadohealth.2020.07.036.

25. Marlene Sokol, "Pinellas Schools Lift Order Requiring Use of Masks," *Tampa Bay Times*, June 10, 2021.

26. Kelly Jo Ross, "Wesclin Parents Oppose Mask Mandate in Schools," *Breese Journal*, Aug. 19, 2021.

27. Strupp, "New State Sex Ed Mandate Draws Fire for Graphic Topics," *Herald-News*, Apr. 6, 2022.

28. Mary Ann Koruth, "NJ Education Chief Defends Sex Ed Lessons," *Central New Jersey Home News*, Apr. 30, 2022.

29. Jaclyn Diaz, "Florida's Governor Signs Controversial Law Opponents Dubbed 'Don't Say Gay,'" NPR, Mar. 28, 2022, https://www.npr.org/2022/03/28/1089221657/dont-say-gay-florida-desantis.

30. Jo Yurcaba, "Break the Law or Out a Student? Florida Teachers Navigate 'Don't Say Gay' Bill," NBC News, Aug. 19, 2022. https://www.nbcnews.com/nbc-out/florida-teachers-navigate-first-year-dont-say-gay-law-rcna43817.

31. Associated Press, "Florida Law Prohibiting Gender Identity, Sexual Orientation Instruction in Grades K-3 Confuses Some Teachers," FOX 13 Tampa Bay, Aug. 15, 2022, https://www.fox13news.com/news/florida-law-prohibiting-gender-identity-sexual-orientation-instruction-in-grades-k-3-confuses-some-teachers.

32. Jo Yurcaba, "DeSantis Signs 'Don't Say Gay' Expansion and Gender-Affirming Care Ban," NBC News, May 17, 2023, https://www.nbcnews.com/nbc-out/out-politics-and-policy/desantis-signs-dont-say-gay-expansion-gender-affirming-care-ban-rcna84698.

33. "Florida State Profile," SIECUS, Jan. 25, 2020, https://siecus.org/stateprofiles/florida-state-profile/.

34. Associated Press, "Florida Officials Pressure Schools to Roll Back Sex Ed Lessons," Sept. 23, 2024, https://apnews.com/article/florida-sex-education-curriculum-5b1a46f5a73e3122f4815cf1d439aef0.

35. Private correspondence.

AFTERWORD

1. American Academy of Pediatrics, "The Importance of Access to Comprehensive Sex Education," last updated Feb. 15, 2024, https://www.aap.org/en/patient-care/adolescent-sexual-health/equitable-access-to-sexual-and-reproductive-health-care-for-all-youth/the-importance-of-access-to-comprehensive-sex-education/.

2. "Texas State Profile," SIECUS, Apr. 5, 2022, https://siecus.org/stateprofiles/texas-state-profile-22/.

INDEX

abortions and abortion laws, 84, 90, 144–45, 210
abstinence: AFLA-supported programs on, 180; attitudes toward, at mid–twentieth century, 72; Bigelow on, 43; effectiveness of, 157; prophylaxis versus, 24; in sex ed curricula, 172–73, 174; SIECUS on, 179; support for, 46, 159, 160, 194; US focus on, 171, 180. *See also* Sex Respect: The Option of True Sexual Freedom (Mast curriculum)
abstinence education: failure of, 179–80, 194; federal funding for, 195–96; in Florida, 211; inaccuracies in, 195; rise of, 175; Satcher on, 194; under Trump, 204
abstinence education, A–H definition of, 190–202; Bush (George W.) and, 193–96; Clinton, welfare reform and sex ed, 190–91; Obama and teen pregnancy prevention, 196–99; Omaha, battles in, 199–202; state workarounds, 192–93
abstinence only: abstinence-only education, federal support for, 190–91; endorsements of, 161; as intellectually dishonest, 213–14; lack of effectiveness of, 190, 194–95, 212; under Obama, 197;

Richard on, 186; Schlafly and, 154–55; support for, 187–88; unsuitability for public schools, 216
abstinence-plus, 216
ACLU (American Civil Liberties Union), 52, 180–82
acquired immune deficiency syndrome. *See* AIDS (acquired immune deficiency syndrome)
Addams, Jane, 17
Adolescent Family Life Act (AFLA, chastity bill): abstinence programs supported by, 180; under Bush (George W.), 193; first AFLA projects, 159–61; funding available under, 159, 160; introduction and passage of, 156–58; questions of legality of, 180–81
adolescents, 198, 214–15. *See also* teenagers; teen pregnancies
Adolescent Sexuality in Contemporary America (Sorensen), 146
Advocates for Youth (AFY), 202, 217
AFSH (American Federation for Sex Hygiene), 13, 14–16, 22
AIDS (acquired immune deficiency syndrome), 168–75
"The Aim and Scope of Sex Education in the High School" (Van Buskirk), 28

01 14

J